Reusable Ada® Components Sourcebook

® Ada is a registered trademark of the Ada Joint Program Office - US Government

The Ada Companion Series

There are currently no better candidates for a co-ordinated, low risk, and synergetic approach to software development than the Ada programming language. Integrated into a support environment, Ada promises to give a solid standards-orientated foundation for higher professionalism in software engineering.

This definitive series aims to be the guide to the Ada software industry for managers, implementors, software producers and users. It will deal with all aspects of the emerging industry: adopting an Ada strategy, conversion issues, style and portability issues, and management. To assist the organised development of an Ada-oriented software components industry, equal emphasis will be placed on all phases of life cycle support.

Some current titles:

Ada for specification: possibilities and limitations
Edited by S.J. Goldsack

Concurrent programming in Ada
A. Burns

Selecting an Ada environment
Edited by T.G.L. Lyons and J.C.D. Nissen

Ada components: Libraries and tools
Proceedings of the 1987 Ada-Europe International Conference
Edited by S. Tafvelin

Ada: the design choice
Proceedings of the 1989 Ada-Europe International Conference
Edited by A. Alvarez

Distibuted Ada: developments and experiences
Proceedings of the Distributed Ada '89 Symposium, Southampton
Edited by J.M. Bishop

Ada: experiences and prospects
Proceedings of the 1990 Ada-Europe International Conferences
Edited by Barry Lynch

Rationale for the Design of the Ada Programming Language
J. Ichbiah, J. Barnes, R. Firth and M. Woodger

Reusable Ada Components Sourcebook

Tony Orme
Consultant

Ian Nussbaum
Dowty-Sema Ltd

and

Chris Mayers
Torus Systems

Published by the Press Syndicate of the University of Cambridge
The Pitt Building, Trumpington Street, Cambridge CB2 1RP
40 West 20th Street, New York, NY 10011, USA
10 Stamford Road, Oakleigh, Victoria 3166, Australia

© Cambrige University Press 1992

First published by CAMBRIDGE University Press 1992

Printed in Great Britain at the University Press, Cambridge

Library of Congress Cataloguing in Publication data available

British Library Cataloguing in Publication data available

ISBN 0 521 40351 0

CONTENTS

Foreword		vi
Preface		viii
Right to Reuse		ix
Components on Discs		x
1.	Introduction	1
2.	How to Use this Book	7
3.	The Components	12
	3.1 Text Handler	12
	3.2 Date & Time	26
	3.3 Universal Integer Arithmetic	42
	3.4 Universal Real Arithmetic	66
	3.5 Flexible Queues	86
	3.6 Trees	108
	3.7 Lists	134
	3.8 Dynamic Tasking	170
	3.8.1 Homogeneous Tasking	172
	3.8.2 Heterogeneous Tasking	187
	3.9 Sets	202
	3.10 Permutations	214
	3.11 Checksum	222
4.	Establishing a Reusable Library	235
5.	Testing of Components	241
Appendices		
A.	Efficiency	251
B.	Generics	253
C.	Portability	255
D.	Exceptions	259
E.	Component Entry Checks	261
F.	Coding Standards and Abbreviations	264
G.	Glossary	266
H.	List of References	271
I.	Index	273

FOREWORD

Modern society spends a considerable amount of effort on writing software. One of the goals of Software Engineering is to move towards a position whereby we can build a software system using as many pre-existing components as possible with little or no modification. This goal of software reuse was publicly stated as long ago as 1968 at a NATO conference; reuse was also one of the major objectives in the design of Ada.

Reusing software has proved difficult for a number of reasons. If software is not written with reuse in mind then it is very likely that it will be almost impossible to reuse. The level of parameterisation in order to make software reusable requires careful judgement. Too little parameterisation will reduce the domain of applicability so that it becomes uneconomic; too much parameterisation will introduce complexity and likely performance overheads (although this is often ameliorated by genericity as in Ada).

If software is written with reuse in mind, then we encounter the difficulty of retrieval. It will be necessary to catalogue the software so that it can be identified. The specification will have to be written in a manner that enables the potential user to ensure that it is appropriate to his or her needs. This has been achieved in the numerical domain of application for years, but this is perhaps a special case.

As with much of the evolution of thinking in software, progress in reuse is being made in a pragmatic way. One of the keys is clearly to encourage programmers to think about the possibility of reuse. It is probably even more important to encourage managers, so that short term gains made by putting together the bare minimum for today's project do not prevent longer term savings obtained by future reuse.

This book provides a helpful and very practical step forward along the line to greater reuse. Its essence is a number of examples of reusable components that can form the basis of a library straight away. The examples are of a general purpose nature and will be of immediate interest for practitioners in most areas of application. Moreover, as well as being of use in their own right, the examples also illustrate the techniques of writing software in a reusable manner. Not only will the book prove invaluable to practising software engineers developing live applications but it has also been written with the needs of the educator in mind. The examples are available separately on disc, and provide solid material for any serious course on Software Engineering.

In conclusion, I would like to congratulate the authors on their efforts and welcome a further valuable contribution to the Ada Companion Series.

John Barnes
Reading
1991

PREFACE

This book was inspired by a seminar on Software Reuse attended by one of the authors, and its development sustained by the belief that the periodic re-invention of wheels should be a thing of the past. The book sets out to provide a foundation of reusable software components for any public or private collection.

All the software herein is written in Ada 83, a language that has withstood the test of time. At the time of going to press, the forthcoming Ada 9X was not sufficiently firm to permit an assessment of its impact on each component. Nevertheless it is anticipated that any backwards incompatibilities will be subtle in nature and very unlikely to affect any of the software. There are a fair number of additions to the standard in 9X. One in particular, the concept of protected records, is welcome and should complement the components well. There was at one point a proposal to include a component in the book with a similar aim of protecting data structures and resources in multitasking environments.

At this juncture it is appropriate to remember those who helped to bring this work into being. They are:

Gerry Fisher, who generously permitted us to reprint his Universal Integer and Universal Real components. A few modifications have been made, so the present authors, rather than Mr. Fisher, should be blamed for any defects or omissions that may appear;

Scott Parris, President of Meridian Software Systems Inc, who provided a review copy of their validated Ada compiler at the outset, without which the book may never have got off the ground;

Karen Zentler-Gordon, now **Karen Nussbaum**, especially for her perseverance in helping the authors to finish the book one week before rushing off to get married to Ian;

Our long-suffering wives, **Kathy Orme** and **Jill Mayers**;

Guy Warner and **John Young** of Dowty-Sema for their help in the loan of equipment to prepare the book's camera copy;

Last but not least, the desk editors at Cambridge University Press, whose understanding of the practical problems facing authors was a boon.

Right to Reuse

At the time of designing, a system designer may specify any of the components in this book provided that he or she is currently in legal possession of a copy of this book.

Similarly at the coding stage a programmer may incorporate part or all of these components in a piece of software provided he or she is currently in legal possession of a copy of this book.

The expressions "system designer" and "programmer" above do not necessarily refer to job titles but to job functions.

Copyright is naturally reserved and on no account should any of the components be photocopied or otherwise reproduced outside a computer system. They may not be published supplied or sold except as an integral part of a much larger application system designed and programmed in accordance with the above paragraphs.

Limits of Liability and Disclaimer of Warranty

We make no warranties, express or implied, that the programs contained in this volume are free of error, or are consistent with any particular standard of merchantability, or that they will meet your requirement for any particular application. They should not be relied on for solving a problem whose incorrect solution would result in injury to a person or loss of property. If you do use the programs in such a manner, it is at your own risk. The authors and publisher, discharge all liability for direct or consequential damages resulting from your use of the programs.

COMPONENTS ON DISCS

A floppy disc version of the components contained within this book is available.

For each of the components, the floppy discs hold:
    Full specification
    Full body (most with additional comments to the book version)
    Full test specification (see section 5)
    Full set of test code (meeting the test specification)
    Where additional code was used in a component body for testing (see section 5) this larger version of the component is also included

All the above is in simple ASCII format files.

The discs are available in either high density 5 1/4 inch IBM PC format, or high density 3 1/2 inch IBM PC format.

The cost of the disc set is 15 pounds for the UK or US$30 elsewhere. A set can be obtained by sending a cheque (personal or business) for the above, made payable through a UK or US bank to Ian Nussbaum. This price includes postage and packing.

Please send orders to:
    Ian Nussbaum
    6 Carlton Road
    New Malden
    Surrey KT3 3AJ
    United Kingdom

Please state with your order; the size of disc you require, and your name and address (preferably on a sticky label).

PLEASE PRINT CLEARLY.

1 INTRODUCTION

1.1 On Re-inventing the Wheel

One of the many frustrations of computer programming is the frequent need to reproduce a common routine. Almost all programmers have faced the task of writing, say, a date verification procedure or a sort for the umpteenth time, and many will have wondered at the effort and cost of these repeated activities. This book represents an attack on the problem, by providing simple but proven program components that may be reused over and over. For reasons given below, Ada is the language chosen to express these components. Examples of use are provided. No specialist knowledge of Ada, beyond a simple understanding of packages, procedures and functions, is required.

It is the authors' intention that the components presented here will be immediately applicable in all areas where computers are used. Moreover they are designed in such a way that they may be used unaltered, or with minor adaptation, in tasking programs (readers not understanding the significance of this need not worry). Mathematical and scientific algorithms have been excluded, on the grounds that they are covered elsewhere (e.g. [NAG 88]) and are in any case specialised and tend to be complex.

The reusable components presented here may also serve as examples of generalised or reusable code.

1.2 Software Production as an Engineering Activity

When contemplating the achievements of our civilization, many examples of engineering spring to mind: the construction of mighty bridges or supersonic airplanes, or perhaps the robotic assembly of cars. It is not surprising that people in computing, faced with the risky and messy business that is software production, should seek inspiration from the successes of engineering.

Reuse was first formally postulated by [McIlroy 69] in terms of mass-produced software components. The latter would be used as the building blocks for new systems. It would therefore be the case that the "production run" for components would be greater than the "production run" for systems. In manufacturing engineering, that only happens in one of two ways. One is the trivial case where, for example, the same nuts and bolts are specified for use in different products. In the other case, where more substantial (and valuable) components are reused, a number of preconditions must apply. The component must be a member of a well-known class of objects whose function is well understood, where that function recurs in designs of different systems, and whose interface with the rest of the system is clear and standard. Additionally, engineers show reluctance to use bought-in components whose performance characteristics are not well-known.

A good example of reuse in the engineering field is the use of outboard motors for power boats, which are produced in different sizes with varying performances. Boat builders, who are not experts at designing or building motors, will design a boat such that it can use standard outboard engines. Any motor with a suitable power profile can then be chosen with confidence that it will fit, due to the standard means of connecting an outboard motor to a boat. The analogy with software probably holds good here; there is a limited number of functions that are well enough understood to be applicable over a range of systems, and even then the software components are likely to vary according to the size of the systems incorporating them.

The components in this book are designed to be comprehensive enough to cover the great majority of possible uses, without the complexities that would arise from trying to make them fit every conceivable need. In some cases, alternatives are proposed so that the user can select the best fit. Also in some cases, there are (clearly-marked) optional parts to give a range of functionality to the component.

1.3 Reusability and Software Engineering

The term "Software Engineering", signifying a technology for producing large, low-cost, high-quality systems quickly and reliably, was first used at a NATO software symposium at Garmisch in 1968. The term has come to mean slightly different things to different people, but reusable components have a bearing on the following aims of Software Engineering:

1.3.1 Reliability
The components presented herein have not only undergone careful review but have been thoroughly tested using validated compilers. Use of the components therefore reduces risk.

1.3.2 Portability
The components have been designed with portability of source code in mind and tested under two different validated compilers (see 1.6.1). Portability is one of the aims of Software Engineering, and will be achieved when there are established a number of software libraries which simultaneously cater for many different computers.

1.3.3 Understandability
Reuse of components leads to familiarity with them and thus aids software engineers in their appreciation of different systems.

1.3.4 Efficiency
Because the components are generalised, they will not always offer the greatest economy of use of resources. In the vast majority of cases of possible use, that will not matter, whether because the usage of resources is not critical, the components are not in a resource-intensive program fragment, or because a marginal increase in efficiency does not justify the extra development effort. Appendix A contains a more comprehensive discussion on the efficiency of the components.

1.4 Ada for Implementing Reusability

Ada was the authors' unanimous choice for implementation language, for the following reasons.

1.4.1 Ada is Standard
Ada is standardised to a much higher degree than any language before it. Subsets and supersets are not permitted to compiler writers (though of course site standards, or the individual programmer, may decide to constrain the use of certain constructs). The authors are therefore confident that the components will work on any true Ada machine.

1.4.2 Generics
Ada has a feature, the generic, that is particularly well suited to software reuse. Most of the components are presented as generics and may easily be invoked --- "instantiated" in the terminology --- to provide the required functionality. Appendix B provides some additional information on the use of generics.

1.4.3 Tasking

Ada is the only standard language to specify tasking and inter-task communication. It is thus the obvious choice for the expression of solutions to concurrency problems.

1.4.4 Portability

Ada has been shown to be highly portable in a number of studies. The portability of Ada means that a single reusable library can serve for a number of different host and target machines (though there will still be differences in certain areas such as screen handling).

1.4.5 Packages

Ada has a feature, shared with only a few languages such as Modula, of being able to encapsulate abstract data types (e.g., trees, stacks, queues, etc) in such a way that the reusers have no need to be aware of the implementation details. Indeed, the latter may be altered without the need for changes outside the package (although recompilation may still be needed).

1.4.6 Universality

Although Ada is still a young language, the momentum gained around it and the weight of its sponsors guarantee its availability on practically all machines.

1.4.7 Other Features

There are other features of the language, such as user-defined types, which, though not peculiar to Ada, help to express a design clearly and unambiguously.

1.5 Management of Reusability

In 1986 Orme reported the results of a survey of 19 Ada sites in the U.S.A. and Europe. Of these, seventeen had reused, or were planning to reuse, Ada code. Eight of the sites were either using or scheduled to use formal reusable libraries. At sites without formal libraries, quantities of Ada code were often available informally.

The following is an extract from Orme's report [Orme 86], on the management of reusability:

> "Reusability has to be managed to work well, but the rewards can be a considerable increase to effective productivity in the

1 - Introduction

organisation. Larger projects may be able to justify a reusable library on their own.

A problem is to identify components for reuse. Some sites formally examine at the design stage for reusability, but at most places it is left to the individual to propose. Experience is found helpful to generalise a design. Excellent documentation is essential before submission to any library.

It is difficult to maintain a reusable library without resources. There must be a formal system for reporting and fixing bugs, otherwise configuration control becomes unmanagable when everyone keeps private versions of public files."

Chapter 4 gives guidance on how to create a reusable software library.

1.6 Quality

In designing the components with their accompanying descriptions, the following considerations were borne in mind, which may be summed up as representing "quality".

1.6.1 Reliability and Portability
To ensure that all components are composed of valid, portable Ada code and nothing else, they have all been compiled successfully, without alteration, by the following two validated (at the time of use) compilers:

- Meridian Ada
- R.R. Software Janus Ada

To ensure that all components behave correctly in use, the executable code generated by the above compilers has been thoroughly tested. On the associated floppy disc (see introductory pages) tests are available with which the component's correct function can be verified before or after modification. For further details, see Chapter 5 - Testing of Components.

1.6.2 Adaptability
Care was taken to ensure that sufficient information is included in each component's description to enable an Ada practitioner, but probably not a novice, adapt or expand each component. In this book, comments have been left in the source of Ada specifications, but fewer have been left in the bodies so as to save space. The more heavily commented bodies are

present on the floppy disc version of the code. Component tests are on the discs, which should really be regarded as a necessity if the components are to be modified.

1.6.3   Understandability
Bearing in mind the maxim that software is written once and read many times, care has been taken in the naming of identifiers, with the use of standardised abbreviations (see Appendix F). See also the above remarks on source comments.

1.6.4   Utility versus Reusability
The authors have opted for the so-called 90 % reusability level rather than the 100 % (i.e. everything possible parameterised and everything possible a generic). Examples are provided to show intended usage.

1.6.5   Other Considerations
To some extent, aiming for generality and understandability works against efficiency. To keep the book to a manageable size, code for recovery from external failure is not included.

2 HOW TO USE THE BOOK

A considerable amount of thought has been invested in consideration of how to maximise the utility of this work. The components have full descriptions and examples. There are sections on many of the pitfalls of reusability, such as efficiency, the use of exceptions and the creation of a reusable library. A floppy disc is available to readers with all the source code of the components, thereby saving manual entry. Furthermore, comprehensive component tests are available on the disc, which will aid in maintenance (i.e. with new compilers, and after any alteration of the components).

Those readers who wish to use the components immediately should skip to section 2.2. Those with slightly more time may wish to understand the issues facing the authors and how they were resolved.

2.1 Different Users

There are a number of different ways in which the components may be used. The needs of many different possible users have been taken into consideration in creating this book.

2.1.1 The Software Librarian
The components may be used to found a reusable library or augment an existing one. In the case of an existing library, it may be necessary to change identifiers or interfaces to match site standards. Each reuser should have a copy of this book, which will serve as part of the documentation.

2.1.2 The Project Manager
The manager of a project may commend the components to the project's head of design, with a view to incorporation in software under development, possibly after modification.

2.1.3 The Design Head of a Project
The head of design (or designated subordinate) may review the detailed design of the software under development to consider where the components may be profitably inserted. Such decisions are always practical, and it is important for the existing software to be at the right level of

complexity. If many desired functions are missing, it is usually easier to write anew than to adapt. For that reason, the components presented here have a wider functionality than would program fragments created for ad hoc purposes.

2.1.4 The Professional Software Engineer

A team leader or team member has a duty to select the most cost-effective means of meeting a given software specification. Naturally he or she will need to be satisfied regarding, in particular, the utility, reliability and adaptability of any proposed off-the-shelf components. Section 1.6 explains how these needs are met.

2.1.5 The Novice

Junior team members are likely to incorporate components with little or no alteration. If alterations are made, however, the effort will be rewarded with a greater understanding of the design and use of such components. The components may well have value as examples of reusable code.

2.1.6 The Trainer

The components have considerable value on training courses, as examples, as foundations for practical exercises, and as a basis on which students can found a reusable library when they return to their normal workplace (provided, of course, that they each possess a copy of this book).

2.2 Component Format

As a first step to reusing code, the specification and description of a candidate component will be examined to see if there is a "fit" with the application requirements. For this reason, the specification and description are at the front of each component, together with two sections called Dependencies and Minimum Implementable Package, indicating what is assumed to be available and what may be omitted.

When a suitable component is tentatively identified, the remainder of the text will be found to describe, amongst other things, any limitations or options available, and will indicate how the component may be altered to suit certain requirements. As stated above, the source code, having been rigorously tested, may be copied and used "as is", or it may be modified to suit different standards or requirements.

The descriptive text at the front of each component will be the starting point for the different readers mentioned in section 2.1. The descriptions are comprised of the following parts:

2.2.1 Description of Component Specification

Description :
A brief description of the facilities offered by the component.

Dependencies :
External dependencies refer to other library elements that are 'WITH'ed, for example standard packages or other components from this book. Internal dependencies are shown when some part of a component depends on another part in any way that is not obvious.

Minimum Implementable Package :
In most of the components, parts may be deleted if not needed. This section indicates the core that must be present for the component to work effectively, or else those items which may be removed.

Component Specification :
The compilable specification. The Ada Language Reference Manual (ALRM) technique for highlighting keywords has been used, together with comments in italics.

Pragmatics :
A commentary on the component, considering its specification and use only.

Restrictions on Use :
Any limitations, particularly on the types with which a generic may be instantiated.

Exceptions :
Description of the exceptions that may be raised within the component, and the circumstances under which they are raised.

Options :
In many cases, changes to the source may easily be incorporated. This section provides some information on such changes.

Example of Use :
An example is presented. For space reasons, the code here may not be stand-alone compilable, but gives sufficient background to illustrate how to use at least some of the component's facilities.

2.2.2 Description of Component Body

Implementation Points :
This part provides an explanation of aspects of the component which are not obvious. It is the starting point for anyone contemplating large modifications, or wishing to gain an understanding of the design used.

Efficiency :
An indication of how the performance of the component is affected by the size of the data or other parameter. Frequently the relationship is non-linear (see Appendix A).

Package Body :
The final section for each component is the body of the source code. There are few comments to save space, but the disc version has additional comments.

2.3 Use of Components in a Multi-tasking Environment

When designing systems that are to use tasking, it is vital to understand the problems associated with passing or sharing information between tasks. It is a significant design decision to have a data object shared between tasks.

The two main problems when sharing data between tasks are those of race conditions and inconsistent values.

The potential for race conditions is a natural result of having shared data. The users of shared data have to recognise that this is the case and ensure that their design is robust in that respect. For example, the following would be TRUE for a variable X accessed only from within a single task:
$$X = X$$
However, if X were shared between more than one task, with other tasks able to alter its value at any time, then the above could not be assumed to be TRUE. This is because the system undertakes two reads from memory, between which the value may have been altered by the other task.

The problem of inconsistent values can occur whenever a shared object is not updated or read in an atomic (i.e. uninterruptible) manner. In such cases the value of the object is likely to be internally inconsistent until the full sequence of changes has been made. If during that time, a copy of the object is taken (under the thread of control of another task) then an inconsistent value is obtained by the reader.

In a situation where there are concurrent readers and writers of unprotected compound objects, the race condition problem would result in the reader not knowing whether to expect the 'old' version or the 'new' version of the object. The inconsistency problem may mean that what is read is neither, just a corrupt value.

The solutions to these types of problems are often language independent. Ada does give some specific support in the form of the rendezvous, although at some run time expense. Most solutions are based upon some form of resource locking technique using tokens, or by avoiding the problem altogether by controlling task rescheduling using critical regions. Particular solutions to these problems have a tendency to be either inefficient (e.g. use of rendezvous) or non-portable (e.g. disabling interrupts or scheduling). The vast majority of code in most systems need not be concerned with concurrent use.

None of the components presented here maintain internal state, and therefore they are suitable for concurrent use in a multi-tasking environment. However **objects created using the components must not be shared** unless one of the previously mentioned protection mechanisms is invoked.

3. THE COMPONENTS

3.1 TEXT HANDLER

Description

This package provides manipulation of variable length strings. The operations provided are equivalent to those of the the standard STRING type with the addition of a LOCATE function which provides the facility to search for a specified sequence of characters in the variable length string object.

The standard type STRING, whilst permitting operations on strings of unconstrained length, does not allow strings to vary in length once they have been declared.

The package supports string-like objects whose length may vary from time to time, although the maximum length is constrained on declaration.

The package is an implementation of the specification given as an example in the ALRM section 7.6.

Dependencies

None.

Minimum Implementable Package

The LOCATE functions do not correspond to operations on the standard STRING type and could be omitted if not needed.

The overloaded subprograms for type CHARACTER could be omitted since characters could be converted to STRINGs before being passed to this package.

Component Specification

This specification is virtually identical to that contained in the ALRM, section 7.6, where it is presented as an example of how packaging can be used. The only difference is that a value for the constant MAXIMUM has been supplied and that the package name has been extended.

```
package TEXT_HANDLER_PKG_is
    MAXIMUM: constant INTEGER := 1000;  -- See Pragmatics
    subtype INDEX is INTEGER range 0 .. MAXIMUM;
    type TEXT (MAXIMUM_LENGTH: INDEX) is limited private;

    function LENGTH (T: TEXT) return INDEX;
    function VALUE  (T: TEXT) return STRING;
    function EMPTY  (T: TEXT) return BOOLEAN;

    function TO_TEXT (S: STRING;    MAX: INDEX) return TEXT;
    function TO_TEXT (C: CHARACTER; MAX: INDEX) return TEXT;
    function TO_TEXT (S: STRING)                return TEXT;
    function TO_TEXT (C: CHARACTER)             return TEXT;

    function "&" (LEFT: TEXT;      RIGHT: TEXT)      return TEXT;
    function "&" (LEFT: TEXT;      RIGHT: STRING)    return TEXT;
    function "&" (LEFT: STRING;    RIGHT: TEXT)      return TEXT;
    function "&" (LEFT: TEXT;      RIGHT: CHARACTER) return TEXT;
    function "&" (LEFT: CHARACTER; RIGHT: TEXT)      return TEXT;

    function "="  (LEFT: TEXT; RIGHT: TEXT) return BOOLEAN;
    function "<"  (LEFT: TEXT; RIGHT: TEXT) return BOOLEAN;
    function "<=" (LEFT: TEXT; RIGHT: TEXT) return BOOLEAN;
    function ">"  (LEFT: TEXT; RIGHT: TEXT) return BOOLEAN;
    function ">=" (LEFT: TEXT; RIGHT: TEXT) return BOOLEAN;

    procedure SET (OBJECT: in out TEXT; VALUE: in TEXT);
    procedure SET (OBJECT: in out TEXT; VALUE: in STRING);
    procedure SET (OBJECT: in out TEXT; VALUE: in
                                                CHARACTER);

    procedure APPEND (TAIL: in TEXT;      TO: in out TEXT);
    procedure APPEND (TAIL: in STRING;    TO: in out TEXT);
    procedure APPEND (TAIL: in CHARACTER; TO: in out TEXT);
```

3.1 - Text Handler

```
      procedure AMEND (OBJECT   : in out TEXT;
                       BY       : in     TEXT;
                       POSITION : in     INDEX);

      procedure AMEND (OBJECT   : in out TEXT;
                       BY       : in     STRING;
                       POSITION : in     INDEX);

      procedure AMEND (OBJECT   : in out TEXT;
                       BY       : in     CHARACTER;
                       POSITION : in     INDEX);

      function LOCATE (FRAGMENT: TEXT;      WITHIN: TEXT)
                                            return INDEX;
      function LOCATE (FRAGMENT: STRING;    WITHIN: TEXT)
                                            return INDEX;
      function LOCATE (FRAGMENT: CHARACTER; WITHIN: TEXT)
                                            return INDEX;
   private
      type TEXT (MAXIMUM_LENGTH: INDEX) is
         record
            POS   : INDEX := 0;
            VALUE : STRING (1 .. MAXIMUM_LENGTH);
         end record;
end TEXT_HANDLER_PKG;
```

Pragmatics

This package does not adhere to the naming standards for other components in this book because the specification is defined in the ALRM.

The package specification in the ALRM shows that the upper limit for the maximum size for all TEXT objects (the constant MAXIMUM) is *implementation dependent*. A somewhat arbitrary value of 1000 characters has been chosen. A value of INTEGER' LAST could be used, but this is usually far larger than necessary, and makes comprehensive testing problematic.

In the following descriptions of the package facilities, three terms are used to describe different attributes of texts. They are defined below. In order to understand these attributes better, it is simplest to consider a text as a variable length array of characters.

3.1 - Text Handler

length of the text   The number of characters in the variable length array.

maximum length of the text   A constraint independently imposed on each text on declaration. This value is the maximum length that a particular text can ever be.

text's string   The set of characters in the text when considered as a simple string.

LENGTH
This function returns the length of the text.

VALUE
This function returns the text's string.

EMPTY
A boolean function which returns TRUE only if the length of the text is zero.

TO_TEXT
Four overloaded functions used to initialise a text. The maximum length of the text returned can be set explicitly or implicitly. In the latter case it defaults to the length of the supplied string ('LENGTH) or character (i.e. 1).

"&"
Five overloaded operators to concatenate texts to each other, to strings or to characters. The length of the text returned is the sum of the lengths of the parameters. The maximum length of the text returned is the sum of the maximum lengths of the parameters, be they text, string (i.e. 'LENGTH) or character (i.e. 1).

Comparison operators
Overloaded operators to enable texts' strings to be compared. The result returned is independent of the maximum sizes of the texts being compared. The results are the same as if the two texts' strings had been directly compared.

SET
As the TEXT type is limited private, and assignments are therefore not allowed, this collection of overloaded procedures is provided to allow texts

to be initialised from strings or characters. Use of SET also allows texts to be copied.

APPEND
Three overloaded procedures to allow a text, string or character to be appended to another text. This operation is carried out directly onto the 'TO' text, and is therefore different from the '&' operator, which generates a new text.

AMEND
Three overloaded procedures to allow part of a text's string to be overwritten by characters, strings or text. The length of the text cannot be altered by this operation. An example of an equivalent operation on a string is:

```
declare
    S : STRING (1..4) := "1234";
begin
    S(2..4) := "BCD";
    -- Equivalent to:
    -- AMEND (S, "BCD", 2)
end;
```

The POSITION parameter specifies the position of the first character to be overwritten in the text's string which is the OBJECT parameter. The BY parameter holds the data which is to overwrite that of the OBJECT parameter.

LOCATE
Three overloaded functions which scan a text's string to establish the position of a match with a string, character or further text. The value zero is returned if the fragment is not found.

Restrictions on use

None

Exceptions

CONSTRAINT_ERROR will be raised if any of the conditions described below occur.

The AMEND procedures are the only ones which explicitly test for the conditions that cause CONSTRAINT_ERROR to be raised. They raise it explicitly when necessary. All other procedures and functions rely on the range checking code introduced by the compiler to raise CONSTRAINT_ERROR. For this reason exception handling should not be disabled by the compilation option **pragma** SUPPRESS.

The package's constant MAXIMUM forms an upper bound for the maximum length of all texts. If when using the TO_TEXT functions or the SET procedures, the resulting text would have a maximum length greater than the package constant MAXIMUM, then a CONSTRAINT_ERROR will be raised.

The "&" operations, which returns a text whose length and maximum length is the sum of the input lengths and maximum lengths respectively. Again, if the resulting text's maximum length is greater than the package constant MAXIMUM, then CONSTRAINT_ERROR is raised.

The APPEND procedures will raise CONSTRAINT_ERROR when an attempt is made to set the length of a text beyond its maximum length.

The AMEND procedure will raise CONSTRAINT_ERROR when an attempt is made to increase the length of the amended text.

Options

Extensive use of the package during testing has shown that a very useful addition is a function which returns the maximum length of a text. The specification for such a function is:

```
function MAXIMUM_LENGTH (T : TEXT) return INDEX;
```

The body for such a function is:

```
function MAXIMUM_LENGTH (T : TEXT) return INDEX is
begin
    return T.MAXIMUM_LENGTH;
end MAX_LENGTH;
```

The procedures and functions could be expanded explicitly to test for CONSTRAINT_ERROR conditions and explicitly raise more specific exceptions.

Many other additions could be made, but this would extend the package well beyond that conceived by the ALRM. The implementation is straightforward, so many enhancements are envisaged.

Example of use

```
with TEXT_HANDLER_PKG;
use  TEXT_HANDLER_PKG;

procedure TEXT_HANDLER_PKG_EXAMPLE is
begin
   declare
      S, T : TEXT (20);
   begin
      SET (S, "This text");
      SET (T, "That text");
      AMEND (S, "That", POSITION => 1);
      -- Now S = T
   end;
end TEXT_HANDLER_PKG_EXAMPLE;
```

A larger example is shown in the ALRM, section 7.6.

Implementation points

This implementation uses array and record aggregates as it is good Ada practice and offers compilers the opportunity to produce efficient code.

However, some compilers generate inefficient code for these constructs; if speed is important, consult your compiler documentation for techniques to avoid this problem. Techniques may include implementation-dependent pragmas, compiler, or linker options.

As implemented, the package assumes that exception handling has not been disabled. To do so would cause use of the package's subprograms to be erroneous in cases where an exception would have been propagated to the calling code, as defined in the exceptions section.

The implementation of the LOCATE functions is simple. A more sophisticated algorithm would be appropriate if WITHIN is likely to be long.

Efficiency

The following table shows how the run time performance is related to the length of the text for each subprogram.

LENGTH	constant
VALUE	text's length
EMPTY	constant
TO_TEXT	length of text or string as applicable
"&"	sum of the lengths of the texts
Comparison operators	sum of the lengths of the texts
SET	resulting text's length
APPEND	resulting text's length
AMEND	length of the amending string
LOCATE	length of the searched text

Package Body

```
package body TEXT_HANDLER_PKG is

   function LENGTH (T : TEXT) return INDEX is
   begin
      return T.POS;
   end LENGTH;


   function VALUE (T : TEXT) return STRING is
   begin
      return T.VALUE (1 .. T.POS);
   end VALUE;


   function EMPTY (T : TEXT) return BOOLEAN is
   begin
      return T.POS = 0;
   end EMPTY;


   function TO_TEXT (S   : STRING;
                     MAX : INDEX) return TEXT is
   begin
      return (MAX, S'LENGTH, S & (1..(MAX-S'LENGTH)=>'~'));
   end TO_TEXT;
```

```
function TO_TEXT (C   : CHARACTER;
                  MAX : INDEX) return TEXT is
begin
   return (MAX, 1, C & (1 .. (MAX - 1) => '~'));
end TO_TEXT;


function TO_TEXT (S : STRING) return TEXT is
begin
   return (S'LENGTH, S'LENGTH, S);
end TO_TEXT;


function TO_TEXT (C : CHARACTER) return TEXT is
begin
   return (1, 1, (1=>C));
end TO_TEXT;


function "&" (LEFT  : TEXT;
              RIGHT : TEXT) return TEXT is
begin
   return (LEFT.MAXIMUM_LENGTH + RIGHT.MAXIMUM_LENGTH,
           LEFT.POS + RIGHT.POS,
           LEFT.VALUE (1 .. LEFT.POS) &
           RIGHT.VALUE (1 .. RIGHT.POS) &
           (1 .. (LEFT.MAXIMUM_LENGTH +
                  RIGHT.MAXIMUM_LENGTH - LEFT.POS -
                  RIGHT.POS) => '~'));
end "&";


function "&" (LEFT  : TEXT;
              RIGHT : STRING) return TEXT is
begin
   return (LEFT.MAXIMUM_LENGTH + RIGHT'LENGTH,
           LEFT.POS + RIGHT'LENGTH,
           LEFT.VALUE (1 .. LEFT.POS) & RIGHT &
           (1 .. (LEFT.MAXIMUM_LENGTH -
                  LEFT.POS) => '~'));
end "&";
```

3.1 - Text Handler

```
function "&" (LEFT  : STRING;
              RIGHT : TEXT) return TEXT is
begin
   return (LEFT'LENGTH + RIGHT.MAXIMUM_LENGTH,
           LEFT'LENGTH + RIGHT.POS,
           LEFT & RIGHT.VALUE (1 .. RIGHT.POS) &
           (1 .. (RIGHT.MAXIMUM_LENGTH -
                  RIGHT.POS) => '~'));
end "&";


function "&" (LEFT  : TEXT;
              RIGHT : CHARACTER) return TEXT is
begin
   return (LEFT.MAXIMUM_LENGTH + 1,
           LEFT.POS + 1,
           LEFT.VALUE (1 .. LEFT.POS) & RIGHT
           & (1 .. (LEFT.MAXIMUM_LENGTH -
                    LEFT.POS) => '~'));
end "&";


function "&" (LEFT  : CHARACTER;
              RIGHT : TEXT) return TEXT is
begin
   return (1 + RIGHT.MAXIMUM_LENGTH,
           1 + RIGHT.POS,
           LEFT & RIGHT.VALUE (1 .. RIGHT.POS) &
           (1 .. (RIGHT.MAXIMUM_LENGTH -
                  RIGHT.POS) => '~'));
end "&";


function "=" (LEFT  : TEXT;
              RIGHT : TEXT) return BOOLEAN is
begin
   return LEFT.POS = RIGHT.POS and then
          LEFT.VALUE (1 .. LEFT.POS) =
          RIGHT.VALUE (1 .. RIGHT.POS);
end "=";
```

```
   function "<" (LEFT  : TEXT;
                 RIGHT : TEXT) return BOOLEAN is
   begin
      return LEFT.VALUE (1 .. LEFT.POS) <
             RIGHT.VALUE (1 .. RIGHT.POS);
   end "<";



   function "<=" (LEFT  : TEXT;
                  RIGHT : TEXT) return BOOLEAN is
   begin
      return LEFT.VALUE (1 .. LEFT.POS) <=
             RIGHT.VALUE (1 .. RIGHT.POS);
   end "<=";



   function ">" (LEFT  : TEXT;
                 RIGHT : TEXT) return BOOLEAN is
   begin
      return LEFT.VALUE (1 .. LEFT.POS) >
             RIGHT.VALUE (1 .. RIGHT.POS);
   end ">";



   function ">=" (LEFT  : TEXT;
                  RIGHT : TEXT) return BOOLEAN is
   begin
      return LEFT.VALUE (1 .. LEFT.POS) >=
             RIGHT.VALUE (1 .. RIGHT.POS);
   end ">=";



   procedure SET (OBJECT : in out TEXT;
                  VALUE  : in     TEXT) is
   begin
      OBJECT.VALUE (1 .. VALUE.POS) :=
         VALUE.VALUE (1 .. VALUE.POS);
      OBJECT.POS := VALUE.POS;
   end SET;
```

3.1 - Text Handler

```
procedure SET (OBJECT : in out TEXT;
               VALUE  : in     STRING) is
begin
   OBJECT.POS := VALUE'LENGTH;
   OBJECT.VALUE (1 .. VALUE'LENGTH) := VALUE;
end SET;


procedure SET (OBJECT : in out TEXT;
               VALUE  : in     CHARACTER) is
begin
   OBJECT.POS := 1;
   OBJECT.VALUE(1) := VALUE;
end SET;


procedure APPEND (TAIL : in     TEXT;
                  TO   : in out TEXT) is
begin
   TO.VALUE (1 .. TO.POS + TAIL.POS) :=
      TO.VALUE (1 .. TO.POS) &
      TAIL.VALUE (1 .. TAIL.POS);
   TO.POS := TO.POS + TAIL.POS;
end APPEND;


procedure APPEND (TAIL : in     STRING;
                  TO   : in out TEXT) is
begin
   TO.VALUE (1 .. TO.POS + TAIL'LENGTH) :=
      TO.VALUE (1 .. TO.POS) & TAIL;
   TO.POS := TO.POS + TAIL'LENGTH;
end APPEND;


procedure APPEND (TAIL: in     CHARACTER;
                  TO  : in out TEXT) is
begin
   TO.VALUE (1 .. TO.POS + 1) := TO.VALUE (1 .. TO.POS)
                                 & TAIL;
   TO.POS := TO.POS + 1;
end APPEND;
```

```
            procedure AMEND (OBJECT   : in out TEXT;
                             BY       : in     TEXT;
                             POSITION : in     INDEX) is
            begin
               if POSITION = 0 or
                  POSITION+BY.POS-1 > OBJECT.POS then
                     raise CONSTRAINT_ERROR;
               elsif BY.POS /= 0 then
                  OBJECT.VALUE (POSITION .. POSITION + BY.POS-1)
                     BY.VALUE (1 .. BY.POS);
               end if;
            end AMEND;


            procedure AMEND (OBJECT   : in out TEXT;
                             BY       : in     STRING;
                             POSITION : in     INDEX) is
            begin
               if POSITION = 0 or
                  POSITION + BY'LENGTH - 1 > OBJECT.POS then
                     raise CONSTRAINT_ERROR;
               elsif BY'LENGTH /= 0 then
                  OBJECT.VALUE (POSITION .. POSITION + BY'LENGTH-
                     := BY;
               end if;
            end AMEND;


            procedure AMEND (OBJECT   : in out TEXT;
                             BY       : in     CHARACTER;
                             POSITION : in     INDEX) is
            begin
               if POSITION in 1 .. OBJECT.POS then
                  OBJECT.VALUE (POSITION) := BY;
               else
                  raise CONSTRAINT_ERROR;
               end if;
            end AMEND;
```

3.1 - Text Handler

```ada
   function LOCATE (FRAGMENT : TEXT;
                    WITHIN   : TEXT) return INDEX is
begin
   if FRAGMENT.POS /= 0 then
      for J in 1 .. WITHIN.POS - FRAGMENT.POS + 1 loop
         if WITHIN.VALUE(J .. J+FRAGMENT.POS-1) =
            FRAGMENT.VALUE (1 .. FRAGMENT.POS) then
            return J;
         end if;
      end loop;
   end if;
   return 0;
end LOCATE;


   function LOCATE (FRAGMENT : STRING;
                    WITHIN   : TEXT) return INDEX is
begin
   if FRAGMENT'LENGTH /= 0 then
      for J in 1..WITHIN.POS - FRAGMENT'LENGTH + 1 loop
         if WITHIN.VALUE (J .. J+FRAGMENT'LENGTH-1) =
            FRAGMENT then
            return J;
         end if;
      end loop;
   end if;
   return 0;
end LOCATE;


   function LOCATE (FRAGMENT : CHARACTER;
                    WITHIN   : TEXT) return INDEX is
begin
   for J in 1 .. WITHIN.POS loop
      if WITHIN.VALUE (J) = FRAGMENT then
         return J;
      end if;
   end loop;
   return 0;
end LOCATE;

end TEXT_HANDLER_PKG;
```

3.2 DATE & TIME

Description

Facilities are provided beyond the standard package CALENDAR (provided with every validated compiler) to allow :
- day names,
- month names,
- times according to the 12 hour and 24 hour clocks,
- display of date and/or time.

Following the Example of Use is a discussion on the handling of dates and times in Ada.

Dependencies

External : on the standard package CALENDAR.
Internal : where two overloaded (i.e. of the same name) subprograms are shown in the package specification, the first depends on the second. Even if only the first is required, the second must not be removed.

Minimum Implementable Package

The types HOUR_TYPE, MINUTE_TYPE and SECOND_TYPE, together with the subprograms SPLIT and PRETTY_TIME that use them, may be removed to the package body. It is not anticipated that these types would be used for arithmetic, but the option is left to the user. Other subprograms may be omitted from the package, but consult the dependencies section before removing any.

Component Specification

```
with CALENDAR;
package DATE_TIME_PKG is

    TIME_ERROR : exception renames CALENDAR.TIME_ERROR;
```

3.2 - Date & Time

```ada
-- TIME_ERROR can be raised by DAY_OF_WEEK, DATE_STRING,
-- and PRETTY_DATE if the actual parameters DAY, MONTH
-- and YEAR do not form a proper date
TWENTY_4_HOUR        : constant BOOLEAN := TRUE;
TWELVE_HOUR          : constant BOOLEAN := FALSE;
DEFAULT_CLOCK        : constant BOOLEAN := TWENTY_4_HOUR;
-- Change default if 12-Hour clock desired

SECONDS_IN_MINUTE : constant := 60;
MINUTES_IN_HOUR   : constant := 60;
SECONDS_IN_HOUR   : constant := MINUTES_IN_HOUR *
                                SECONDS_IN_MINUTE;
SECONDS_IN_DAY    : constant := 24 * SECONDS_IN_HOUR;

type DAY_OF_WEEK_TYPE is (SUN,MON,TUE,WED,THU,FRI,SAT);

subtype TWENTY_4_HOUR_TYPE is INTEGER range 0 .. 23;
                   -- N.B. 24-Hour clock
subtype TWELVE_HOUR_TYPE   is INTEGER range 1 .. 12;
                   -- N.B. 12-Hour clock
subtype MINUTE_TYPE is INTEGER range 0 .. 59;
subtype SECOND_TYPE is INTEGER range 0 .. 59;
type TIME_OF_DAY_TYPE
    (TWENTY_4_HOUR_CLOCK : BOOLEAN := DEFAULT_CLOCK) is
  record
      DUPLICATE_INDICATOR : BOOLEAN := FALSE;
                   -- For when clock is put back
      SECOND              : SECOND_TYPE;
      MINUTE              : MINUTE_TYPE;
      case TWENTY_4_HOUR_CLOCK is
         when TRUE  => HOUR_OF_24 : TWENTY_4_HOUR_TYPE;
         when FALSE => HOUR_OF_12 : TWELVE_HOUR_TYPE;
                       PM         : BOOLEAN;
                       -- TRUE for p.m., FALSE for a.m.
      end case;
  end record;

function DAY_OF_WEEK (DATE  : CALENDAR.TIME)
                              return DAY_OF_WEEK_TYPE;
function DAY_OF_WEEK (YEAR  : CALENDAR.YEAR_NUMBER;
                      MONTH : CALENDAR.MONTH_NUMBER;
                      DAY   : CALENDAR.DAY_NUMBER)
                              return DAY_OF_WEEK_TYPE;
```

3.2 - Date & Time

```
function DATE_STRING
         (DATE             : CALENDAR.TIME;
          CENTURY_DISPLAY  : BOOLEAN := FALSE)
                             return STRING;
function DATE_STRING
         (YEAR             : CALENDAR.YEAR_NUMBER;
          MONTH            : CALENDAR.MONTH_NUMBER;
          DAY              : CALENDAR.DAY_NUMBER;
          CENTURY_DISPLAY  : BOOLEAN := FALSE)
                             return STRING;
```
-- Compile-time options in the package body cause the date to be returned
-- in a string either in the American form "MM/DD/YY" or in the European
-- form "DD/MM/YY". The CENTURY_DISPLAY parameter, if set to
-- TRUE, enables the century to be displayed also, i.e. "MM/DD/YYYY"
-- or "DD/MM/YYYY" respectively.
```
function PRETTY_DATE (DATE  : CALENDAR.TIME)
                             return STRING;
function PRETTY_DATE (YEAR  : CALENDAR.YEAR_NUMBER;
                      MONTH : CALENDAR.MONTH_NUMBER;
                      DAY   : CALENDAR.DAY_NUMBER)
                             return STRING;
```
-- PRETTY_DATE returns a string in the form: "Wednesday, 24th February 198
-- in a string just large enough to hold the characters. Century is always displaye
-- The code in the package body may easily be changed to display in a language
-- other than English.

```
procedure SPLIT
          (SECONDS      : in     CALENDAR.DAY_DURATION;
           TIME_OF_DAY  : in out TIME_OF_DAY_TYPE);
function JOIN (TIME_OF_DAY : TIME_OF_DAY_TYPE)
           return CALENDAR.DAY_DURATION;
function PRETTY_TIME
          (SECONDS             : CALENDAR.DAY_DURATION;
           TWENTY_4_HOUR_CLOCK : BOOLEAN := DEFAULT_CLOC
                                 return STRING;
function PRETTY_TIME (TIME_OF_DAY : TIME_OF_DAY_TYPE)
                                 return STRING;
```
-- PRETTY_TIME returns, for an input in the 24 hour variant, a nine-character
-- string in the form: "HH:MM:SS " or, for an input in the 12 hour variant a
-- thirteen-character string in the form: "HH:MM:SS x.m.", where x.m is either
-- a.m. or p.m. If the DUPLICATE_INDICATOR is TRUE, an asterisk is
-- placed immediately after the seconds i.e. "HH:MM:SS*"
```
end DATE_TIME_PKG;
```

Pragmatics

As with package CALENDAR, this package may be used for any dates and times during the years 1901 - 2099. Specification of an invalid date or time results in the raising of an exception.

A constant DEFAULT_CLOCK is provided, so that either the twelve or twenty-four hour clocks will be assumed when no other indication is available. Variables of TIME_OF_DAY_TYPE can still be explicitly declared with either variant.

Restrictions on use

As with package CALENDAR, years are restricted to the range 1901 - 2099.

Exceptions

TIME_ERROR is raised within the package if an invalid date or time is specified as an input parameter. Where TIME_ERROR is raised by a CALENDAR function invoked from within the package, it is propagated to the caller without being handled.

Options

Options are explicitly provided to display:
- dates either in American or European numeric form,
- years with or without the century, e.g. "1992" or "92",
- times according to either the 12-hour or the 24-hour clock.

It is straightforward to alter the procedures and functions herein to return dates in a language other than English.

Those interested in a wider range of years than 1901 - 2099 are referred to a readable discussion of Time and the Calendar in [Abell 75]. This package could certainly be modified for dates outside the range but the user must also provide his own CALENDAR package capable of handling such a range.

In Europe, different delimiters are used to separate the components of a date, e.g. in Britain and France the end of June 1991 is known as 30/06/91, in Germany 30.06.91, and in Italy 30-06-91. In the package body a constant (called DATE_DELIMITER) is provided which may be changed to suit the national requirement. Similarly a constant called TIME_DELIMITER is provided for national differences in specifying times.

Note that the functions and procedures provided also work with a mixture of 12-hour and 24-hour clock types; changing the option DEFAULT_CLOCK purely changes the default.

Example of use

```
with CALENDAR, DATE_TIME_PKG;
   .
   .
   NOW      : CALENDAR.TIME;
   YEAR     : CALENDAR.YEAR_NUMBER;
   MONTH    : CALENDAR.MONTH_NUMBER;
   DAY      : CALENDAR.DAY_NUMBER;
   SECONDS  : CALENDAR.DAY_DURATION;
   .
   .
   NOW := CALENDAR.CLOCK;
   TEXT_IO.PUT ("Today's date is ");
   TEXT_IO.PUT (DATE_TIME_PKG.PRETTY_DATE (NOW));
   TEXT_IO.PUT ("  and the time is ");
   CALENDAR.SPLIT (NOW, YEAR, MONTH, DAY, SECONDS);
   TEXT_IO.PUT
            (DATE_TIME_PKG.PRETTY_TIME (SECONDS) (1 .. 5))
   -- Prints just the hours and minutes -- hh:mm
```

Handling of Dates and Times

The standard package CALENDAR, provided with every validated compiler, has certain deficiencies. While years, month numbers and day numbers are catered for, month names and days of the week are not. Time-of-day is not well supported. There is a (implementation-dependent) type called TIME which combines date and time expressed in seconds since midnight. There is no mention of hours and minutes.

This package, DATE_TIME_PKG, rectifies these omissions. It is expected that CALENDAR will still be used for date and time calculations (such as:

3.2 - Date & Time

what is the date one week from now? Has a milestone date passed since this program was last run?). However, use should be made of the facilities provided here for display (or input) purposes. If required, procedures can be added to perform arithmetic on HOUR_TYPE, MINUTE_TYPE and SECOND_TYPE.

Where records must be ordered chronologically, a field of type CALENDAR.TIME is usually to be preferred as the sort key, on the grounds of efficiency.

The range of nearly 200 years covered by CALENDAR, 1901 to 2099, is unusual in that within it all years divisible by four are leap years. That is not true, for example, of 1900 and 2100. Where dates outside the CALENDAR range are to be used, and particularly for historians dealing with periods before the Gregorian calendar was introduced in different countries, it is wise to consult a specialised reference such as [Parise 82].

It is anticipated that the user of these routines will wish to standardise either on the 12 hour or the 24 hour clock. Railway timetables which use the 24 hour system use both 0000 and 2400 to represent midnight. For consistency 0000 is to be preferred, because for example nobody refers to 60 minutes past the hour. The package body therefore implements 0000 and not 2400.

In most countries, one hour per year is duplicated as clocks are put back at the end of the official Summer Time. There are no means of recording that in CALENDAR, but an indicator is provided here, in the TIME_OF_DAY_TYPE record, for those applications (military, emergency services, airline, etc) where such precision is vital. It is envisaged that, where the same time occurs twice one hour apart, applications will mark the second occurrence. However, it is emphasized that any interpretation may be placed upon times marked with an asterisk, and that in any case the application is responsible for turning the DUPLICATE_INDICATOR on or off - the component has no knowledge of Summer Times. Note that the SPLIT procedure must set the indicator off by default. The PRETTY_TIME function returns an asterisk to indicate a duplicate time.

To cope with the world's different time zones, certain applications may need to use CALENDAR.TIME in a record together with a time zone indication. A function could be provided to convert between the zones. These facilities are too specialised to be provided here.

To synchronise the man-made time system with the Earth's rotation, leap seconds are occasionally introduced. Usually they take the form of an extra second just before midnight - i.e. 11:59:60 p.m. Due to constraints in the CALENDAR package, standard Ada cannot cope with that time, and nor can DATE_TIME_PKG.

It will be noticed that some of the variable names in DATE_TIME_PKG do not follow Appendix F: Where a type from CALENDAR has been used, the corresponding variable name from CALENDAR has been used here also.

The constants SECONDS_IN_MINUTE, MINUTES_IN_HOUR, etc used in the body of the package, are provided in the package specification in case they are of use outside the conversion routines supplied.

It should be noted that DAY_OF_WEEK_TYPE in reality is a cyclical type (in that Sunday follows Saturday, etc, and there is no general agreement as to the first day of the week). However, it is mapped to an enumeration type which is linear. The position of Sunday as first day of the week should NOT be changed as some of the routines depend on it. Furthermore, it is dangerous to make use of ranges of this type. For example, the innocent-looking declaration:
   type WEEKEND **is array** (DAY_OF_WEEK_TYPE range SAT .. SUN)
     of ITEM_TYPE;
will be compiled apparently successfully but variables of this type will yield a null array at run time.

Implementation Points

The type DD_TYPE is useful in calculating times. Although it may appear that the upper bound of this discrete type should be declared in terms of CALENDAR.DAY_DURATION'LAST, type conversion problems are raised which can only be resolved by looking at the integer types available on the given target machine. In the interests of portability as well as clarity, the upper bound is defined in terms of a constant.

The generic function STR_N_CHAR is a generally useful routine for forcing an input string to a given size.

The DAY_OF_WEEK function makes use of two facts:
- Jan 1st advances one day of the week every year (two days after a leap year);

3.2 - Date & Time

- The first of each month always occurs a given number of days of the week after Jan 1st (again with a correction to be made in leap years).

Therefore the value of the variable INX is kept to a figure always below 1000 and it is safe to use a predefined type such as integer. It will be observed that, just before the remainder by 7 operation, +1 is added to the expression to be remaindered. That +1 is actually the sum of two quantities: -1 because (DAY - 1) should be added to obtain the difference from the 1st of the month; and +2 because Jan 1st 1901 was a Tuesday (index 2 in the array).

Efficiency

The performance of each of the subprograms is unrelated to the value of the dates.

Package Body

```
package body DATE_TIME_PKG is

    DATE_DELIMITER : constant CHARACTER := '/';
    -- May be changed, e.g. to '.' in Germany or '-' in Italy
    TIME_DELIMITER : constant CHARACTER := ':';
    -- May be changed, e.g. to '.' in Italy

    generic
        STRING_SIZE : POSITIVE;
    function STR_N_CHAR (S : STRING) return STRING;

    function STR_N_CHAR (S : STRING) return STRING is
        -- STR_N_CHAR takes a string that should be numeric. If the first element
        -- is blank, it is replaced by a zero. A string STRING_SIZE long is always
        -- returned. May return a strange result if S > (STRING_SIZE+1) or S
        -- contains characters other than numbers and a leading blank
        subtype SN_TYPE is STRING (1 .. STRING_SIZE);
        ZEROES : constant STRING (1 .. STRING_SIZE) :=
                                               (others => '0');
        COPY   : STRING (1 .. STRING_SIZE);
    begin
        if S'LENGTH = STRING_SIZE then
            COPY := S;
```

```
      elsif S'LENGTH > STRING_SIZE then
         COPY := S (2 .. STRING_SIZE + 1);
      else
         COPY := ZEROES (1 .. STRING_SIZE - S'LENGTH) & S;
      end if;
      if COPY (1) = ' ' then
         COPY (1) := '0';
      end if;
      return COPY;
   end STR_N_CHAR;

   function STR_2_CHAR is new STR_N_CHAR (2);
   function STR_4_CHAR is new STR_N_CHAR (4);

   procedure CHECK_DATE (YEAR  : in CALENDAR.YEAR_NUMBER;
                         MONTH : in CALENDAR.MONTH_NUMBER;
                         DAY   : in CALENDAR.DAY_NUMBER) i
   -- CHECK_DATE either returns (if a valid date is provided)
   -- or raises TIME_ERROR (if the date is invalid)
   begin
      if DAY < 29 then
         return;
      elsif MONTH = 2 then
         if DAY = 29 and (YEAR rem 4) = 0 then
            return;
         end if;
      elsif DAY = 31 then
         if not (MONTH = 4 or MONTH = 6 or MONTH = 9 or
                 MONTH = 11) then
            return;
         end if;
      else
         -- DAY = 29 or 30, MONTH /= February
         return;
      end if;
      raise TIME_ERROR;
   end CHECK_DATE;

   -- Now we come to the routines declared in the package spec
   function DAY_OF_WEEK (YEAR  : CALENDAR.YEAR_NUMBER;
                         MONTH : CALENDAR.MONTH_NUMBER;
                         DAY   : CALENDAR.DAY_NUMBER)
                               return DAY_OF_WEEK_TYPE i
```

3.2 - Date & Time

```
    DAYS_IN_MONTH : constant array
       (CALENDAR.MONTH_NUMBER) of INTEGER :=
       (0, 3, 3, 6, 1, 4, 6, 2, 5, 0, 3, 5);
    -- This gives the number of days by which the 1st of any month will
    -- differ from the day-of-the-week of Jan 1st. E.g. Feb 1st (month 2)
    -- will always be 3 days of the week after Jan 1st. A correction of +1
    -- day must be made in leap years for months after February.
    INX  : INTEGER;          -- Range 0 .. 248;
    LEAP : BOOLEAN := (YEAR rem 4) = 0;
begin
    -- Jan 1st 1901 was a Tuesday.
    -- After a leap year Jan 1st advances 2 days of the week.
    -- After a non-leap year Jan 1st advances 1 day of the week
    CHECK_DATE (YEAR, MONTH, DAY);
    INX := (YEAR - 1901) * 5 / 4;
    if LEAP and MONTH > 2 then
        INX := INX + 1;
        -- Correction applied in leap year
    end if;
    INX := (INX + DAYS_IN_MONTH (MONTH) + DAY + 1) rem 7;
    return DAY_OF_WEEK_TYPE'VAL (INX);
end DAY_OF_WEEK;



function DAY_OF_WEEK (DATE : CALENDAR.TIME)
                            return DAY_OF_WEEK_TYPE is
    YEAR    : CALENDAR.YEAR_NUMBER;
    MONTH   : CALENDAR.MONTH_NUMBER;
    DAY     : CALENDAR.DAY_NUMBER;
    SECONDS : CALENDAR.DAY_DURATION;
begin
    CALENDAR.SPLIT (DATE, YEAR, MONTH, DAY, SECONDS);
    return DAY_OF_WEEK (YEAR, MONTH, DAY);
end DAY_OF_WEEK;



function DATE_STRING
        (YEAR             : CALENDAR.YEAR_NUMBER;
         MONTH            : CALENDAR.MONTH_NUMBER;
         DAY              : CALENDAR.DAY_NUMBER;
         CENTURY_DISPLAY  : BOOLEAN := FALSE)
                            return STRING is
```

```
      type FORM_TYPE is (AMERICAN_FORM, EUROPEAN_FORM);
      -- American form is mm/dd/yy
      -- European form is dd/mm/yy
      FORM : constant FORM_TYPE := EUROPEAN_FORM;
      S    : STRING (1 .. 6);

   begin
      CHECK_DATE (YEAR, MONTH, DAY);
      if FORM = AMERICAN_FORM then
         S := STR_2_CHAR
                 (CALENDAR.MONTH_NUMBER'IMAGE (MONTH)) &
              '/' & STR_2_CHAR
                 (CALENDAR.DAY_NUMBER'IMAGE (DAY)) & '/';
      else     -- European form
         S := STR_2_CHAR (CALENDAR.DAY_NUMBER'IMAGE(DAY))
              DATE_DELIMITER & STR_2_CHAR
                 (CALENDAR.MONTH_NUMBER'IMAGE (MONTH)) &
              DATE_DELIMITER;
      end if;
      if CENTURY_DISPLAY then
         return S & STR_4_CHAR
                 (CALENDAR.YEAR_NUMBER'IMAGE (YEAR));
      else
         return S & STR_2_CHAR
                 (CALENDAR.YEAR_NUMBER'IMAGE (YEAR rem 100)
      end if;
   end DATE_STRING;


   function DATE_STRING
             (DATE            : CALENDAR.TIME;
              CENTURY_DISPLAY : BOOLEAN := FALSE)
                              return STRING is
      YEAR    : CALENDAR.YEAR_NUMBER;
      MONTH   : CALENDAR.MONTH_NUMBER;
      DAY     : CALENDAR.DAY_NUMBER;
      SECONDS : CALENDAR.DAY_DURATION;
   begin
      CALENDAR.SPLIT (DATE, YEAR, MONTH, DAY, SECONDS);
      return DATE_STRING
             (YEAR, MONTH, DAY, CENTURY_DISPLAY);
   end DATE_STRING;
```

3.2 - Date & Time

```ada
function PRETTY_DATE (YEAR  : CALENDAR.YEAR_NUMBER;
                      MONTH : CALENDAR.MONTH_NUMBER;
                      DAY   : CALENDAR.DAY_NUMBER)
                              return STRING is
   subtype LEN_TYPE is POSITIVE range 1 .. 9;
   type NINE_CHAR_REC_TYPE is
      record
         L : LEN_TYPE;
         S : STRING (LEN_TYPE);
      end record;
   MONTH_NAMES : constant array (CALENDAR.MONTH_NUMBER)
   of NINE_CHAR_REC_TYPE := ((7, "January  "),
                             (8, "February "),
                             (5, "March    "),
                             (5, "April    "),
                             (3, "May      "),
                             (4, "June     "),
                             (4, "July     "),
                             (6, "August   "),
                             (9, "September"),
                             (7, "October  "),
                             (8, "November "),
                             (8, "December "));
   DAY_NAMES : constant array (DAY_OF_WEEK_TYPE)
   of NINE_CHAR_REC_TYPE := ((6, "Sunday   "),
                             (6, "Monday   "),
                             (7, "Tuesday  "),
                             (9, "Wednesday"),
                             (8, "Thursday "),
                             (6, "Friday   "),
                             (8, "Saturday "));
   -- Do not rearrange the start of the week.  These days
   -- must agree with DAY_OF_WEEK_TYPE

   S : STRING (1 .. 2);
   D : constant DAY_OF_WEEK_TYPE :=
            DAY_OF_WEEK (YEAR, MONTH, DAY);
begin
   CHECK_DATE (YEAR, MONTH, DAY);
   -- Set S with the two characters to be used after the DAY of the month
   if    (DAY / 10)   = 1 then S := "th";
   elsif (DAY mod 10) = 1 then S := "st";
   elsif (DAY mod 10) = 2 then S := "nd";
```

```
      elsif (DAY mod 10) = 3 then S := "rd";
      else                        S := "th";
      end if;
      return DAY_NAMES (D).S (1 .. DAY_NAMES (D).L) & ','
             CALENDAR.DAY_NUMBER'IMAGE (DAY) & S & ' ' &
             MONTH_NAMES (MONTH).
             S (1 .. MONTH_NAMES (MONTH).L) & ' ' &
             STR_4_CHAR(CALENDAR.YEAR_NUMBER'IMAGE (YEAR)
   end PRETTY_DATE;


   function PRETTY_DATE (DATE : CALENDAR.TIME)
                              return STRING is
      YEAR    : CALENDAR.YEAR_NUMBER;
      MONTH   : CALENDAR.MONTH_NUMBER;
      DAY     : CALENDAR.DAY_NUMBER;
      SECONDS : CALENDAR.DAY_DURATION;
   begin
      CALENDAR.SPLIT (DATE, YEAR, MONTH, DAY, SECONDS);
      return PRETTY_DATE (YEAR, MONTH, DAY);
   end PRETTY_DATE;


   procedure SPLIT
              (SECONDS     : in     CALENDAR.DAY_DURATION;
               TIME_OF_DAY : in out TIME_OF_DAY_TYPE) is
      S    : CALENDAR.DAY_DURATION := SECONDS;
      MS   : CALENDAR.DAY_DURATION;
      H, M : INTEGER;

   begin
      if S >= CALENDAR.DAY_DURATION (SECONDS_IN_DAY) then
      -- Cater for 2400 Hours
         S := 0.0;
      end if;
      M := INTEGER (S / SECONDS_IN_MINUTE);
      MS := CALENDAR.DAY_DURATION (M) * SECONDS_IN_MINUTE
      if MS > S then
         M  := M - 1;
         MS := MS -
               CALENDAR.DAY_DURATION (SECONDS_IN_MINUTE);
      end if;
```

3.2 - Date & Time

```
      S                      := S - MS;
      TIME_OF_DAY.SECOND := INTEGER (S);
      H                      := M / MINUTES_IN_HOUR;
      TIME_OF_DAY.MINUTE := M - (H * MINUTES_IN_HOUR);
      if TIME_OF_DAY.TWENTY_4_HOUR_CLOCK then
         TIME_OF_DAY.HOUR_OF_24 := H;
      else                                 -- 12-hour clock
         if H >= 12 then
         -- N.B. Noon is treated as p.m.
            TIME_OF_DAY.PM := TRUE;
            H := H - 12;
         else
            TIME_OF_DAY.PM := FALSE;
         end if;
         if H = 0 then
            H := 12;
         end if;
         TIME_OF_DAY.HOUR_OF_12 := H;
      end if;
   end SPLIT;


   function JOIN  (TIME_OF_DAY : TIME_OF_DAY_TYPE)
                           return CALENDAR.DAY_DURATION is
   begin
      if TIME_OF_DAY.TWENTY_4_HOUR_CLOCK then
         return CALENDAR.DAY_DURATION
              (TIME_OF_DAY.SECOND + (TIME_OF_DAY.MINUTE *
              SECONDS_IN_MINUTE)) + CALENDAR.DAY_DURATION
              (TIME_OF_DAY.HOUR_OF_24) * SECONDS_IN_HOUR;
      else
         if TIME_OF_DAY.PM then
            return CALENDAR.DAY_DURATION
                 (TIME_OF_DAY.SECOND + (TIME_OF_DAY.MINUTE *
                 SECONDS_IN_MINUTE)) + CALENDAR.DAY_DURATION
                 (TIME_OF_DAY.HOUR_OF_12 rem 12 + 12) *
                 SECONDS_IN_HOUR;
         else
            return CALENDAR.DAY_DURATION
                 (TIME_OF_DAY.SECOND + (TIME_OF_DAY.MINUTE *
                 SECONDS_IN_MINUTE)) + CALENDAR.DAY_DURATION
                 (TIME_OF_DAY.HOUR_OF_12 rem 12) *
                 SECONDS_IN_HOUR;
```

```ada
         end if;
      end if;
   end JOIN;

   function PRETTY_TIME (TIME_OF_DAY : TIME_OF_DAY_TYPE)
                                     return STRING is
      CH  : CHARACTER := ' ';
      TOD : TIME_OF_DAY_TYPE renames TIME_OF_DAY;
   begin
      if TOD.DUPLICATE_INDICATOR then
         CH := '*';
      end if;
      if TOD.TWENTY_4_HOUR_CLOCK then
         return STR_2_CHAR (TWENTY_4_HOUR_TYPE'IMAGE
            (TOD.HOUR_OF_24)) & TIME_DELIMITER &
            STR_2_CHAR (MINUTE_TYPE'IMAGE (TOD.MINUTE))
            TIME_DELIMITER & STR_2_CHAR (SECOND_TYPE'IMA
            (TOD.SECOND)) & CH;
      elsif TOD.PM then
         return STR_2_CHAR (TWELVE_HOUR_TYPE'IMAGE
            (TOD.HOUR_OF_12)) & TIME_DELIMITER &
            STR_2_CHAR (MINUTE_TYPE'IMAGE (TOD.MINUTE))
            TIME_DELIMITER & STR_2_CHAR (SECOND_TYPE'IMA
            (TOD.SECOND)) & CH & "p.m.";
      else
         return STR_2_CHAR (TWELVE_HOUR_TYPE'IMAGE
            (TOD.HOUR_OF_12)) & TIME_DELIMITER &
            STR_2_CHAR (MINUTE_TYPE'IMAGE (TOD.MINUTE))
            TIME_DELIMITER & STR_2_CHAR (SECOND_TYPE'IMA
            (TOD.SECOND)) & CH & "a.m.";
      end if;
   end PRETTY_TIME;

   function PRETTY_TIME
           (SECONDS              : CALENDAR.DAY_DURATION;
            TWENTY_4_HOUR_CLOCK : BOOLEAN := DEFAULT_CLO
                                 return STRING is
      TOD : TIME_OF_DAY_TYPE (TWENTY_4_HOUR_CLOCK);
   begin
      SPLIT (SECONDS, TOD);
      return PRETTY_TIME (TOD);
   end PRETTY_TIME;
```

end DATE_TIME_PKG;

3.3 UNIVERSAL INTEGER ARITHMETIC

Description

This package provides all the normal facilities of integer arithmetic on arbitrarily large values. This package and the Universal Real component (3.4) have extended the work of Gerry Fisher in [Fisher 84].

The range of the predefined Ada type INTEGER is implementation-dependent. On some compilers it is only -32768..32767. Some compilers provide types LONG_INTEGER and LONG_LONG_INTEGER, but some do not. Hence the provision below of Universal Integers, composed of an array of INTEGERs, the dimensions of which are dependent on the value stored.

This package is portable to all machines from 8-bit INTEGER size upwards. (Note, however, that in the very rare case of 8-bit INTEGERs, a one-line change has to be made as indicated in Implementation Points). Moreover, the amount of data stored in each INTEGER is dependent on the size of INTEGERs on the target machine, so inefficiencies are not introduced for the sake of portability.

The maximum value that can be stored in an Universal Integer is one less than ten to the power of an exponent calculated as follows (for common INTEGER sizes):

INTEGER Size (bits)	Exponent	Storage Occupied by Largest Universal Integer (bytes)
8	127	127 B
16	65,534	64 kB
24	25,165,821	24 MB
32	8,589,934,588	8096 MB

Due to practical limitations of storage, above about 20 bits the largest possible value is of theoretical interest only.

Dependencies

None.

Minimum Implementable Package

Many of the facilities are optional in that they may be removed without affecting the rest of the package (however, if implementing the Universal Real Arithmetic component (3.4), note that it depends on this one).

Functions SIGN, ORDER_OF and "mod" may be readily omitted. The functions IMAGE and/or VALUE may also be omitted if not needed.

Component Specification

```
package UNIVERSAL_INTEGER_ARITHMETIC_PKG is
   type UNIVERSAL_INTEGER is private;

   I_ZERO : constant UNIVERSAL_INTEGER;
   I_ONE  : constant UNIVERSAL_INTEGER;
   I_TEN  : constant UNIVERSAL_INTEGER;

   function "+"   (LEFT, RIGHT : UNIVERSAL_INTEGER)
                     return UNIVERSAL_INTEGER;
   function "-"   (LEFT, RIGHT : UNIVERSAL_INTEGER)
                     return UNIVERSAL_INTEGER;
   function "*"   (LEFT, RIGHT : UNIVERSAL_INTEGER)
                     return UNIVERSAL_INTEGER;
   function "/"   (LEFT, RIGHT : UNIVERSAL_INTEGER)
                     return UNIVERSAL_INTEGER;
   function "mod" (LEFT, RIGHT : UNIVERSAL_INTEGER)
                     return UNIVERSAL_INTEGER;
   function "rem" (LEFT, RIGHT : UNIVERSAL_INTEGER)
                     return UNIVERSAL_INTEGER;
   function "**"  (LEFT  : UNIVERSAL_INTEGER;
                   RIGHT : INTEGER)
                     return UNIVERSAL_INTEGER;
   function "-"   (RIGHT : UNIVERSAL_INTEGER)
                     return UNIVERSAL_INTEGER;
   function "abs" (RIGHT : UNIVERSAL_INTEGER)
                     return UNIVERSAL_INTEGER;
```

3.3 - Universal Integer Arithmetic

```ada
    function ">="    (LEFT, RIGHT: UNIVERSAL_INTEGER)
                     return BOOLEAN;
    function ">"     (LEFT, RIGHT: UNIVERSAL_INTEGER)
                     return BOOLEAN;
    function "<="    (LEFT, RIGHT: UNIVERSAL_INTEGER)
                     return BOOLEAN;
    function "<"     (LEFT, RIGHT: UNIVERSAL_INTEGER)
                     return BOOLEAN;
    function EQ      (LEFT, RIGHT: UNIVERSAL_INTEGER)
                     return BOOLEAN;

    -- SIGN returns 0, -1 or +1 according to the sign of the parameter
    function SIGN    (RIGHT : UNIVERSAL_INTEGER)
                     return INTEGER;

    -- ORDER_OF returns the exponent of the first power of ten smaller than the
    -- absolute value of the parameter supplied: thus if RIGHT may be expressed in
    -- a convenient decimal notation as -9748 * 10 ** 49072, then ORDER_OF
    -- gives 49075.  Raises NUMERIC_ERROR if parameter is zero.
    function ORDER_OF (RIGHT : UNIVERSAL_INTEGER)
                     return UNIVERSAL_INTEGER;

    function TO_INTEGER (FROM_UNIVERSAL_INTEGER :
                         UNIVERSAL_INTEGER) return INTEGER;
    function TO_UNIVERSAL_INTEGER (FROM_INTEGER : INTEGER)
                     return UNIVERSAL_INTEGER;

    function IMAGE (VALUE : UNIVERSAL_INTEGER)
                     return STRING;
    function VALUE (IMAGE : STRING)
                     return UNIVERSAL_INTEGER;
private
    type VECTOR is array (POSITIVE range <>) of INTEGER;
    type UNIVERSAL_INTEGER is access VECTOR;

    I_ZERO  : constant UNIVERSAL_INTEGER
              := new VECTOR' (1=>0);
    I_ONE   : constant UNIVERSAL_INTEGER
              := new VECTOR' (1=>1);
    I_TEN   : constant UNIVERSAL_INTEGER
              := new VECTOR' (1=>10);
end UNIVERSAL_INTEGER_ARITHMETIC_PKG;
```

Pragmatics

The operations defined on Universal Integers are those defined in section 4 of the ALRM, with additions: IMAGE, VALUE, SIGN, ORDER_OF, and the conversion functions to and from standard INTEGERs.

The EQ function corresponds to the predefined equality "=" on standard INTEGERs. "=" must not be used to compare Universal Integers.

The IMAGE and VALUE functions correspond to the 'IMAGE and 'VALUE attributes of standard integer types. Note that they necessarily make use of the predefined type STRING, which means they cannot be used with any number whose absolute value is equal to or greater than 10 ** (POSITIVE'LAST).

SIGN returns -1, 0 or +1, depending on the sign of the parameter supplied.

ORDER_OF returns the exponent of the greatest power of ten no larger than the absolute value of the parameter supplied. This is mathematically equivalent to the integer part (the characteristic) of the logarithm (to the base 10) of the absolute value of the parameter.

An attempt to evaluate an uninitialised Universal Integer should be regarded as erroneous. It will usually raise a CONSTRAINT_ERROR but no reliance should be placed on that.

Restrictions on use

None

Exceptions

Ada requires certain operations on INTEGER values to raise the predefined exceptions CONSTRAINT_ERROR and NUMERIC_ERROR. This package raises the same exceptions in equivalent situations: for example, dividing a Universal Integer by zero will raise NUMERIC_ERROR.

Because of the flexibility of Universal Integers, it is almost impossible to get an overflow condition, which results, with conventional representations, in NUMERIC_ERROR. However, if Universal Integers of sufficient magnitude are added or multiplied together, then an overflow will be signalled by CONSTRAINT_ERROR (assuming that STORAGE_ERROR is not raised first). The table of maximum Universal Integer values, in the description section, should be consulted to decide if an overflow would likely occur in a given application.

The exceptions (other than STORAGE_ERROR) raised by specific functions under different circumstances are:

CONSTRAINT_ERROR :
"+","*"   -   Universal Integer Overflow (in theory)
"**"   -   Negative Exponent
VALUE   -   Non-numeric supplied

NUMERIC_ERROR:
TO_INTEGER   -   INTEGER Overflow
"/", "rem", "mod"   -   Division by zero
ORDER_OF   -   Zero parameter

N.B. Refer to Appendix D regarding the use of NUMERIC_ERROR.

Options

None.

Example of use

An (inefficient) program to calculate factorials from 1! to 15! :

```
with UNIVERSAL_INTEGER_ARITHMETIC_PKG, TEXT_IO;
use  UNIVERSAL_INTEGER_ARITHMETIC_PKG, TEXT_IO;
procedure TF is
   function FACTORIAL (X : POSITIVE)
            return UNIVERSAL_INTEGER is
      F, N  : UNIVERSAL_INTEGER := I_ONE;
   begin
      for I in 1 .. X loop
         F := F * N;
         N := N + I_ONE;
      end loop;
      return F;
   end FACTORIAL;
```

```
begin
   for J in 1 .. 15 loop
      PUT_LINE ("The factorial of" & INTEGER'IMAGE(J)
                    & " is" & IMAGE(FACTORIAL(J)));
   end loop;
end TF;
```

Implementation points

Universal integers are stored as vectors of ordinary integers. Rather than storing just one decimal digit in each integer, this package stores N decimal digits, where N is automatically calculated so that the maximum possible product obtained by multiplying two together will still fit into an ordinary integer.

Suppose a given compiler provides type INTEGER range -32768 .. 32767. The square of 99 is less than INTEGER'LAST, while the square of 999 is not. Therefore in this case UNIVERSAL_INTEGER will store decimal digits in pairs, with 99 as the largest value stored in each element of the vector. For example the value 599,668,234 will be stored as:

   +5 99 66 82 34

The sign is always stored in the first element of the vector.
Every element of the vector has a number in the range 0 .. (BASE-1), with two exceptions: (1) the first element, in order to incorporate the sign, has the range -(BASE-1) .. +(BASE-1), and (2) temporarily, in a multiplication or other operation.

The Universal Integer constant I_TEN has many uses and is exported by the package for that reason. However, if the number of bits (including sign) in the standard INTEGER is 14 or less, then only one decimal digit is stored per INTEGER and therefore the declaration of I_TEN in the package specification must be changed to incorporate two vector elements as follows:

```
I_TEN : constant UNIVERSAL_INTEGER
             := new VECTOR'(1 => 1, 2 => 0);
-- only when standard INTEGERs are 14 bits or less
```

The standard (one element) definition of I_TEN would in fact work with 8-bit arithmetic except for the function EQ which would, for example, return FALSE to the call EQ (I_TEN, TO_UNIVERSAL_INTEGER (10)). Because of the problems of using 8-bit arithmetic, it is not advised to export Universal Arithmetic constants of absolute value greater than 10 if package portability is required.

It is not possible to declare, in the front of the package body, Universal Integer constants in terms of the results of a call to TO_UNIVERSAL_INTEGER, because that function has not been elaborated at that point. Hence, for example, the declaration of I_16 inside the function VALUE.

The limits on the size of Universal Integers, quoted in the Description, arise out of the fact that it is not possible to create a vector with more than POSITIVE'LAST elements (see the declaration of VECTOR).

This implementation is geared towards simplicity rather than speed. Any Ada implementation of this package is likely to be much slower than using the predefined INTEGER types, unless specially handled by a particular Ada compiler.

Note that it is not possible to declare EQ as an "=" operator because the UNIVERSAL_INTEGER type is a private type rather than a limited private type. The "=" operator must not be used; it will not yield the same value as EQ.

Efficiency

The relationship between runtime performance and size of operand for the various subprograms is as follows (for large values of n, the Universal Integer operand) :

	Time dependent on:
TO_UNIVERSAL_INTEGER, SIGN, ORDER_OF	Constant
TO_INTEGER, IMAGE, ABS, unary "-" EQ (when operands are in fact equal)	$\log n$
">", "<", "<=", ">=", "+", "-"	$\log(\max(n_1, n_2))$
VALUE	length of string

3.3 - Universal Integer Arithmetic

"*"   log(n1) * log(n2)

"/", REM, MOD   log (n1)
(n1 = Dividend)

The time for operation "**" (Exponentiation) depends on :
(1) the square of the logarithm of the Universal Integer to be exponentiated, and
(2) a function of the exponent that is better than x**2 but not as good as x.log(x).

Package Body

```
package body UNIVERSAL_INTEGER_ARITHMETIC_PKG is
   BASE_D   : constant := (INTEGER'WIDTH - 2) / 2;
   BASE     : constant := 10 ** BASE_D;
   BASE_SQ  : constant := BASE * BASE;
   INT_D    : constant := 1 + (INTEGER'WIDTH - 2)/BASE_D;

   I_TWO    : constant UNIVERSAL_INTEGER
                     := new VECTOR'(1=>2);

   function TO_UNIVERSAL_INTEGER (V : VECTOR;
                                  S : BOOLEAN := FALSE)
                     return UNIVERSAL_INTEGER is
      -- Constructs a universal integer from a vector and a sign; the vector need not
      -- be normalised (see below). The boolean S is true if the number is negative.

      T : UNIVERSAL_INTEGER;
   begin
      -- The representation used in this package requires that all universal integer
      -- values be normalised, i.e. the first digit of any number, other than zero,
      -- must be non-zero.

      for J in V'RANGE loop
         if V(J) /= 0 then
            -- Ensure lower bound = 1
            T := new VECTOR(1..V'LAST -J + 1);
            for K in T.all'RANGE loop
               T.all(K) := V(J+K-1);
            end loop;
            if S then
```

3.3 - Universal Integer Arithmetic

```
               T(1) := - T(1);
            end if;
            return T;
         end if;
      end loop;
      return I_ZERO;
   end TO_UNIVERSAL_INTEGER;



   function TO_UNIVERSAL_INTEGER (FROM_INTEGER : INTEGER)
                         return UNIVERSAL_INTEGER is
      Y : VECTOR(1..INT_D) := (others => 0);
      Z : INTEGER;
   begin
      if FROM_INTEGER < BASE
      and then FROM_INTEGER > -BASE then
         return new VECTOR'(1 => FROM_INTEGER);
      end if;

      Z := FROM_INTEGER;

      for J in reverse Y'RANGE loop
         Y(J) := abs (Z rem BASE);
         Z    := Z / BASE;
      end loop;

      return TO_UNIVERSAL_INTEGER (Y, FROM_INTEGER < 0);
   end TO_UNIVERSAL_INTEGER;



   function TO_INTEGER
               (FROM_UNIVERSAL_INTEGER : UNIVERSAL_INTEGE
                return INTEGER is
      Y: INTEGER;
   begin
      if FROM_UNIVERSAL_INTEGER'LENGTH = 1 then
         return FROM_UNIVERSAL_INTEGER (1);
      end if;

      Y := 0;

      for J in FROM_UNIVERSAL_INTEGER'RANGE loop
         -- Convert to a negative integer.
```

3.3 - Universal Integer Arithmetic

```
        -- NUMERIC_ERROR may be raised here if magnitude of X is too large.
        Y := Y * BASE - abs FROM_UNIVERSAL_INTEGER(J);
    end loop;

    if FROM_UNIVERSAL_INTEGER(1) < 0 then
        -- negative
        return Y;
    else
        -- positive
        -- NUMERIC_ERROR is raised here only if X =-(INTEGER'FIRST)
        -- and the range is asymmetric.
        return -Y;
    end if;
end TO_INTEGER;


function "+" (LEFT, RIGHT: UNIVERSAL_INTEGER)
            return UNIVERSAL_INTEGER is
    M, K, R       : INTEGER;
    LEFT_LENGTH   : constant INTEGER := LEFT'LENGTH;
    RIGHT_LENGTH  : constant INTEGER := RIGHT'LENGTH;
begin

    if LEFT_LENGTH = 1 and then RIGHT_LENGTH = 1 then
        return TO_UNIVERSAL_INTEGER(LEFT(1) + RIGHT(1));
    end if;

    if LEFT_LENGTH < RIGHT_LENGTH then
        M := RIGHT_LENGTH + 1;
    else
        M := LEFT_LENGTH + 1;
    end if;

    declare
        U : VECTOR(1..M) := (1 .. M - LEFT_LENGTH => 0)
                & abs LEFT(1) & LEFT (2..LEFT_LENGTH);
        V : VECTOR(1..M) := (1 .. M - RIGHT_LENGTH => 0)
                & abs RIGHT(1) & RIGHT (2..RIGHT_LENGTH);

        LEFT_SIGN  : constant BOOLEAN := LEFT(1)  < 0;
        RIGHT_SIGN : constant BOOLEAN := RIGHT(1) < 0;
    begin
        if LEFT_SIGN = RIGHT_SIGN then
```

```
        K := 0;

        for J in reverse 1 .. M loop
           R := U(J) + V(J) + K;
           if R >= BASE then
              R := R - BASE;
              K := 1;
           else
              K := 0;
           end if;
           U(J) := R;
        end loop;

        return TO_UNIVERSAL_INTEGER (U, LEFT_SIGN);
    else
        -- signs different, subtract smaller from larger
        K := 0;

        for J in reverse 1 .. M loop
           R := U(J) - V(J) + K;
           if R < 0 then
              R := R + BASE;
              K := -1;
           else
              K := 0;
           end if;
           U(J) := R;
        end loop;

        if K = 0 then  -- LEFT has the larger magnitude
           return TO_UNIVERSAL_INTEGER(U, LEFT_SIGN);
        else    -- RIGHT has the larger magnitude, so recomplement
           K := 1;

           for J in reverse 1 .. M loop
              R := BASE - 1 - U(J) + K;
              if R = BASE then
                 R := 0;
                 K := 1;
              else
                 K := 0;
              end if;
              U(J) := R;
```

3.3 - Universal Integer Arithmetic

```ada
            end loop;
            return TO_UNIVERSAL_INTEGER (U, RIGHT_SIGN);
         end if;
      end if;
   end;
end "+";



function "-" (LEFT, RIGHT: UNIVERSAL_INTEGER)
             return UNIVERSAL_INTEGER is
begin
   return LEFT + (-RIGHT);
end "-";



function "*" (LEFT, RIGHT: UNIVERSAL_INTEGER)
             return UNIVERSAL_INTEGER is
   LEFT_LENGTH  : constant INTEGER := LEFT'LENGTH;
   RIGHT_LENGTH : constant INTEGER := RIGHT'LENGTH;
begin
   if LEFT_LENGTH = 1 and then RIGHT_LENGTH = 1 then
      return TO_UNIVERSAL_INTEGER(LEFT(1) * RIGHT(1));
   end if;

   declare
      W   : VECTOR(1 .. LEFT_LENGTH + RIGHT_LENGTH)
               := ( others => 0);
      K, R : INTEGER;
      B   : constant BOOLEAN := (LEFT(1) < 0)
                                   xor (RIGHT(1) < 0);
   begin
      for J in reverse RIGHT'RANGE loop
         K := 0;
         for I in reverse LEFT'RANGE loop
            R := abs (LEFT(I) * RIGHT(J)) + W(I+J)+ K;
            W(I+J) := R rem BASE;
            K      := R /    BASE;
         end loop;
         W(J) := K;
      end loop;
      return TO_UNIVERSAL_INTEGER (W, B);
   end;
end "*";
```

3.3 - Universal Integer Arithmetic

```ada
function "/" (LEFT, RIGHT: UNIVERSAL_INTEGER)
              return UNIVERSAL_INTEGER is
   M             : INTEGER;
   LEFT_LENGTH   : INTEGER;
   RIGHT_LENGTH  : INTEGER;
   E             : INTEGER;
   D, R, T       : INTEGER;
   QE            : INTEGER;     -- Quotient digit estimate
   V1, V2        : INTEGER;
begin
   LEFT_LENGTH  := LEFT'LENGTH;
   RIGHT_LENGTH := RIGHT'LENGTH;

   if LEFT_LENGTH = 1 and RIGHT_LENGTH = 1 then
      -- integer divide catches zero divisor
      return TO_UNIVERSAL_INTEGER (LEFT(1) / RIGHT(1));
   elsif LEFT_LENGTH < RIGHT_LENGTH then
      return I_ZERO;
   elsif RIGHT_LENGTH = 1 then
      -- Single 'digit' divisor is treated separately for efficiency.
      R  := 0;
      V1 := abs RIGHT(1);
      if V1 = 0 then    -- divisor is zero
         raise NUMERIC_ERROR;
      end if;

      declare
         Q : VECTOR (1..LEFT_LENGTH);
      begin
         for J in LEFT'RANGE loop
            T := R * BASE + abs LEFT(J);
            Q(J) := T / V1;
            R := T rem V1;
         end loop;

         return TO_UNIVERSAL_INTEGER (Q, (LEFT(1) < 0)
                   xor (RIGHT(1) < 0));
      end;
   end if;
```

-- At this point the length of the dividend is at least 2 and at least as great
-- as the length of the divisor. A full long division is needed. The algorithm
-- used here is from [Knuth 81], Section 4.3.1, Algorithm D.

3.3 - Universal Integer Arithmetic

-- *The first step is to multiply both the divisor and dividend by a scale factor*
-- *to ensure that the first digit of the divisor is at least BASE / 2.*
-- *This condition is required by the quotient digit estimation algorithm*
-- *used in the division loop. Note that this may increase the size of the*
-- *dividend by one digit, and thus the scaled dividend is placed in U.*

```
M := LEFT_LENGTH - RIGHT_LENGTH + 1;

declare
    U: VECTOR (1 .. LEFT_LENGTH + 1);   -- dividend
    V: VECTOR (1 .. RIGHT_LENGTH);      -- divisor
    Q: VECTOR (1 .. M);                 -- quotient
begin

    U := 0 & abs LEFT (1) & LEFT (2..LEFT_LENGTH);
    V := abs RIGHT (1) & RIGHT (2..RIGHT_LENGTH);

    V1 := V(1);

    D := BASE / (V1 + 1);      -- scale factor

    if D > 1 then              -- scale dividend and divisor

        R := 0;
        for J in reverse U'RANGE loop
            T := U(J) * D + R;
            U (J) := T rem BASE;
            R := T / BASE;
        end loop;

        R := 0;
        for J in reverse V'RANGE loop
            T := V(J) * D + R;
            V (J) := T rem BASE;
            R := T / BASE;
        end loop;

    end if;
```

-- *This is the major loop, corresponding to long division steps.*

```
    V1 := V(1);
    V2 := V(2);
```

3.3 - Universal Integer Arithmetic

```
for J in Q'RANGE loop
    -- Guess the next quotient digit QE by dividing the first two
    -- remaining dividend digits by the high order divisor digit.
    -- This estimate is never low and is at most 2 high.

    T := U(J) * BASE + U(J+1);
    if U(J) /= V1 then
        QE := T / V1;
    else
        QE := BASE - 1;
    end if;

    -- Now refine this guess so that it is almost always correct and is
    -- at worst one too high.

    while V2*QE > (T - QE*V1) * BASE + U(J+2) lo
        QE := QE - 1;
    end loop;

    -- Using QE as the quotient digit, multiply the divisor by QE and
    -- subtract from the remaining dividend.

    R := 0;
    for K in reverse V'RANGE loop
        T := U(J+K) - QE * V(K) + R;
        E := T rem BASE;
        R := T / BASE;
        if E < 0 then
            E := E + BASE;
            R := R - 1;
        end if;
        U(J+K) := E;
    end loop;

    U(J) := U(J) + R;

    -- If QE was off by one, then U(J) went negative when the last ca
    -- was added. So we correct the error by subtracting 1 from the
    -- quotient digit and adding back the divisor to the relevant portic
    -- of the dividend.
    if U(J) < 0 then
        QE := QE - 1;
        R := 0;
```

```ada
            for K in reverse V'RANGE loop
               T := U(J+K) + V(K) + R;
               if T > BASE then
                  T := T - BASE;
                  R := 1;
               else
                  R := 0;
               end if;
               U(J+K) := T;
            end loop;
            U(J) := U(J) + R;
         end if;

         -- Store the next quotient digit.
         Q(J) := QE;
      end loop;
      return TO_UNIVERSAL_INTEGER (Q, (LEFT(1) < 0)
            xor (RIGHT(1) < 0));
   end;
end "/";



function "mod" (LEFT, RIGHT: UNIVERSAL_INTEGER)
             return UNIVERSAL_INTEGER is
   R: constant UNIVERSAL_INTEGER := LEFT rem RIGHT;
begin
   if (LEFT(1) < 0) = (RIGHT(1)<0) or else R(1) = 0 then
      return R;
   else
      return RIGHT + R;
   end if;
end "mod";



function "rem" (LEFT, RIGHT: UNIVERSAL_INTEGER)
             return UNIVERSAL_INTEGER is
begin
   if LEFT'LENGTH = 1 and then RIGHT'LENGTH = 1 then
      return TO_UNIVERSAL_INTEGER(LEFT(1) rem RIGHT(1));
   else
      return LEFT - (LEFT/RIGHT) * RIGHT;
   end if;
end "rem";
```

3.3 - Universal Integer Arithmetic

```ada
function "**" (LEFT  : UNIVERSAL_INTEGER;
               RIGHT : INTEGER)
               return UNIVERSAL_INTEGER is
   R : UNIVERSAL_INTEGER := I_ONE;
   V : INTEGER := RIGHT;
   T : UNIVERSAL_INTEGER := abs LEFT;
begin
   if RIGHT < 0 then
      raise CONSTRAINT_ERROR;
   elsif RIGHT = 0 then
      return I_ONE;
   elsif LEFT(1) = 0 then
      return I_ZERO;
   end if;
   -- Starting the variable R at 1 and T at LEFT, loop through the binary
   -- digits of V, squaring T each time and multiplying the result R by the
   -- current value of T each time a 1-bit is found.
   while V /= 0 loop
      if V rem 2 = 1 then      -- V is odd
         R := R * T;
      end if;
      T := T * T;
      V := V / 2;
   end loop;
   -- The result is positive if RIGHT is even, the sign of LEFT if RIGHT is o

   if LEFT(1) < 0 and then RIGHT rem 2 = 1 then
      R(1) := - R(1);
   end if;
   return R;
end "**";



function "-" (RIGHT: UNIVERSAL_INTEGER)
              return UNIVERSAL_INTEGER is
begin
   return new VECTOR'(-RIGHT(1) & RIGHT(2..RIGHT'LAST)
end "-";



function "abs" (RIGHT: UNIVERSAL_INTEGER)
                return UNIVERSAL_INTEGER is
begin
```

3.3 - Universal Integer Arithmetic

```
      return new VECTOR'(abs RIGHT(1) &
                         RIGHT(2..RIGHT'LAST));
end "abs";


function ">=" (LEFT, RIGHT: UNIVERSAL_INTEGER)
            return BOOLEAN is
   Z : constant UNIVERSAL_INTEGER := LEFT - RIGHT;
begin
   return Z(1) >= 0;
end ">=";


function ">" (LEFT, RIGHT: UNIVERSAL_INTEGER)
            return BOOLEAN is
   Z : constant UNIVERSAL_INTEGER := LEFT - RIGHT;
begin
   return Z(1) > 0;
end ">";


function "<=" (LEFT, RIGHT: UNIVERSAL_INTEGER)
            return BOOLEAN is
   Z : constant UNIVERSAL_INTEGER := LEFT - RIGHT;
begin
   return Z(1) <= 0;
end "<=";


function "<" (LEFT, RIGHT: UNIVERSAL_INTEGER)
            return BOOLEAN is
   Z : constant UNIVERSAL_INTEGER := LEFT - RIGHT;
begin
   return Z(1) < 0;
end "<";


function EQ (LEFT, RIGHT: UNIVERSAL_INTEGER)
            return BOOLEAN is
begin
   return LEFT.all = RIGHT.all;
end EQ;
```

```
function IMAGE (VALUE: UNIVERSAL_INTEGER)
               return STRING is
   M    : INTEGER := VALUE'LENGTH * BASE_D + 1;
   S    : STRING (1 .. M);
   Y    : UNIVERSAL_INTEGER := abs VALUE;
   J, D : INTEGER;
begin
   if VALUE(1) = 0 then
      return " 0";
   end if;

   J := M;

   while Y(1) /= 0 loop
      D := TO_INTEGER(Y rem I_TEN);
      Y := Y / I_TEN;
      S(J) := CHARACTER'VAL(CHARACTER'POS('0') + D);
      J := J - 1;
   end loop;

   if VALUE(1) < 0 then
      S(J) := '-';
   else
      S(J) := ' ';
   end if;

   D := M - J + 1;
   S (1 .. D) := S (J .. M);   -- Ensures string starts at index 1
   return S (1 .. D);
end IMAGE;


function VALUE (IMAGE : STRING)
               return UNIVERSAL_INTEGER is
   I_16      : constant UNIVERSAL_INTEGER
                        := TO_UNIVERSAL_INTEGER (16);
   NUM       : UNIVERSAL_INTEGER := I_ZERO;
   NUM_BASE  : UNIVERSAL_INTEGER := I_ZERO;
   V         : UNIVERSAL_INTEGER;
   EXP       : INTEGER := 0;
   J, VV     : INTEGER;
   SIGNED    : BOOLEAN := FALSE;
   HAS_EXP   : BOOLEAN := FALSE;
```

3.3 - Universal Integer Arithmetic

```
BASED_LIT : BOOLEAN := FALSE;
BETWEEN   : BOOLEAN := FALSE;   -- True if between sharps
CH        : CHARACTER;

function NUMERIC (C : CHARACTER) return BOOLEAN is
begin
   if (C in '0'..'9') or (C in 'A'..'F')
     or (C in 'a'..'f') then
      return TRUE;
   else
      return FALSE;
   end if;
end NUMERIC;

procedure PROCESS_LETTER (C : CHARACTER) is
begin                  -- Only capital letters are passed
   if BETWEEN then     -- in between the sharps
      V := TO_UNIVERSAL_INTEGER
        (CHARACTER'POS (C) -
         CHARACTER'POS ('A') + 10);
      if V >= NUM_BASE then
         raise CONSTRAINT_ERROR;
      end if;
      NUM := NUM * NUM_BASE + V;
   else   -- Must be an exponent
      if C /= 'E' then
         raise CONSTRAINT_ERROR;
      end if;
      if HAS_EXP or else
        (IMAGE(J-1) not in '0' .. '9'
         and IMAGE(J-1) /= '#') then
         raise CONSTRAINT_ERROR;
      end if;
      HAS_EXP := TRUE;
      if not BASED_LIT then
         NUM_BASE := I_TEN;      -- default base is 10
      end if;
      if IMAGE (J+1) = '+' then
         J := J + 1;
         if IMAGE (J+1) not in '0' .. '9' then
            raise CONSTRAINT_ERROR;
         end if;
      elsif IMAGE (J+1) not in '0' .. '9' then
```

```ada
            raise CONSTRAINT_ERROR;
         end if;
      end if;
   end PROCESS_LETTER;

begin
   if IMAGE'LENGTH = 0 then
      raise CONSTRAINT_ERROR;
   end if;

   J  := IMAGE'FIRST;
   CH := IMAGE (J);
   while CH = ' ' loop
      J  := J + 1;
      CH := IMAGE (J);
   end loop;

   if CH = '-' or CH = '+' then
      J := J + 1;
      if IMAGE (J) not in '0' .. '9' then
         raise CONSTRAINT_ERROR;
      end if;
      SIGNED := CH = '-';
   end if;

   while J <= IMAGE'LAST loop
      CH := IMAGE(J);
      case CH is
         when '0' .. '9' =>
            VV := CHARACTER'POS(CH) -
                  CHARACTER'POS('0');
            if HAS_EXP then
               EXP := EXP * 10 + VV;
            else
               V := TO_UNIVERSAL_INTEGER (VV);
               if BASED_LIT then
                  if V >= NUM_BASE then
                     raise CONSTRAINT_ERROR;
                  else
                     NUM := NUM * NUM_BASE + V;
                  end if;
               else
                  NUM := NUM * I_TEN + V;
```

3.3 - Universal Integer Arithmetic

```ada
         end if;
      end if;

   when '_' =>
      if not NUMERIC (IMAGE (J-1))
        or else not NUMERIC (IMAGE (J+1)) then
         raise CONSTRAINT_ERROR;
      end if;

   when 'a' .. 'f' =>
      PROCESS_LETTER (
        CHARACTER'VAL (CHARACTER ' POS(CH) -
        (CHARACTER'POS('a') -
         CHARACTER'POS('A'))));

   when 'A' .. 'F' =>
      PROCESS_LETTER (CH);

   when ' ' =>
      exit;    -- exit the while loop

   when '#' =>
      if BASED_LIT then
         if not BETWEEN then
            -- third sharp
            raise CONSTRAINT_ERROR;
         else
            -- second sharp
            if IMAGE (J-1) = '#' then
               -- two sharps together
               raise CONSTRAINT_ERROR;
            end if;
            BETWEEN := FALSE;
         end if;
      else                           -- first sharp
         if NUM < I_TWO or NUM > I_16 then
            raise CONSTRAINT_ERROR;
         end if;
         BASED_LIT := TRUE;
         BETWEEN   := TRUE;   -- Between sharps
         NUM_BASE  := NUM;
         NUM := I_ZERO;
      end if;
```

```ada
            when others =>
                raise CONSTRAINT_ERROR;
         end case;
         J := J + 1;
      end loop;

      if BETWEEN then   -- only one sharp found
         raise CONSTRAINT_ERROR;
      end if;

      if HAS_EXP then
         NUM := NUM * NUM_BASE ** EXP;
      end if;

      if SIGNED then
         NUM := - NUM;
      end if;
      return NUM;
   end VALUE;


   function SIGN (RIGHT: UNIVERSAL_INTEGER)
                  return INTEGER is
   begin
      if RIGHT (1) = 0 then
         return 0;
      elsif RIGHT (1) < 0 then
         return -1;
      else
         return +1;
      end if;
   end SIGN;


   function ORDER_OF (RIGHT: UNIVERSAL_INTEGER)
                      return UNIVERSAL_INTEGER is
      R1 : constant INTEGER := abs RIGHT (1);
      I  : INTEGER := BASE;
      C  : INTEGER := BASE_D;
   begin
      if R1 = 0 then
         raise NUMERIC_ERROR;
      end if;
```

3.3 - Universal Integer Arithmetic

```
      while I > R1 loop
         I := I / 10;  -- result is always 1 or a multiple of 10
         C := C - 1;
      end loop;
      return  TO_UNIVERSAL_INTEGER (RIGHT'LENGTH - 1)
              * TO_UNIVERSAL_INTEGER (BASE_D)
              + TO_UNIVERSAL_INTEGER (C);
   end ORDER_OF;

end UNIVERSAL_INTEGER_ARITHMETIC_PKG;
```

3.4   UNIVERSAL REAL ARITHMETIC

Description

This package provides all the normal facilities of real (floating-point) arithmetic on arbitrarily large values. It depends on the Universal Integer package shown above.

Reals are stored in the rational form A/B, where A and B are Universal Integers. Extremely small numbers may be stored with very high precision, while retaining full arithmetic capabilities.

This package is portable to all machines from 8-bit INTEGER size upwards.

The largest value that can be stored in an Universal Real is the same as for Universal Integers. The smallest positive values that may be stored are the reciprocals of those values.

Dependencies

This component depends on the Universal Integer package, which it WITHs in.

Minimum Implementable Package

Many of the facilities are optional in that they may be removed without affecting the rest of the package.

The functions SIGN and ORDER_OF may be readily left out. So may NUMERATOR and DENOMINATOR. The functions IMAGE and/or VALUE may also be omitted if not needed.

3.4 - Universal Real Arithmetic

Component Specification

```ada
with UNIVERSAL_INTEGER_ARITHMETIC_PKG, SYSTEM;
use  UNIVERSAL_INTEGER_ARITHMETIC_PKG;

package UNIVERSAL_REAL_ARITHMETIC_PKG is
   type UNIVERSAL_REAL is private;

   R_ZERO: constant UNIVERSAL_REAL;
   R_ONE : constant UNIVERSAL_REAL;
   R_TEN : constant UNIVERSAL_REAL;

   function "+"  (LEFT, RIGHT : UNIVERSAL_REAL)
                    return UNIVERSAL_REAL;
   function "-"  (LEFT, RIGHT : UNIVERSAL_REAL)
                    return UNIVERSAL_REAL;
   function "*"  (LEFT, RIGHT : UNIVERSAL_REAL)
                    return UNIVERSAL_REAL;
   function "/"  (LEFT, RIGHT : UNIVERSAL_REAL)
                    return UNIVERSAL_REAL;

   function "**" (LEFT  : UNIVERSAL_REAL;
                  RIGHT : INTEGER) return UNIVERSAL_REAL;

   function "*"  (LEFT  : UNIVERSAL_INTEGER;
                  RIGHT : UNIVERSAL_REAL)
                    return UNIVERSAL_REAL;
   function "*"  (LEFT  : UNIVERSAL_REAL;
                  RIGHT : UNIVERSAL_INTEGER)
                    return UNIVERSAL_REAL;

   function "/"  (LEFT  : UNIVERSAL_REAL;
                  RIGHT : UNIVERSAL_INTEGER)
                    return UNIVERSAL_REAL;

   function "-"  (RIGHT : UNIVERSAL_REAL)
                    return UNIVERSAL_REAL;

   function "abs"(RIGHT : UNIVERSAL_REAL)
                    return UNIVERSAL_REAL;

   function ">=" (LEFT, RIGHT : UNIVERSAL_REAL)
                    return BOOLEAN;
```

3.4 - Universal Real Arithmetic

```
function ">"   (LEFT, RIGHT : UNIVERSAL_REAL)
                  return BOOLEAN;
function "<="  (LEFT, RIGHT : UNIVERSAL_REAL)
                  return BOOLEAN;
function "<"   (LEFT, RIGHT : UNIVERSAL_REAL)
                  return BOOLEAN;
function EQ    (LEFT, RIGHT : UNIVERSAL_REAL)
                  return BOOLEAN;
```

-- SIGN returns -1, 0 or +1
```
function SIGN (RIGHT : UNIVERSAL_REAL) return INTEGER;
```

-- ORDER_OF returns the exponent of the first power of ten smaller
-- than abs(RIGHT)
```
function ORDER_OF (RIGHT : UNIVERSAL_REAL)
                                     return UNIVERSAL_INTEGER;
```

-- The following function converts to Universal Integer by rounding
```
function TO_UNIVERSAL_INTEGER
           (FROM_UNIVERSAL_REAL : UNIVERSAL_REAL)
                                     return UNIVERSAL_INTEGER;

function TO_UNIVERSAL_REAL
           (NUMERATOR, DENOMINATOR : UNIVERSAL_INTEGER)
                                     return UNIVERSAL_REAL;
function TO_UNIVERSAL_REAL
           (FROM_UNIVERSAL_INTEGER : UNIVERSAL_INTEGER)
                                     return UNIVERSAL_REAL;

function NUMERATOR   (RIGHT : UNIVERSAL_REAL)
                                     return UNIVERSAL_INTEGER;
function DENOMINATOR (RIGHT : UNIVERSAL_REAL)
                                     return UNIVERSAL_INTEGER;
```

-- MIN_DIGITS must be at least 2
```
function IMAGE (VALUE      : UNIVERSAL_REAL;
                MIN_DIGITS : INTEGER
                           := SYSTEM.MAX_DIGITS)
                                     return STRING;
function VALUE (IMAGE : STRING) return UNIVERSAL_REAL;
```

3.4 - Universal Real Arithmetic

```
private
   type UNIVERSAL_REAL is
      record
         NUM: UNIVERSAL_INTEGER;
         DEN: UNIVERSAL_INTEGER;
      end record;

   R_ZERO : constant UNIVERSAL_REAL := (I_ZERO, I_ONE);
   R_ONE  : constant UNIVERSAL_REAL := (I_ONE , I_ONE);
   R_TEN  : constant UNIVERSAL_REAL := (I_TEN , I_ONE);

end UNIVERSAL_REAL_ARITHMETIC_PKG;
```

Pragmatics

The operations defined on Universal Reals are those defined on floating point variables in section 4 of the ALRM, with additions: IMAGE, VALUE, SIGN, ORDER_OF, and the conversion functions to and from Universal Integers.

The EQ function corresponds to the predefined equality "=" on standard Floating Point.

The IMAGE and VALUE functions are analogous to the 'IMAGE and 'VALUE attributes of standard integer types (they are not defined in the ALRM for non-discrete types).

VALUE takes a string parameter defined in the same way as real literals (ALRM 2.4), with the following improvement. The radix point (if supplied) need not be the second character in a decimal or based literal; the only requirement is that it be embedded in digits.

IMAGE provides a string in the form of a decimal literal with exponent (see ALRM 2.4.1) and is preceded by a minus sign if appropriate. The precision with which the mantissa is supplied depends on an integer parameter that defaults to the compiler-dependent quantity SYSTEM.MAX_DIGITS (which is the maximum precision in a standard float).

SIGN returns -1, 0 or +1, depending on the sign of the parameter supplied.

ORDER_OF returns the exponent of the greatest power of ten no larger than the absolute value of the parameter supplied. This is mathematically equivalent to the integer part (the characteristic) of the logarithm (to the base ten) of the absolute value of the parameter.

An attempt to evaluate an Universal Real which has a zero denominator will result in NUMERIC_ERROR. An attempt to evaluate an uninitialised Universal Real should be regarded as erroneous, in the same way as the evaluation of any other uninitialised type. Normally such a use will result in CONSTRAINT_ERROR, but that should not be relied upon.

In order to economise on space, the numerator and denominator of Universal Reals are always divided by their greatest common divisors before storing. However, users should be aware that large amounts of storage can be taken up by great precision as well as by great magnitude. For example, if X = 10 ** 9_999, then the number represented by (X-1)/X is very close to one but will require twenty kilobytes of storage.

Restrictions on use

None

Exceptions

This package raises exceptions in equivalent situations to standard floats: for example, dividing a Universal Real by zero will raise NUMERIC_ERROR.

Because of the flexibility of Universal Reals, it is almost impossible to get an overflow condition which results, with conventional representations, in NUMERIC_ERROR. However, if Universal Reals of sufficient magnitude (or sufficient precision and without common factors in numerator and denominator) are operated on, then an overflow can occur which will be signalled by CONSTRAINT_ERROR (assuming that STORAGE_ERROR is not raised first).

The specific exceptions that may be raised, other than STORAGE_ERROR, are:

CONSTRAINT_ERROR :
Many functions   -   Universal Real Overflow (in theory)
VALUE   -   Non-numeric literal

3.4 - Universal Real Arithmetic

NUMERIC_ERROR:
TO_UNIVERSAL_REAL - Zero denominator
"/"   - Division by zero
"**"   - Zero to a negative Exponent
ORDER_OF   - Zero parameter

Options

The package could be extended by a number of mathematical functions, including reciprocal, lowest common denominator, etc.

Example of use

A square root approximation function :

```
with UNIVERSAL_INTEGER_ARITHMETIC_PKG,
     UNIVERSAL_REAL_ARITHMETIC_PKG;
use  UNIVERSAL_INTEGER_ARITHMETIC_PKG,
     UNIVERSAL_REAL_ARITHMETIC_PKG;
function SQRT (X : UNIVERSAL_REAL;
               I : INTEGER ) return UNIVERSAL_REAL is
-- Using Newton-Raphson. The algorithm can be shown to converge from
-- above provided that the first guess at the root of X is above it. The processing
-- continues until the approximation ESTIMATE to the root of X is such that
-- the interval between two successive approximations is less than: ( 10 ** I )
    I_TWO : constant UNIVERSAL_INTEGER
                        := TO_UNIVERSAL_INTEGER (2);
    EPS   : constant UNIVERSAL_REAL := R_TEN ** I;
    LAST_EST, ESTIMATE : UNIVERSAL_REAL;
begin
    if SIGN (X) /= +1 then
       raise NUMERIC_ERROR;
    end if;
    ESTIMATE := (X + R_ONE) / I_TWO;
    loop
       LAST_EST := ESTIMATE;
       ESTIMATE := (ESTIMATE + X/ESTIMATE) / I_TWO;
       exit when (LAST_EST - ESTIMATE) < EPS;
    end loop;
    return ESTIMATE;
end SQRT;
```

Implementation points

Universal reals are stored as pairs of universal integers representing numerator and denominator. The sign is always stored in the numerator. The largest value that can theoretically be stored in a Universal Real is exactly the same as for a Universal Integer, when that value will be in the numerator and I_ONE in the denominator.
No changes need be made to the Universal Real package to cope with the differing sizes of integer representations on different machines.

It is not possible to declare, in the front of the package body, Universal Real constants in terms of the results of a call to TO_UNIVERSAL_REAL, because that function has not been elaborated at that point.

Note that it is not possible to declare EQ as an "=" operator because the UNIVERSAL_REAL type is a private type rather than a limited private type. The "=" operator must not be used; it will not yield the same value as EQ.

The 'VALUE attribute is not defined in the ALRM for non-discrete types. The VALUE function provided here caters for strings that may or may not contain a radix point. If the point is considered mandatory for the Universal Real package, then the statements following
  case *'.'* =>
in the middle of function VALUE should be changed to:
  raise CONSTRAINT_ERROR;

Rounding of values, where appropriate, is per the ALRM. The 'IMAGE attribute is not defined in the ALRM for non-discrete types: as implemented, IMAGE truncates rather than rounds.

Efficiency

The relationship between runtime performance and size of operand for the various subprograms is as follows (for large values of num, the numerator, and den, the denominator):

	Time dependent on:
TO_UNIVERSAL_REAL (single parameter), SIGN, NUMERATOR, DENOMINATOR	Constant

3.4 - Universal Real Arithmetic

TO_UNIVERSAL_REAL (double parameter)	log(num) * log(den)
ORDER_OF, ABS, unary "-", TO_UNIVERSAL_INTEGER	log(num)
EQ,">","<","<=",">=","+","-"	log(num1)*log(den2) + log(num2)*log(den1) + log(den1)*log(den2)
VALUE	length of string
"*"	log(num1) * log(num2) + log(den1) * log(den2)
"/"	log(num1) * log(den2) + log(num2) * log(den1)

The time for IMAGE depends on a function that is better than d^2, where d is the number of digits required.

The time for operation "**" (Exponentiation) depends on
(1) $\log^2(\text{num}) + \log^2(\text{den})$
(2) a function of the exponent that is better than x^2 but not as good as $x.\log(x)$.

N.B. For multiplication and division operations between Universal Reals and Universal Integers, there is no second denominator den2, and so log(den2) may be taken as equal to zero (which consequently simplifies the appropriate expression).

Package Body

```
with UNIVERSAL_INTEGER_ARITHMETIC_PKG;
pragma ELABORATE (UNIVERSAL_INTEGER_ARITHMETIC_PKG);

package body UNIVERSAL_REAL_ARITHMETIC_PKG is

    I_TWO : constant UNIVERSAL_INTEGER
                    := TO_UNIVERSAL_INTEGER(2);
    I_16  : constant UNIVERSAL_INTEGER
                    := TO_UNIVERSAL_INTEGER(16);
    R_TWO : constant UNIVERSAL_REAL := (I_TWO, I_ONE);
```

```
function TO_UNIVERSAL_REAL
          (NUMERATOR, DENOMINATOR : UNIVERSAL_INTEGER)
                              return UNIVERSAL_REAL
```

-- Constructs a universal real as the ratio of two universal integers.
-- Raises NUMERIC_ERROR when value of DENOMINATOR is zero

-- Every real number produced as a result of an operation defined in
-- this package must have a positive denominator, and the numerator
-- and denominator must be reduced to lowest terms. This ensures
-- uniqueness of representation

```
    R, Y, Z :   UNIVERSAL_INTEGER;

begin
    if EQ (DENOMINATOR, I_ZERO) then
        raise NUMERIC_ERROR;
    elsif EQ (NUMERATOR, I_ZERO) then
        return R_ZERO;
    end if;

    -- Now reduce to lowest terms; that is, find the greatest
    -- common divisor of numerator and denominator

    Y := abs NUMERATOR;
    Z := abs DENOMINATOR;

    loop
        R := Y rem Z;
        exit when EQ (R, I_ZERO);
        Y := Z;
        Z := R;
    end loop;

    if SIGN (DENOMINATOR) >= 0 then
        return ( NUMERATOR/Z,  DENOMINATOR/Z);
    else
        return (-NUMERATOR/Z, -DENOMINATOR/Z);
    end if;

end TO_UNIVERSAL_REAL;
```

3.4 - Universal Real Arithmetic

```
function TO_UNIVERSAL_INTEGER
          (FROM_UNIVERSAL_REAL: UNIVERSAL_REAL)
                              return UNIVERSAL_INTEGER is
   I      :  constant UNIVERSAL_INTEGER
                    := FROM_UNIVERSAL_REAL.NUM /
                       FROM_UNIVERSAL_REAL.DEN;
   R      :  constant UNIVERSAL_REAL := (I, I_ONE);
   R_HALF :  constant UNIVERSAL_REAL := (I_ONE, I_TWO);
begin
   if EQ (FROM_UNIVERSAL_REAL.NUM, I_ZERO) then
      return I_ZERO;
   elsif SIGN (FROM_UNIVERSAL_REAL.NUM) = -1
   and then FROM_UNIVERSAL_REAL -R <= -R_HALF then
      return I - I_ONE;
   elsif SIGN (FROM_UNIVERSAL_REAL.NUM) = +1
   and then FROM_UNIVERSAL_REAL - R >=  R_HALF then
      return I + I_ONE;
   else
      return I;
   end if;
end TO_UNIVERSAL_INTEGER;


function TO_UNIVERSAL_REAL
          (FROM_UNIVERSAL_INTEGER :  UNIVERSAL_INTEGER)
                              return UNIVERSAL_REAL is
begin
   return (FROM_UNIVERSAL_INTEGER, I_ONE);
end TO_UNIVERSAL_REAL;


function "+" (LEFT, RIGHT : UNIVERSAL_REAL)
                              return UNIVERSAL_REAL is
begin
   return TO_UNIVERSAL_REAL
          (LEFT.NUM*RIGHT.DEN + RIGHT.NUM*LEFT.DEN,
                               LEFT.DEN*RIGHT.DEN);
end "+";


function "-" (LEFT, RIGHT: UNIVERSAL_REAL)
                              return UNIVERSAL_REAL is
begin
```

```
      return LEFT + (-RIGHT);
   end "-";


   function "*" (LEFT, RIGHT: UNIVERSAL_REAL)
                                      return UNIVERSAL_REAL
   begin
      return TO_UNIVERSAL_REAL (LEFT.NUM * RIGHT.NUM,
                                LEFT.DEN * RIGHT.DEN);
   end "*";


   function "/" (LEFT, RIGHT: UNIVERSAL_REAL)
                                      return UNIVERSAL_REAL
   begin
      return TO_UNIVERSAL_REAL (LEFT.NUM*RIGHT.DEN,
                                LEFT.DEN*RIGHT.NUM);
   end "/";



   function "**"(LEFT  : UNIVERSAL_REAL;
                RIGHT : INTEGER) return UNIVERSAL_REAL i
   begin
      if RIGHT = 0 then
         return R_ONE;
      elsif RIGHT > 0 then
         return TO_UNIVERSAL_REAL (LEFT.NUM ** RIGHT,
                                   LEFT.DEN ** RIGHT);
      else
         return TO_UNIVERSAL_REAL (LEFT.DEN ** (-RIGHT),
                                   LEFT.NUM ** (-RIGHT));
      end if;
   end "**";



   function "*" (LEFT  : UNIVERSAL_INTEGER;
                 RIGHT : UNIVERSAL_REAL)
                                      return UNIVERSAL_REAL i
   begin
      return TO_UNIVERSAL_REAL (RIGHT.NUM * LEFT,
                                RIGHT.DEN);
   end "*";
```

3.4 - Universal Real Arithmetic

```
function "*" (LEFT  : UNIVERSAL_REAL;
              RIGHT : UNIVERSAL_INTEGER)
                              return UNIVERSAL_REAL is
begin
    return TO_UNIVERSAL_REAL (LEFT.NUM * RIGHT,
                              LEFT.DEN);
end "*";


function "/" (LEFT  : UNIVERSAL_REAL;
              RIGHT : UNIVERSAL_INTEGER)
                              return UNIVERSAL_REAL is
begin
    return TO_UNIVERSAL_REAL (LEFT.NUM,
                              LEFT.DEN * RIGHT);
end "/";


function "-" (RIGHT : UNIVERSAL_REAL)
                              return UNIVERSAL_REAL is
begin
   return (-RIGHT.NUM, RIGHT.DEN);
end "-";


function "abs" (RIGHT : UNIVERSAL_REAL)
                              return UNIVERSAL_REAL is
begin
   return (abs RIGHT.NUM, RIGHT.DEN);
end "abs";


function ">=" (LEFT, RIGHT : UNIVERSAL_REAL)
                              return BOOLEAN is
   Z : constant UNIVERSAL_REAL := LEFT - RIGHT;
begin
   return SIGN (Z.NUM) /= -1;
end ">=";


function ">"  (LEFT, RIGHT : UNIVERSAL_REAL)
                                 return BOOLEAN is
   Z : constant UNIVERSAL_REAL := LEFT - RIGHT;
```

```ada
begin
   return SIGN (Z.NUM) = +1;
end ">";


function "<=" (LEFT, RIGHT : UNIVERSAL_REAL)
                                          return BOOLEAN i
   Z : constant UNIVERSAL_REAL := LEFT - RIGHT;
begin
   return SIGN (Z.NUM) /= +1;
end "<=";


function "<" (LEFT, RIGHT : UNIVERSAL_REAL)
                                          return BOOLEAN i
   Z : constant UNIVERSAL_REAL := LEFT - RIGHT;
begin
   return SIGN (Z.NUM) = -1;
end "<";


function EQ (LEFT, RIGHT : UNIVERSAL_REAL)
                                          return BOOLEAN is
   Z : constant UNIVERSAL_REAL := LEFT - RIGHT;
begin
   return EQ (Z.NUM, I_ZERO);
end EQ;


function NUMERATOR (RIGHT : UNIVERSAL_REAL)
                                 return UNIVERSAL_INTEGER
begin
   return RIGHT.NUM;
end NUMERATOR;


function DENOMINATOR (RIGHT : UNIVERSAL_REAL)
                                 return UNIVERSAL_INTEGER
begin
    return RIGHT.DEN;
end DENOMINATOR;
```

3.4 - Universal Real Arithmetic

```ada
function SIGN (RIGHT : UNIVERSAL_REAL)
                              return INTEGER is
begin
   return SIGN (RIGHT.NUM);
end SIGN;


function ORDER_OF (RIGHT : UNIVERSAL_REAL)
                              return UNIVERSAL_INTEGER is
begin
   if EQ (RIGHT.DEN, I_ZERO) then
      raise NUMERIC_ERROR;
   end if;
   if abs RIGHT.NUM >= RIGHT.DEN then
      return ORDER_OF (RIGHT.NUM / RIGHT.DEN);
   else
      return - I_ONE - ORDER_OF ((RIGHT.DEN - I_ONE)
                                 / RIGHT.NUM);
   end if;
end ORDER_OF;


function IMAGE
           (VALUE      : UNIVERSAL_REAL;
            MIN_DIGITS : INTEGER := SYSTEM.MAX_DIGITS)
                              return STRING is
   R : UNIVERSAL_REAL := VALUE;
   N : UNIVERSAL_INTEGER;

   function ZEROES (N : NATURAL) return STRING is
      Z : STRING (1 .. N) := (others => '0');
   begin
      return Z;
   end ZEROES;

   function MANTISSA_STRING (S : STRING) -- containing integer
                              return STRING is
   -- This returns S with a full stop (period) after the first character
   begin
      return S (1 .. 2) & '.' & S (3 .. S'LAST);
   end MANTISSA_STRING;
```

```
    function EXPONENT_STRING (S : STRING)  -- containing intege
                                          return STRING
begin
   if S (1) = ' ' then
      return 'E' & S (2 .. S'LAST);
   else
      return 'E' & S;
   end if;
end EXPONENT_STRING;

function POWER_OF_TEN (U : UNIVERSAL_INTEGER)
                              return UNIVERSAL_REAL i
   ILAST : constant UNIVERSAL_INTEGER :=
                    TO_UNIVERSAL_INTEGER (INTEGER'LAST
   IREM  : UNIVERSAL_INTEGER := abs (U);
   I     : UNIVERSAL_INTEGER := I_ONE;
begin

   -- It is possible for U to exceed INTEGER'LAST
   while IREM >= ILAST loop
      I := I * I_TEN ** INTEGER'LAST;
      IREM := IREM - ILAST;
   end loop;
   if IREM /= I_ZERO then
      I := I * I_TEN ** TO_INTEGER (IREM);
   end if;
   if SIGN (U) /= -1 then
      return TO_UNIVERSAL_REAL (I, I_ONE);
   else
      return TO_UNIVERSAL_REAL (I_ONE, I);
   end if;
end POWER_OF_TEN;

begin  -- IMAGE
   if MIN_DIGITS < 2 then
     raise CONSTRAINT_ERROR;
   end if;
   if EQ (R.NUM, I_ZERO) then
     return " 0." & ZEROES (MIN_DIGITS - 1) & "E0";
   end if;
   N := ORDER_OF (R);
   R := R * POWER_OF_TEN
           (TO_UNIVERSAL_INTEGER (MIN_DIGITS - 1) - N);
```

3.4 - Universal Real Arithmetic

```ada
    return MANTISSA_STRING (IMAGE (R.NUM / R.DEN)) &
           EXPONENT_STRING (IMAGE (N));
end IMAGE;


function VALUE (IMAGE: STRING) return UNIVERSAL_REAL is

    NUM        : UNIVERSAL_INTEGER := I_ZERO;
    DEN        : UNIVERSAL_INTEGER := I_ONE;
    NUM_BASE   : UNIVERSAL_INTEGER := I_TEN;  -- Default
    V          : UNIVERSAL_INTEGER;
    EXP        : INTEGER := 0;
    J, VV      : INTEGER;
    PLACES     : INTEGER := 0;  -- Count of figures after radix point
    SIGNED     : BOOLEAN := FALSE;
    POINTED    : BOOLEAN := FALSE;  -- True if radix point found
    HAS_EXP    : BOOLEAN := FALSE;
    NEG_EXP    : BOOLEAN := FALSE;
    BASED_LIT  : BOOLEAN := FALSE;
    BETWEEN    : BOOLEAN := FALSE;  -- True if between sharps
    CH         : CHARACTER;

    function NUMERIC (C : CHARACTER) return BOOLEAN is
    begin
        if (C in '0'..'9') or (C in 'A'..'F') or
           (C in 'a'..'f') then
            return TRUE;
        else
            return FALSE;
        end if;
    end NUMERIC;

    procedure PROCESS_LETTER (C : CHARACTER) is
    begin      -- Only capital letters are passed in
        if BETWEEN then  -- Between the sharps
            V := TO_UNIVERSAL_INTEGER
                   (CHARACTER'POS (C) - CHARACTER'POS ('A')
                    + 10);
            if V >= NUM_BASE then
                raise CONSTRAINT_ERROR;
            end if;
            NUM := NUM * NUM_BASE + V;
            if POINTED then
```

```ada
                    PLACES := PLACES + 1;
                end if;
            else    -- Must be an exponent
                if C /= 'E' then
                    raise CONSTRAINT_ERROR;
                end if;
                if HAS_EXP or else
                    (IMAGE(J-1) not in '0' .. '9' and
                     IMAGE(J-1) /= '#') then
                    raise CONSTRAINT_ERROR;
                end if;
                HAS_EXP := TRUE;
                if not BASED_LIT then
                    NUM_BASE := I_TEN;      -- default base is 10
                end if;
                if IMAGE (J+1) = '+' then
                    J := J + 1;
                    if IMAGE (J+1) not in '0' .. '9' then
                        raise CONSTRAINT_ERROR;
                    end if;
                elsif IMAGE (J+1) = '-' then
                    J := J + 1;
                    NEG_EXP := TRUE;
                    if IMAGE (J+1) not in '0' .. '9' then
                        raise CONSTRAINT_ERROR;
                    end if;
                elsif IMAGE (J+1) not in '0' .. '9' then
                    raise CONSTRAINT_ERROR;
                end if;
            end if;
        end PROCESS_LETTER;

begin     -- VALUE
    if IMAGE'LENGTH = 0 then
        raise CONSTRAINT_ERROR;
    end if;

    J := IMAGE'FIRST;
    CH := IMAGE (J);
    while CH = ' ' loop
        J := J + 1;
        CH := IMAGE (J);
    end loop;
```

3.4 - Universal Real Arithmetic

```ada
if CH = '-' or CH = '+' then
   J := J + 1;
   if IMAGE (J) not in '0' .. '9' then
      raise CONSTRAINT_ERROR;
   end if;
   SIGNED := CH = '-';
end if;

while J <= IMAGE'LAST loop
   CH := IMAGE(J);

   case CH is
      when '0' .. '9' =>
         VV := CHARACTER'POS(CH) -
               CHARACTER'POS('0');
         if HAS_EXP then
            EXP := EXP * 10 + VV;
         else
            V := TO_UNIVERSAL_INTEGER (VV);
            if BASED_LIT then
               if V >= NUM_BASE then
                  raise CONSTRAINT_ERROR;
               else
                  NUM := NUM * NUM_BASE + V;
               end if;
            else
               NUM := NUM * I_TEN + V;
            end if;
            if POINTED then
               PLACES := PLACES + 1;
            end if;
         end if;

      when '.' =>
         -- Check to ensure that the period is followed by a digit,
         -- preceded by a digit, that a previous radix point
         -- has not been seen, that the period is not in an exponent
         if not NUMERIC (IMAGE (J+1))
           or else not NUMERIC (IMAGE (J-1))
           or else POINTED
           or else HAS_EXP then
             raise CONSTRAINT_ERROR;
```

```ada
      end if;
      POINTED := TRUE;

   when '_' =>
      if not NUMERIC (IMAGE (J-1))
      or else not NUMERIC (IMAGE (J+1)) then
         raise CONSTRAINT_ERROR;
      end if;

   when 'a' .. 'f' =>
      PROCESS_LETTER (
        CHARACTER'VAL (CHARACTER'POS(CH) -
        (CHARACTER'POS('a') -
        CHARACTER'POS('A'))));

   when 'A' .. 'F' =>
      PROCESS_LETTER (CH);

   when ' ' =>
      exit;    -- exit the while loop

   when '#' =>
      if BASED_LIT then
         if not BETWEEN then   -- third sharp
            raise CONSTRAINT_ERROR;
         else                       -- second sharp
            if IMAGE (J-1) = '#' then
               -- two sharps together
               raise CONSTRAINT_ERROR;
            end if;
            BETWEEN := FALSE;
         end if;
      else                    -- first sharp
         if NUM < I_TWO or NUM > I_16 then
            raise CONSTRAINT_ERROR;
         end if;
         if POINTED then
            -- radix point not permitted in radix
            raise CONSTRAINT_ERROR;
         end if;
         BASED_LIT := TRUE;
         BETWEEN   := TRUE;   -- Between sharps
         NUM_BASE  := NUM;
```

3.4 - Universal Real Arithmetic

```
                    NUM := I_ZERO;

              end if;

          when others =>
              raise CONSTRAINT_ERROR;
        end case;
        J := J + 1;
     end loop;

     if BETWEEN then   -- only one sharp
        raise CONSTRAINT_ERROR;
     end if;

     if POINTED then
        DEN := NUM_BASE ** PLACES;
     end if;

     if HAS_EXP then
        if NEG_EXP then
           DEN := DEN * NUM_BASE ** EXP;
        else
           NUM := NUM * NUM_BASE ** EXP;
        end if;
     end if;

     if SIGNED then
        NUM := - NUM;
     end if;
     return TO_UNIVERSAL_REAL (NUM , DEN);
  end VALUE;

end UNIVERSAL_REAL_ARITHMETIC_PKG;
```

3.5 FLEXIBLE QUEUES

Description

This component provides routines to manipulate three kinds of data storage construct:

Stack - Provides storage on a last-in-first-out (LIFO) basis, i.e. the item most recently added is the next item retrieved.

Queue - Sometimes known as a pipe, a queue provides storage on a first-in-first-out (FIFO) basis, i.e. the earliest item added is the next item retrieved.

Deque - (Pronounced "deck") provides a combination of queue and stack access methods. Items can be placed or retrieved from either "end" of the deque.

The term "flexible queue" is used to refer to any of these three storage constructs. Within the code, the term "flexi-queue" is sometimes used.

Three main sets of facilities are provided. They are :

Data Manipulation	- Adding and removing items from a flexible queue, and flushing all items.
Queue Characteristics	- Enquiring whether the flexible queue is empty or full, how many items are held within it, and an ability to set a maximum permissible number of items held.
Collection of Statistics	- Reading statistics about the flexible queue, e.g. the number of times it has been accessed, and what its average length has been since the statistics were last read.

In addition, it is possible to control the manner in which heap memory is recycled.

3.5 - Flexible Queues

The data type of the objects held in each of the storage constructs is supplied through a generic parameter.

Dependencies

External : None.
Internal : The first three subprograms within the package body are used throughout the rest of the code.

Minimum Implementable Package

Statistics gathering may be removed.

The package can be reduced so as to support only a single storage construct.

Component Specification

Two package specifications are shown in this section. The reasons for the use of two packages in this implementation of the facility is described in the section on pragmatics.

```
package FQ_TYPES_PKG is
   type FQ_CLASS_TYPE is (QUEUE_CLASS,
                          STACK_CLASS,
                          DEQUE_CLASS);
end FQ_TYPES_PKG;



with FQ_TYPES_PKG;
use  FQ_TYPES_PKG;
generic
   FQ_CLASS : FQ_CLASS_TYPE;
   AUTOMATIC_DEALLOCATION_ENABLED : BOOLEAN;
   type ITEM_TYPE is private;   -- The item being stored

package FQ_PACKAGE is
   STATS_ERROR         : exception;
   TYPE_ERROR          : exception;
   PUSH_ERROR          : exception;
```

```ada
POP_ERROR              : exception;
LEN_LIMIT_ERROR        : exception;

type STATS_TYPE is
   record
      TIMES_ACCESSED : NATURAL := 0;
      MAX_LEN        : NATURAL := 0;
      MIN_LEN        : NATURAL := 0;
      MEAN_LEN       : FLOAT   := 0.0;  -- Sum of lengths / times
                                        -- accessed since last
                                        -- statistics read
      MS_DIFF_LEN : FLOAT      := 0.0;  -- Mean square difference
                                        -- between actual and me
                                        -- flexi-queue length
   end record;


type FQ_TYPE is limited private;

type TOP_OR_BOTTOM_TYPE is (TOP,BOTTOM);

procedure PUSH_Q (Q            : in out FQ_TYPE;
                  PUSHED_ITEM  : in     ITEM_TYPE);

procedure PUSH_DEQ
             (DEQ          : in out FQ_TYPE;
              PUSHED_ITEM  : in     ITEM_TYPE;
              END_OF_DEQ   : in     TOP_OR_BOTTOM_TYP

procedure PUSH_STACK (STACK        : in out FQ_TYPE;
                      PUSHED_ITEM  : in     ITEM_TYPE)

procedure POP_Q (Q            : in out FQ_TYPE;
                 POPPED_ITEM  :    out ITEM_TYPE);

procedure POP_DEQ
             (DEQ          : in out FQ_TYPE;
              POPPED_ITEM  :    out ITEM_TYPE;
              END_OF_DEQ   : in     TOP_OR_BOTTOM_TYP

procedure POP_STACK (STACK        : in out FQ_TYPE;
                     POPPED_ITEM  :    out ITEM_TYPE);
```

3.5 - Flexible Queues

```ada
function IS_EMPTY   (FQ : in FQ_TYPE) return BOOLEAN;
function IS_FULL    (FQ : in FQ_TYPE) return BOOLEAN;

procedure FLUSH     (FQ : in out FQ_TYPE);

procedure SET_LEN_LIMIT (FQ      : in out FQ_TYPE;
                         MAX_LEN : in     POSITIVE);

function CURRENT_LEN (FQ : in FQ_TYPE) return NATURAL;

procedure DEALLOCATE (FQ : in out FQ_TYPE);
-- Must be used before allowing the flexi-queue to pass out of scope

procedure READ_STATS  (FQ        : in out FQ_TYPE;
                       OUT_STATS :    out STATS_TYPE);

private
   type ITEM_HOLDER_TYPE;
   type ITEM_HOLDER_REF_TYPE is access ITEM_HOLDER_TYPE;
   type ITEM_HOLDER_TYPE is
      record
         ITEM         : ITEM_TYPE;
         FORWARD_REF  : ITEM_HOLDER_REF_TYPE;
         BACKWARD_REF : ITEM_HOLDER_REF_TYPE;
      end record;
   -- See Implementation points

   type INT_STATS_TYPE is
      record
         FAILED : BOOLEAN := FALSE;  -- See pragmatics
         MS_LEN : FLOAT   := 0.0;    -- Mean square of number of
                                     -- current items
      end record;
   -- Holds the internal statistical values that are not available to
   -- the users, but necessary for the calculations

   type FQ_TYPE is
      record
         LEN       : INTEGER := 0;            -- Current number of items held
                                              -- in the flexi-queue
         LEN_LIMIT : INTEGER := INTEGER'LAST; -- Maximum permissible
                                              -- number of items
```

```
            STATS       : STATS_TYPE;       -- Running stats values
            INT_STATS   : INT_STATS_TYPE;   -- Implementation
                                            -- specific statistics
                                            -- working values
            TOP_REF     : ITEM_HOLDER_REF_TYPE;  -- See impl. point
            BOTTOM_REF  : ITEM_HOLDER_REF_TYPE;  --  "   "    "
            SPARE_REF   : ITEM_HOLDER_REF_TYPE;  --  "   "    "
      end record;
end FQ_PACKAGE;
```

Pragmatics

Use of two packages
The main generic package requires a generic parameter to control its operation regarding the use of Queues, Stacks or Deques. In order to utilise an enumeration type for this parameter, rather than an integer, an enumeration type has been defined, and made visible to both the generic specification and body, and to the instantiating code. The simplest implementation is to place the generic unit inside a further package which contains the type declarations. However, in testing this implementation, it was found that certain validated compilers (or rather their linkers) were not happy with this construction. When faced with the choice between portability and "good" Ada programming style, the former was considered to be more important here.

Dynamic Memory Usage
The routine DEALLOCATE should be used prior to a flexible queue object passing out of scope. See Implementation Points.

Errors Generated By Statistics Gathering
The statistics part of the package can suffer from numeric overflow problems (see below). If one occurs, it does not affect the data storage aspect of the component. The exception STATS_ERROR will be raised during a subsequent call to the READ_STATS procedure. Within the body of the READ_STATS procedure, an attempt is made to reset all the working values, as well as the flag indicating the existence of the error. This ensures that the calculations refer to the characteristics of the flexible queue since the last call to READ_STATS.

There are only two conditions that can cause these problems with the statistics calculations: The first is when the number of accesses that have occurred since the last call to read the statistics is greater than

3.5 - Flexible Queues

INTEGER'LAST. This situation is a distinct possibility. The second cause of a numeric overflow error can occur during the calculation of the internal working values, specifically the new mean square flexible queue length. If the square of the flexible queue's current length is greater than FLOAT'LAST then a numeric overflow error will be raised. This can only occur with compilers where FLOAT'LAST < (INTEGER'LAST)^2. This was not the case on any of the compilers used to test the component. It would have to be a very strange compiler implementation to allow this situation to exist, but it is conceivable. Examination of compiler documentation should establish if the condition can occur.

If the length of the flexible queue when READ_STATS is called is such that its square can not be held in a type FLOAT, then the error condition can not be cleared. This is because the working value (mean square length) cannot be reset without an overflow occurring. Sufficient items must be removed, and another READ_STATS performed, or else the use of the statistics should be abandoned. As it can be determined from the compiler documentation whether or not this problem can arise, the package was not made to be resilient to this type of problem.

None of these "errors" affect the data holding characteristics of the flexible queue.

Restrictions on use

The generic package FQ_PACKAGE may not be instantiated for unconstrained types, nor for types which are **limited private.**

Exceptions

Five exceptions may be raised by the generic package.

STATS_ERROR   Only raised during a READ_STATS call. If raised, it indicates that the statistics calculations could not be completed. The data storage facilities are not impaired. The error flag is cleared after having raised this exception, provided the square of the current length of the flexible queue is less then FLOAT'LAST.

TYPE_ERROR   Raised by attempting to use a push or pop procedure for a package which was instantiated for a different class of flexible queue than was indicated by that particular procedure.

PUSH_ERROR   Raised by a call to any of the push procedures when a flexible queue already has its maximum number of entries, as controlled by the SET_LEN_LIMIT routine.

POP_ERROR   Raised when attempting to remove an item off a flexible queue when it is empty, using a pop procedure.

LEN_LIMIT_ERROR   Raised when attempting to set the maximum length of a flexible queue to a value less than the current length.

In cases where more than one of the above error conditions occurs, the precedence is from the first to the last as shown above.

In addition to the exceptions declared in the package described above, CONSTRAINT_ERROR can be raised by attempting to set a length limit of 0 or less. Finally, adding items to a flexible queue uses memory, hence a STORAGE_ERROR may be raised by the RTS.

Options

Additional statistics gathering capability can be added. If this is undertaken, then the subprograms which require alteration are :
   UPDATE_STATS
   READ_STATS
   DEALLOCATE
In addition, if a new working variable is required, then this must be added to the declaration of the record type INT_STATS_TYPE. Also the data type STATS_TYPE may be altered.

The runtime overhead of statistics gathering may be removed by editing UPDATE_STATS, or by removing the calls to this procedure within the package body.

Example of Use

The following example is taken from the area of real time computer operating systems. It illustrates the use of some of the simpler facilities provided by the FQ_PACKAGE in handling a set of objects, called processes. A process is a job which a real time operating system must provide with a resource, such as the computer's processing capability. Associated with each process is a level of priority.

A procedure (BLOCK) is supplied which would be called when the current process has had its quota of computer processing time.

A second procedure (NEXT_PROCESS) is supplied which returns the identifier of the process of the highest priority which has been blocked for the longest time. This would be called having blocked the current process, in order to establish which process should now be started.

Within the body of the PROCESS_QUEUE_PACKAGE, an array of queues is declared, one for each priority level. When BLOCK is called, the identifier is pushed on to the relevant queue. By scanning from high to low priority, looking for a queue which holds a process identifier, the next process is selected.

```
package PROCESS_QUEUE_PACKAGE is
    -- Maintains a set of priority queues, that are used to hold process IDs for
    -- a multi-user environment. Twenty priority levels are provided, 1..20,
    -- where the NEXT_PROCESS function returns the oldest, highest priority
    -- PROCESS_ID that has been stored

    subtype NAME_TYPE     is STRING (1..10);
    subtype PRIORITY_TYPE is INTEGER range 1..20;
    type    PROCESS_TYPE  is
       record
          NAME     : NAME_TYPE;
          PRIORITY : PRIORITY_TYPE;
       end record;

    procedure BLOCK (PROCESS : in PROCESS_TYPE);
    function  NEXT_PROCESS return PROCESS_TYPE;

end;
```

```ada
with FQ_PACKAGE;
with FQ_TYPES_PKG;

package body PROCESS_QUEUE_PACKAGE is

   package Q_PACKAGE is new FQ_PACKAGE
      (FQ_TYPES_PKG.QUEUE_CLASS,TRUE,PROCESS_TYPE);
   use Q_PACKAGE;
   PROCESS_QUEUES : array (PRIORITY_TYPE) of FQ_TYPE;

   procedure BLOCK (PROCESS : in PROCESS_TYPE ) is
   begin
      PUSH_Q (PROCESS_QUEUES (PROCESS.PRIORITY), PROCESS)
   end;

   function NEXT_PROCESS return PROCESS_TYPE is
      NEXT : PROCESS_TYPE;
   begin
      for I in PRIORITY_TYPE
      loop
         if not IS_EMPTY (PROCESS_QUEUES (I))
         then
            POP_Q (PROCESS_QUEUES(I), NEXT);
            return NEXT;
         end if;
      end loop;
   end;
begin
   null;
end;
```

Implementation Points

Use of AUTOMATIC_DEALLOCATION_ENABLED parameter
When the parameter AUTOMATIC_DEALLOCATION_ENABLED in the generic specification is set to TRUE, this causes the package to invoke an instance of the compiler provided UNCHECKED_DEALLOCATION subprogram whenever an item is removed from a flexible queue. If it is set to FALSE, then the package retains items within the structure of each flexible queue object, and preferentially uses these recycled items whenever a subsequent item is added to the flexible queue. Thus, when set to

3.5 - Flexible Queues

FALSE, the memory allocated to the flexible queue object cannot exceed the value reached when the maximum number of items were held in the object. No progressive use of heap (heap creep) can occur, as the implementation does not rely upon invocations of UNCHECKED_DEALLOCATION. Thus the RTS is not relied upon for effective garbage collection.

This does, however, mean that even when all the stored items have been popped off the flexible queue (or even flushed), memory is still allocated to the flexible queue object, in the form of item holders. Prior to the object passing out of scope, it is very important that these holders are recycled back into the heap storage by the RTS. The only way to do this is to call the subprogram DEALLOCATE, provided within the generic package.

As a matter of good programming technique, it is strongly recommended that subprogram DEALLOCATE should always be called before the flexible queue object passes out of scope, irrespective of the value supplied to the AUTOMATIC_DEALLOCATION_ENABLED generic parameter.

Use of Pointers

The flexible queue object data type (FQ_TYPE) uses three access types in order to store the items.

An item holder type is declared which holds one instance of an item, and has forward and backward access types, capable of pointing to further item holders.

The three access types within the flexible queue object are used as follows:

- BOTTOM_REF points to the first of a double linked list of item holders.

- TOP_REF points to the last of the same double linked list.

- The item holder's FORWARD_REF access type is used in the direction of BOTTOM_REF to TOP_REF. The item holder's BACKWARD_REF access type links in the opposite direction.

- The two end pointers in the double linked list are left as **null**.

- SPARE_REF is used as the bottom of a list of (spare) item holders, using only the FORWARD_REF access types. In this list, all the BACKWARD_REF access types are set to **null**.

Efficiency

The performance of the facilities is largely dependent upon the length of the flexible queue, i.e. how many items are contained within the object.

For each subprogram, the following table shows how the run time performance is related to the size of the flexible queue, i.e. the number of items it contains (denoted as 'n').

PUSH_Q	constant
PUSH_DEQ	constant
PUSH_STACK	constant
POP_Q	constant
POP_DEQ	constant
POP_STACK	constant
IS_EMPTY	constant
IS_FULL	constant
FLUSH	n
SET_LEN_LIMIT	constant
CURRENT_LEN	constant
DEALLOCATE	see note below
READ_STATS	constant

Note: If the generic parameter controlling memory recycling, AUTOMATIC_DEALLOCATION_ENABLED, has been set to FALSE then popped items will be kept within the flexible queue. DEALLOCATE's performance is dependent upon the total number of items which are held in the queue object, both those for current items, and those which are being recycled due to the automatic deallocation choice.

Package Body

```
with UNCHECKED_DEALLOCATION;
package body FQ_PACKAGE is

   type UPDATE_TYPE is
        (PUSH_UPDATE, POP_UPDATE, FLUSH_UPDATE);

   procedure UPDATE_STATS (FQ      : in out FQ_TYPE;
                           UPDATE  : in     UPDATE_TYPE )
       SCALE           : FLOAT;
```

3.5 - Flexible Queues

```
   NEW_MEAN           : FLOAT;
   NEW_MS_LEN         : FLOAT;
   NEW_MS_DIFF_LEN    : FLOAT;
   FQ_STATES          : INTEGER;
begin
   if FQ.INT_STATS.FAILED
   then
      return;
   end if;

   FQ.STATS.TIMES_ACCESSED := FQ.STATS.TIMES_ACCESSED+1;
   FQ_STATES               := FQ.STATS.TIMES_ACCESSED+1;
   case UPDATE is
      when PUSH_UPDATE =>
         -- Update Max length
         if FQ.LEN > FQ.STATS.MAX_LEN
         then
            FQ.STATS.MAX_LEN := FQ.LEN;
         end if;

      when POP_UPDATE =>
         -- Update min length
         if FQ.LEN < FQ.STATS.MIN_LEN
         then
            FQ.STATS.MIN_LEN := FQ.LEN;
         end if;

      when FLUSH_UPDATE =>
         -- Update min length
            FQ.STATS.MIN_LEN := 0;
   end case;

   SCALE   :=  (FLOAT(FQ_STATES) - 1.0)/
               (FLOAT(FQ_STATES));

   -- Determine new mean length value
   NEW_MEAN := SCALE * FQ.STATS.MEAN_LEN +
               (FLOAT(FQ.LEN) / FLOAT(FQ_STATES));

   -- Determine new mean square length
   NEW_MS_LEN := SCALE * FQ.INT_STATS.MS_LEN +
                 ((FLOAT(FQ.LEN) / FLOAT(FQ_STATES)) *
                 FLOAT(FQ.LEN));
```

```
        -- Hence determine new mean square difference
        NEW_MS_DIFF_LEN := NEW_MS_LEN - NEW_MEAN * NEW_MEAN

        -- There has been no numerical overflow so update statistics values
        FQ.INT_STATS.MS_LEN     := NEW_MS_LEN;
        FQ.STATS.MEAN_LEN       := NEW_MEAN;
        FQ.STATS.MS_DIFF_LEN    := NEW_MS_DIFF_LEN;

    exception
        -- Any numeric or constraint error means that the statistics calculations
        -- have failed in some manner. The flag in the internal statistics field
        -- of the flexi-queue is set to stop future calculations, and to cause an
        -- exception to be raised when READ_STATS is called

        when NUMERIC_ERROR | CONSTRAINT_ERROR =>
            FQ.INT_STATS.FAILED := TRUE;
end UPDATE_STATS;


procedure ITEM_HOLDER_DEALLOCATE
    is new UNCHECKED_DEALLOCATION (ITEM_HOLDER_TYPE,
                                   ITEM_HOLDER_REF_TYPE


procedure PUSH
        (FQ              : in out FQ_TYPE;
         PUSHED_ITEM     : in     ITEM_TYPE;
         END_OF_FQ       : in     TOP_OR_BOTTOM_TYPE) is

    NEW_ITEM_HOLDER_REF : ITEM_HOLDER_REF_TYPE;

begin

    -- Make sure there is no overflow of the flexi-queue
    if FQ.LEN >= FQ.LEN_LIMIT
    then
        raise PUSH_ERROR;
    end if;

    -- Increment length and update the statistics
    FQ.LEN := FQ.LEN + 1;
    UPDATE_STATS (FQ, PUSH_UPDATE);
```

3.5 - Flexible Queues

```
-- Start the insertion by first obtaining an ITEM_HOLDER, preferably
-- from the spare list. If there are none, then create one
if FQ.SPARE_REF = null
then
    NEW_ITEM_HOLDER_REF := new ITEM_HOLDER_TYPE;
else
    -- Free an ITEM_HOLDER, maintaining the pointers
    NEW_ITEM_HOLDER_REF := FQ.SPARE_REF;
    FQ.SPARE_REF        := FQ.SPARE_REF.FORWARD_REF;
end if;

-- Put the item into the freed item holder
NEW_ITEM_HOLDER_REF.ITEM := PUSHED_ITEM;

-- Now insert the item holder into the flexi-queue's double linked list
case END_OF_FQ is
    when BOTTOM =>
        if FQ.BOTTOM_REF = null
        then
            FQ.BOTTOM_REF := NEW_ITEM_HOLDER_REF;
            FQ.TOP_REF    := NEW_ITEM_HOLDER_REF;
        else
            NEW_ITEM_HOLDER_REF.FORWARD_REF :=
                FQ.BOTTOM_REF;
            FQ.BOTTOM_REF.BACKWARD_REF :=
                NEW_ITEM_HOLDER_REF;
            FQ.BOTTOM_REF := NEW_ITEM_HOLDER_REF;
        end if;
    when TOP =>
        if FQ.TOP_REF = null
        then
            FQ.TOP_REF    := NEW_ITEM_HOLDER_REF;
            FQ.BOTTOM_REF := NEW_ITEM_HOLDER_REF;
        else
            FQ.TOP_REF.FORWARD_REF :=
                NEW_ITEM_HOLDER_REF;
            NEW_ITEM_HOLDER_REF.BACKWARD_REF :=
                FQ.TOP_REF;
            FQ.TOP_REF := NEW_ITEM_HOLDER_REF;
        end if;
end case;
end PUSH;
```

3.5 - Flexible Queues

```ada
procedure POP
            (FQ                     : in out FQ_TYPE;
             POPPED_ITEM           :     out ITEM_TYPE;
             END_OF_FQ              : in     TOP_OR_BOTTOM_TYPE)
   POPPED_ITEM_HOLDER_REF : ITEM_HOLDER_REF_TYPE;
begin

   -- Make sure that there is an item to pop
   if FQ.LEN = 0
   then
      raise POP_ERROR;
   end if;

   -- Decrement the length and update the statistics
   FQ.LEN := FQ.LEN - 1;
   UPDATE_STATS (FQ, POP_UPDATE);

   -- Remove the item holder from the flexi-queue's double linked list
   case END_OF_FQ is
      when TOP =>
          POPPED_ITEM_HOLDER_REF := FQ.TOP_REF;
          FQ.TOP_REF := FQ.TOP_REF.BACKWARD_REF;
          if FQ.TOP_REF /= null
          then
             FQ.TOP_REF.FORWARD_REF := null;
          else
             FQ.BOTTOM_REF := null;
          end if;

      when BOTTOM =>
          POPPED_ITEM_HOLDER_REF := FQ.BOTTOM_REF;
          FQ.BOTTOM_REF := FQ.BOTTOM_REF.FORWARD_REF;
          if FQ.BOTTOM_REF /= null
          then
             FQ.BOTTOM_REF.BACKWARD_REF := null;
          else
             FQ.TOP_REF := null;
          end if;
   end case;

   -- Copy the item into the return parameter
   POPPED_ITEM := POPPED_ITEM_HOLDER_REF.ITEM;
```

3.5 - Flexible Queues

```
-- Put the empty item holder into the flexi-queue's spare list or use the
-- RTS's UNCHECKED_DEALLOCATION function, depending upon
-- the memory management option selected
if AUTOMATIC_DEALLOCATION_ENABLED
then
   ITEM_HOLDER_DEALLOCATE (POPPED_ITEM_HOLDER_REF);
else
   POPPED_ITEM_HOLDER_REF.BACKWARD_REF := null;
   POPPED_ITEM_HOLDER_REF.FORWARD_REF  :=
      FQ.SPARE_REF;
   FQ.SPARE_REF := POPPED_ITEM_HOLDER_REF;
end if;
end POP;


procedure PUSH_Q (Q            : in out FQ_TYPE;
               PUSHED_ITEM : in      ITEM_TYPE) is
begin
   if FQ_CLASS = QUEUE_CLASS
   then
      PUSH (Q, PUSHED_ITEM, BOTTOM);
   else
      raise TYPE_ERROR;
   end if;
end PUSH_Q;


procedure PUSH_DEQ
         (DEQ          : in out FQ_TYPE;
          PUSHED_ITEM : in      ITEM_TYPE;
          END_OF_DEQ  : in      TOP_OR_BOTTOM_TYPE) is
begin
   if FQ_CLASS = DEQUE_CLASS
   then
      PUSH (DEQ, PUSHED_ITEM, END_OF_DEQ);
   else
      raise TYPE_ERROR;
   end if;
end PUSH_DEQ;
```

```ada
   procedure PUSH_STACK
                     (STACK        : in out FQ_TYPE;
                      PUSHED_ITEM  : in     ITEM_TYPE) is
   begin
      if FQ_CLASS = STACK_CLASS
      then
         PUSH (STACK, PUSHED_ITEM, TOP);
      else
         raise TYPE_ERROR;
      end if;
   end PUSH_STACK;


   procedure POP_Q (Q            : in out FQ_TYPE;
                    POPPED_ITEM  : out    ITEM_TYPE) is
   begin
      if FQ_CLASS = QUEUE_CLASS
      then
         POP (Q, POPPED_ITEM, TOP);
      else
         raise TYPE_ERROR;
      end if;
   end POP_Q;


   procedure POP_DEQ
              (DEQ          : in out FQ_TYPE;
               POPPED_ITEM  : out    ITEM_TYPE;
               END_OF_DEQ   : in     TOP_OR_BOTTOM_TYPE) is
   begin
      if FQ_CLASS = DEQUE_CLASS
      then
         POP (DEQ, POPPED_ITEM, END_OF_DEQ);
      else
         raise TYPE_ERROR;
      end if;
   end POP_DEQ;


   procedure POP_STACK (STACK        : in out FQ_TYPE;
                        POPPED_ITEM  :    out ITEM_TYPE) is
   begin
      if FQ_CLASS = STACK_CLASS
```

3.5 - Flexible Queues

```
       then
          POP (STACK, POPPED_ITEM, TOP);
       else
          raise TYPE_ERROR;
       end if;
    end POP_STACK;


    function IS_EMPTY (FQ : in FQ_TYPE) return BOOLEAN is
    begin
       return FQ.LEN = 0;
    end IS_EMPTY;


    function IS_FULL (FQ : in FQ_TYPE) return BOOLEAN is
    begin
       return FQ.LEN = FQ.LEN_LIMIT;
    end IS_FULL;


    procedure FLUSH (FQ : in out FQ_TYPE) is
       FLUSHED_ITEM_HOLDER_REF : ITEM_HOLDER_REF_TYPE;
    begin
       -- Set the current flexi-queue length to zero and maintain statistics
       FQ.LEN := 0;
       UPDATE_STATS (FQ, FLUSH_UPDATE);
       -- Either transfer all of the items held on the flexi-queue's double linked list
       -- onto the spare list, or use the RTS's UNCHECKED_DEALLOCATION
       -- function, depending upon the memory management option selected
       loop
          exit when FQ.TOP_REF = null;
          if AUTOMATIC_DEALLOCATION_ENABLED
          then
             FLUSHED_ITEM_HOLDER_REF := FQ.TOP_REF;
             FQ.TOP_REF := FQ.TOP_REF.BACKWARD_REF;
             if FQ.TOP_REF /= null then
                FQ.TOP_REF.FORWARD_REF := null;
             end if;
             ITEM_HOLDER_DEALLOCATE
               (FLUSHED_ITEM_HOLDER_REF);
          else
             FQ.TOP_REF.FORWARD_REF := FQ.SPARE_REF;
             FQ.SPARE_REF := FQ.TOP_REF;
```

```
              FQ.TOP_REF      := FQ.TOP_REF.BACKWARD_REF;
              FQ.SPARE_REF.BACKWARD_REF := null;
              if FQ.TOP_REF /= null
              then
                  FQ.TOP_REF.FORWARD_REF := null;
              else
                  FQ.BOTTOM_REF := null;
              end if;
          end if;
      end loop;
end FLUSH;


procedure SET_LEN_LIMIT (FQ      : in out FQ_TYPE;
                         MAX_LEN : in     POSITIVE) is
begin
    if MAX_LEN < FQ.LEN
    then
        raise LEN_LIMIT_ERROR;
    end if;
    FQ.LEN_LIMIT := MAX_LEN;
end SET_LEN_LIMIT;


function  CURRENT_LEN
          (FQ : in FQ_TYPE) return NATURAL is
begin
    return FQ.LEN;
end CURRENT_LEN;


procedure DEALLOCATE (FQ : in out FQ_TYPE) is
    DEAD_ITEM_REF : ITEM_HOLDER_REF_TYPE;
begin
    -- Deallocate all item holders on the spare list
    loop
        exit when FQ.SPARE_REF = null;
        DEAD_ITEM_REF := FQ.SPARE_REF;
        FQ.SPARE_REF  := FQ.SPARE_REF.FORWARD_REF;
        ITEM_HOLDER_DEALLOCATE (DEAD_ITEM_REF);
    end loop;
```

3.5 - Flexible Queues

```ada
-- Deallocate all the item holders on the double linked list
loop
   exit when FQ.BOTTOM_REF = null;
   DEAD_ITEM_REF := FQ.BOTTOM_REF;
   FQ.BOTTOM_REF := FQ.BOTTOM_REF.FORWARD_REF;
   if FQ.BOTTOM_REF /= null
   then
       FQ.BOTTOM_REF.BACKWARD_REF := null;
   end if;
   ITEM_HOLDER_DEALLOCATE (DEAD_ITEM_REF);
end loop;

-- Clear all flexi-queue fields back to the start point
FQ := (TOP_REF       => null,
       BOTTOM_REF    => null,
       SPARE_REF     => null,
       LEN           => 0,
       LEN_LIMIT     => INTEGER'LAST,
       INT_STATS     => (FAILED          => FALSE,
                         MS_LEN          => 0.0 ),
       STATS         => (TIMES_ACCESSED  => 0,
                         MAX_LEN         => 0,
                         MIN_LEN         => 0,
                         MEAN_LEN        => 0.0,
                         MS_DIFF_LEN     => 0.0));
end DEALLOCATE;


procedure READ_STATS (FQ         : in out FQ_TYPE;
                      OUT_STATS  :    out STATS_TYPE) is
   TEMP_INT_STATS : INT_STATS_TYPE;
begin
   -- Return the accumulated statistics, and reset all the internal
   -- values so that they are calculated from a fresh start

   OUT_STATS := FQ.STATS;

   FQ.STATS := (TIMES_ACCESSED => 0,
                MAX_LEN        => FQ.LEN,
                MIN_LEN        => FQ.LEN,
                MEAN_LEN       => FLOAT(FQ.LEN),
                MS_DIFF_LEN    => 0.0);
```

3.5 - Flexible Queues

```
            -- Calculate the new mean square length to enable trapping
            -- of the error that may be raised due to integer overflow

            TEMP_INT_STATS := (FAILED => FALSE,
                              MS_LEN => FLOAT(FQ.LEN) *
                                        FLOAT(FQ.LEN));

            -- If the FQ.INT_STATS.FAILED flag is set to TRUE, then this indicates
            -- that an error has occurred in the calculation of the statistics since the
            -- last call to this routine. Clear the internal statistics values indicating
            -- the flag, and raise STATS_ERROR
            if FQ.INT_STATS.FAILED
            then
                FQ.INT_STATS := TEMP_INT_STATS;
                raise STATS_ERROR;
            else
                FQ.INT_STATS := TEMP_INT_STATS;
            end if;

        exception

            when NUMERIC_ERROR | CONSTRAINT_ERROR =>

                -- This exception handler will only be entered if the MS_LEN cannot
                -- be set to FQ_LEN squared. See implementation points
                FQ.INT_STATS := (FAILED => TRUE,
                                 MS_LEN => 0.0);
        end READ_STATS;

begin
    null;
end FQ_PACKAGE;
```

3.6 TREES

Description

This package provides the facility to manipulate trees of objects. The package does not assume or maintain any relationship between the structure of a tree and the "value" of the items held within each node of the tree. The topology of a tree is controlled directly by the user of this package.

The type of the object held at each node, plus the degree of the tree (number of branches coming from a node) are provided as generic actual parameters to this generic package.

The facilities provided by the package are split into four categories as follows:

    Tree manipulation   - to alter the structure of the tree.
    Data value manipulation - to alter or read the data values associated with a particular node in the tree.
    Pointer Manipulation - to point at different nodes in a tree.
    Condition Test - exception avoidance
    Management facilities - memory management control and safety control

A data type, POSITION_TYPE, is defined. This provides the facility to refer to a particular node within the tree by declaring an object of this type and causing it to point to a particular location in the tree. There is a significant difficulty (see pragmatics) in using position objects following deletion of a node or restructuring of the tree. The program therefore has a default mode where <u>all</u> position objects become unusable if the structure of the tree is altered. In this mode each position object has to be reset before use. This mode can be suppressed, but at the users risk.

A wide range of exceptions may be raised by the package due to the extensive run time protection present.

3.6 - Trees

Dependencies

External : None.
Internal : The routines make extensive cross calls in order to keep the replication of code to a minimum.

Minimum Implementable Package

The boolean functions may be removed. They are present to enable the user of the package to avoid raising exceptions.

EXTRACT_TREE and INSERT_TREE may be removed if not required.

In principle, the WRITE_DATA procedure could be removed, as the INSERT_NODE procedure allows for the initialisation of a node's value item. However, the size of this routine is so small that there is little benefit from its removal.

Component Specification

```
generic
   type DATA_TYPE is private;
   DEGREE        : POSITIVE;  -- Must be 2 or greater
package GENERIC_UNSORTED_TREE_PKG is
   subtype CHILD_TYPE is NATURAL range 0..DEGREE;
   SELF         : constant CHILD_TYPE := 0;
   FIRST_CHILD  : constant CHILD_TYPE := 1;
   LAST_CHILD   : constant CHILD_TYPE := DEGREE;

   type TREE_REF_TYPE is private;
   type POSITION_TYPE is private;

   -- Tree Manipulation Subprograms

   procedure CREATE_TREE  (TREE : in out TREE_REF_TYPE);

   procedure DESTROY_TREE (TREE : in out TREE_REF_TYPE);

   procedure DUPLICATE_TREE
                  (POSITION : in      POSITION_TYPE;
                   TO_TREE  : in out TREE_REF_TYPE);
```

```
procedure INSERT_NODE (POSITION : in out POSITION_TYPE
                       CHILD    : in      CHILD_TYPE;
                       DATA     : in      DATA_TYPE);

procedure DELETE_NODE
              (POSITION : in POSITION_TYPE;
               CHILD    : in CHILD_TYPE := SELF);

procedure EXTRACT_TREE
              (POSITION : in      POSITION_TYPE;
               CHILD    : in      CHILD_TYPE := SELF;
               TO_TREE  : in out  TREE_REF_TYPE);

procedure INSERT_TREE
              (POSITION  : in     POSITION_TYPE;
               CHILD     : in     CHILD_TYPE;
               FROM_TREE : in out TREE_REF_TYPE);
```

-- *Data Manipulation Subprograms*

```
procedure READ_DATA   (POSITION : in      POSITION_TYPE
                       DATA     :     out DATA_TYPE);

procedure WRITE_DATA  (POSITION : in      POSITION_TYPE
                       DATA     : in      DATA_TYPE);
```

-- *Pointer Manipulation Subprograms*

```
procedure SET_TO_ROOT (TREE     : in      TREE_REF_TYPE,
                       POSITION :     out POSITION_TYPE)

procedure GOTO_PARENT (POSITION : in out POSITION_TYPE)

procedure GOTO_CHILD  (POSITION : in out POSITION_TYPE;
                       CHILD    : in     CHILD_TYPE);
```

-- *Condition Testing Subprograms*

```
function CHILD_EXISTS (POSITION : in POSITION_TYPE;
                       CHILD    : in CHILD_TYPE)
                              return BOOLEAN;
```

3.6 - Trees

```ada
function TREE_HAS_BEEN_CREATED
        (TREE : in TREE_REF_TYPE)         return BOOLEAN;

function IS_OBSOLETE
        (POSITION : in POSITION_TYPE) return BOOLEAN;

function POSITION_HAS_BEEN_SET
        (POSITION : in POSITION_TYPE) return BOOLEAN;
```

-- *Management Facilities Subprograms*

```ada
procedure WHICH_TREE (POSITION : in       POSITION_TYPE;
                      TO_TREE  : in out TREE_REF_TYPE);

procedure VERSION_CHECK (TREE    : in out TREE_REF_TYPE;
                         ENABLED : in       BOOLEAN);

function VERSION_CHECK_ENABLED
        (TREE : TREE_REF_TYPE) return BOOLEAN;

procedure DEALLOCATE   (TREE : in out TREE_REF_TYPE);
```

-- *Exceptions*

```ada
NODE_DOES_NOT_EXIST_ERROR   : exception;
NODE_ALREADY_EXISTS_ERROR   : exception;
CHILDREN_EXIST_ERROR        : exception;
INVALID_CHILD_ERROR         : exception;
POSITION_NOT_SET_ERROR      : exception;
TREE_CREATION_ERROR         : exception;
DEST_TREE_CREATED_ERROR     : exception;
AT_ROOT_ERROR               : exception;
OBSOLETE_POSITION_ERROR     : exception;
```

private

```ada
    type NODE_TYPE;
    type NODE_REF_TYPE is access NODE_TYPE;
    type CHILDREN_REF_TYPE is array
       (CHILD_TYPE range FIRST_CHILD .. LAST_CHILD)
       of NODE_REF_TYPE;
```

```
    type NODE_TYPE is record
        DATA          : DATA_TYPE;
        PARENT_REF    : NODE_REF_TYPE;      -- null for root node
        CHILDREN_REF  : CHILDREN_REF_TYPE;  -- Array of pointers
                                            -- to children
    end record;

    type VERSION_TYPE is new INTEGER;
    type TREE_TYPE is record
        ROOT    : NODE_REF_TYPE;  -- Null when no root node
        VERSION : VERSION_TYPE := VERSION_TYPE'FIRST;
        CHECKING_ENABLED : BOOLEAN := TRUE;
    end record;

    type TREE_REF_TYPE is access TREE_TYPE;
    type POSITION_TYPE is record
        NODE_REF  : NODE_REF_TYPE;  -- Null prior to SET_TO_ROOT
        VERSION   : VERSION_TYPE;
        TREE_COPY : TREE_REF_TYPE;  -- Null prior to SET_TO_ROOT
    end record;
end GENERIC_UNSORTED_TREE_PKG;
```

Pragmatics

An explanation of terms associated with trees is given later.

Tree Manipulation Subprograms

CREATE_TREE
Called to initialise tree objects. Necessary before a tree can be used for any of the other subprograms, except TREE_HAS_BEEN_CREATED.

DESTROY_TREE
The opposite of CREATE_TREE, it removes all items in the tree. To reuse the tree object requires a call to the CREATE_TREE procedure.

DUPLICATE_TREE
Takes an initialised tree and creates a duplicate of part or all of that tree. The root of the new tree is specified by the value of the POSITION parameters. The destination tree, TO_TREE, must not have been initialised.

INSERT_NODE
This routine inserts a single node into a spare slot in a tree. At the same time, data is inserted into the new node. The position at which the node is inserted is specified by the value of the POSITION and CHILD parameters. To insert the first, or root, node, the position object must be set to point to an empty tree. In this case, the CHILD parameter is ignored.

DELETE_NODE
This routine removes a node from the tree. The node to be removed is specified by the value of the POSITION and CHILD parameters. The node must have no occupied children.

EXTRACT_TREE
This routine prunes a branch from a tree, at a position specified by the values of the POSITION and CHILD parameters. It creates a new tree with the pruned part. By using CHILD set to SELF, and a position set to point at the root node, the entire tree may be extracted.

INSERT_TREE
This routine takes a tree and transfers its nodes into another tree at a point specified by the value of the POSITION and CHILD parameters. The source tree is empty on return from this subprogram.

Data Value Manipulation Subprograms

READ_DATA
This routine returns a copy of the data value stored in a particular node specified by the value of the POSITION parameter.

WRITE_DATA
This routine overwrites the data value stored in a particular node specified by the value of the POSITION parameter.

Pointer Manipulation Subprograms

SET_TO_ROOT
This routine is the means by which position objects are initialised. The value of the position object returned is such that it can be considered to point to the root node of the specific tree. If the tree has no nodes, then the object can point to a non-existent node. An empty tree is the only case where a position object is permitted to point to an unoccupied position in a tree.

GOTO_PARENT
This routine is used to alter the node to which a position object is pointing. When called, the position object's value is altered such that it points to the node's parent.

GOTO_CHILD
This routine is used to alter the node to which a position object is pointing. When called, the position object's value is altered such that it points to the child of the node specified. This child must be occupied by a node. It is not possible to use this routine to cause a position object to point to an empty node in the tree.

Condition Test Subprograms

CHILD_EXISTS
This boolean function checks whether the particular child of a node is occupied, as specified by the values of the POSITION and CHILD parameters.

TREE_HAS_BEEN_CREATED
This boolean function checks whether a tree object has been initialised (see CREATE_TREE above).

IS_OBSOLETE
This boolean function checks whether the tree pointed to by the POSITION parameter has had its structure altered such as to render unusable all POSITION objects pointing to that tree (see Pointing to a Node below).

POSITION_HAS_BEEN_SET
This boolean function checks whether a position object has been initialised to point to a tree (see SET_TO_ROOT above).

Management Facilities Subprograms

WHICH_TREE
This routine returns a copy of the tree object to which a position object has been set (see SET_TO_ROOT above).

VERSION_CHECK
This routine enables or disables the checking of whether or not a tree has had its structure altered, and hence allows or disallows the raising of OBSOLETE_POSITION_ERROR (see Pointing to a Node below). By default, version checking is enabled.

3.6 - Trees

VERSION_CHECK_ENABLED
This boolean function checks whether version checking is enabled (see VERSION_CHECK above).

DEALLOCATE
This routine is used to ensure that all the memory allocated to a tree is recycled back into the RTS's heap, by forcing UNCHECKED_DEALLOCATION to be invoked, in accordance with the standards employed in this book (see Appendix F). The routine is superfluous with the current implementation, as the DELETE_ITEM procedure calls the necessary routines as standard. However, if an internal memory recycling technique is introduced (see Options) then this routine will be required.

Pointing to a node
The user of this package may declare any number of position objects for a particular tree. If more than one of these "pointers" are set up to point to a particular node, and the node is deleted, then there is a problem: How should the user be protected from using the now invalid pointers ?

It was decided in the implementation of this package, that a safe mechanism would be built in. Any call to a routine which successfully alters the structure of the tree, renders unusable all pointers for that tree. Whilst this approach is safe, it may be considered as an excessive protection feature, especially when initially building up the structure of a tree. Where the user is willing to take on board the problems associated with this use of multiple and obsolete pointers, this protection feature can be disabled.

Tree Terminology

There are a number of terms that are associated with trees that are worth explaining. The keywords in bold are illustrated further below.

A **tree** is formed from a hierarchy of connected **nodes.** The node at the top of a tree is called the **root node**. Every node, apart from the root node, has a node above it, called its **parent,** and it is therefore the **child** of its parent. A node may be the parent of several nodes, but there is a fixed upper limit to the number. This limit is constant for an entire tree, and it called the tree's **degree** (sometimes called the tree's order). The ordering and positions of child nodes with regard to their parent is significant. Each child node has an associated **child number** allocated from the parent. This number is in a range of from one to the degree of the tree, inclusive.

An illustration of each of the terms is given below:

Tree	:	The diagram as a whole, of degree 3
Nodes	:	Each of the boxes
Root node	:	'A' is the root node of the tree
Parent	:	'A' is the parent of 'B'
	:	'B' is the parent of 'E'
	:	'H' is the parent of 'I', 'J' and 'K'
Child	:	'B', 'C' and 'D' are child nodes of 'A'
	:	'F' is the child of 'C'
	:	'I', 'J' and 'K' are each child nodes of 'H'
Degree	:	The tree is of degree 3
Child Number	:	'E' is child 1 of 'B'
	:	'F' is child 2 of 'C'
	:	'H' is child 3 of 'D'

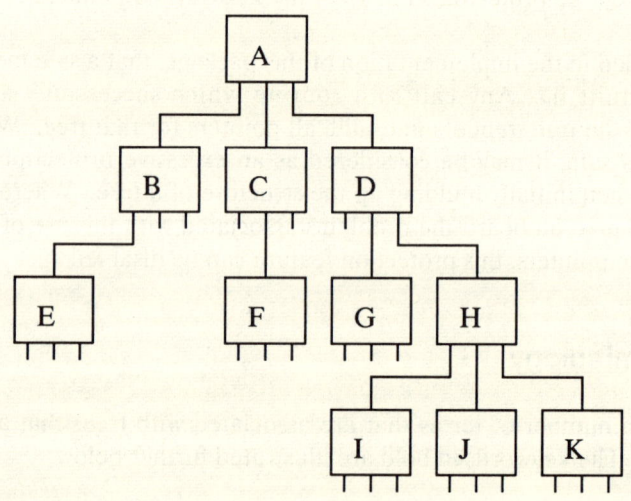

3.6 - Trees

Restrictions on Use

The generic formal parameter DATA_TYPE is private. The implementation imposes the restriction that the generic actual parameter must be a constrained data type.

The generic formal parameter DEGREE must be fulfilled by a value of 2 or greater.

Exceptions

There is a large number of exceptions declared within the generic package. They are necessary as, for any particular procedure call, a number of different problems may occur. The approach taken is that each particular exception raised must be able to resolve down to a particular problem.

A description of the meaning of each of the exceptions is given below, followed by a table which shows which exceptions may be raised by each subprogram. The table refers to the exceptions by number as indicated below:

1   TREE_CREATION_ERROR
Raised when attempting to initialise a tree object more than once or to destroy/deallocate a tree which has not yet been initialised.

2   POSITION_NOT_SET_ERROR
Raised when using a position object before it has been set to point to a tree, or when a tree object has not been initialised when it should have been.

3   OBSOLETE_POSITION_ERROR
Raised when attempting to use a position after the structure of the tree has been altered. This will only be raised if the version checking facility is enabled (as it is by default).

4   NODE_DOES_NOT_EXIST_ERROR
Raised when attempting to access or refer to a location in a tree which does not have a node present.

5   DEST_TREE_CREATED_ERROR
Raised by routines which attempt to set up destination trees with structures, or copies of structures taken from other trees, when the destination tree has already been created.

6 INVALID_CHILD_ERROR
Raised by insertion routines (tree or node) which have CHILD set to SELF except when inserting at the root node position in an empty tree.

7 NODE_ALREADY_EXISTS_ERROR
Raised when attempting to insert a node or tree where a node exists.

8 CHILDREN_EXIST_ERROR
Raised when attempting to delete a node which still has children. If a branch has to be removed, then EXTRACT_TREE should be used.

9 AT_ROOT_ERROR
Raised when attempting to change a pointer to refer to the root's parent.

Subprogram Name	\multicolumn{9}{c}{Exception Numbers}
	1	2	3	4	5	6	7	8	9
CREATE_TREE	X								
DESTROY_TREE	X								
DUPLICATE_TREE		X	X		X				
INSERT_NODE		X	X			X	X		
DELETE_NODE		X	X	X				X	
EXTRACT_TREE		X	X		X				
INSERT_TREE		X	X			X	X		
READ_DATA		X	X	X					
WRITE_DATA		X	X	X					
SET_TO_ROOT	X								
GOTO_PARENT		X	X	X					X
GOTO_CHILD		X	X	X					
CHILD_EXISTS		X	X	X					
IS_OBSOLETE		X							
POSITION_HAS_BEEN_SET									
TREE_HAS_BEEN_CREATED									
WHICH_TREE		X			X				
VERSION_CHECK									
VERSION_CHECK_ENABLED									
DEALLOCATE	X								

3.6 - Trees

A cross in the matrix above indicates that the relevant subprogram may raise the relevant exception. The precedence is such that if more than one exception raising condition is present, then the lower number exception shall be raised.

CONSTRAINT_ERROR will be raised during elaboration if an attempt is made to instantiate the package for a value of DEGREE < 2. In addition CONSTRAINT_ERROR will be raised if a value for a CHILD parameter is used which is less then zero or greater than the value of DEGREE used in the actual generic parameter. STORAGE_ERROR may be raised for the normal reasons, especially during node or tree insertion operations.

Options

As has been illustrated in the Flexible Queues component, it is not difficult to ensure that a dynamic data structure object incurs no progressive usage of heap. The safest technique is to recycle the dynamically used objects (nodes, in the tree's case) within the tree itself. In order to facilitate the inclusion of this option, there are only two routines concerned with the creation and deallocation of these internal dynamic objects, being CREATE_NODE and DEALLOCATE_NODE. If the code within these two units were to be suitably altered, in conjunction with the data type definition of the tree object, then the absence of progressive heap usage could be guaranteed. The final memory recycling would need to be performed in the DEALLOCATE subprogram.

Example of Use

Staff who work within a company organisation are often structured in a hierarchy, where each member of staff has a single person to whom they report and have a number of people reporting to them. A tree structure may be used to capture the relationship between members of staff. The following example shows a number of the facilities provided by the generic package applied to a tree representing a company organisation.

A data type is declared (STAFF_TYPE) which holds a minimum of information. A local procedure has been defined which prints out details of a person's position within an organisation. The setting up of the organisation has been hard coded into the main body of the example procedure before a couple of calls to the local procedure.

```ada
with TEXT_IO;   use TEXT_IO;
with GENERIC_UNSORTED_TREE_PKG;

procedure TREE_EXAMPLE is

   MAX_NO_OF_TEAM_MEMBERS : constant := 10;
   subtype NAME_TYPE is STRING (1..20);
   subtype JOB_TYPE  is STRING (1..20);
   type STAFF_TYPE is record
      NAME : NAME_TYPE ;
      JOB  : JOB_TYPE  ;
   end record;

   package ORGANISATION_PKG is new
           GENERIC_UNSORTED_TREE_PKG
           (STAFF_TYPE, MAX_NO_OF_TEAM_MEMBERS);
   use ORGANISATION_PKG;
begin
   declare
      ORGANISATION   : TREE_REF_TYPE;
      STAFF_POINTER  : POSITION_TYPE;

      procedure PUT_POSITION_IN_ORGANISATION
              (STAFF_POSITION : POSITION_TYPE) is
         TEMP_POS      : POSITION_TYPE;
         STAFF_DETAILS : STAFF_TYPE ;
      begin
         PUT ("Position in organisation of ");
         READ_DATA (STAFF_POSITION, STAFF_DETAILS);
         PUT_LINE (STAFF_DETAILS.NAME);
         TEMP_POS := STAFF_POSITION;
         begin
            GOTO_PARENT (TEMP_POS);
            READ_DATA (TEMP_POS, STAFF_DETAILS);
            PUT      ("Your Superior is ");
            PUT      (STAFF_DETAILS.NAME);
            PUT_LINE (STAFF_DETAILS.JOB);
         exception
            when AT_ROOT_ERROR =>
               PUT ("You are the boss"); NEW_LINE;
         end ;
         PUT_LINE ("Team members :");
         for EACH_TEAM_MEMBER in 1..MAX_NO_OF_TEAM_MEMBEI
```

3.6 - Trees

```
        loop
            if CHILD_EXISTS (STAFF_POSITION,
                             EACH_TEAM_MEMBER) then
                TEMP_POS := STAFF_POSITION;
                GOTO_CHILD (TEMP_POS, EACH_TEAM_MEMBER);
                READ_DATA  (TEMP_POS, STAFF_DETAILS);
                PUT        (STAFF_DETAILS.NAME);
                PUT_LINE   (STAFF_DETAILS.JOB);
            end if;
        end loop;
        NEW_LINE;
    end ;

begin
    -- Set up the organisation
    CREATE_TREE    (ORGANISATION);
    VERSION_CHECK  (ORGANISATION, FALSE);
    SET_TO_ROOT    (ORGANISATION, STAFF_POINTER);
    INSERT_NODE    (STAFF_POINTER, SELF,
      ("George Boson       ","Chairman           "));
    SET_TO_ROOT    (ORGANISATION, STAFF_POINTER);
    INSERT_NODE    (STAFF_POINTER, 1,
      ("Peter Makemore     ","Head of Accounts   "));
    ...    Insert the nodes to represent the organisation
    VERSION_CHECK (ORGANISATION, TRUE);

    -- Print out the organisation surrounding the boss and the head of accounts
    SET_TO_ROOT    (ORGANISATION, STAFF_POINTER);
    PUT_POSITION_IN_ORGANISATION (STAFF_POINTER);
    GOTO_CHILD     (STAFF_POINTER, 1);
    PUT_POSITION_IN_ORGANISATION (STAFF_POINTER);
    end;
end TREE_EXAMPLE;
```

Implementation Points

Considerable thought has been expended on the life cycle of a tree. Questions such as "should the root node exist automatically on tree creation?", "How should pointers be used?" and "How should pointers be used to allow the insertion of the first node and deletion of the last?" have been considered.

The apparently inelegant solution of allowing a CHILD_TYPE option of SELF (being the value 0), and of making CHILD_TYPE only a subtype, were taken in order to simplify the use of the package, even though it does reduce the compile time error checking potential of the package.

The duplication of the functionality provided by the subprograms DESTROY_TREE and DEALLOCATE_TREE is present in order to differentiate between the two different concepts: Reversing the CREATE_TREE operation, and that of heap memory recovery.

Efficiency

The relationship between the run time performance of the facilities provided in the package, against the number of nodes in the tree (termed n) is as follows:

DESTROY_TREE	n
DUPLICATE_TREE	n
DEALLOCATE	n

All other routines' performance is unrelated to the number of nodes in the tree.

Package Body

```
with UNCHECKED_DEALLOCATION;
package body GENERIC_UNSORTED_TREE_PKG is

   procedure CHECK_POSITION
            (POSITION : in POSITION_TYPE) is
   begin
      if POSITION.TREE_COPY = null then
         raise POSITION_NOT_SET_ERROR;
      end if;
      if POSITION.TREE_COPY.CHECKING_ENABLED then
         if POSITION.TREE_COPY.VERSION
         /= POSITION.VERSION then
            raise OBSOLETE_POSITION_ERROR;
         end if;
      end if;
   end;
```

3.6 - Trees

```ada
procedure ALLOCATE_TREE (TREE : out TREE_REF_TYPE) is
-- Allocates the tree object. This may be altered to recycle
-- tree objects, in conjunction with DEALLOCATE_TREE.
begin
    TREE := new TREE_TYPE;
end ALLOCATE_TREE;


procedure DEALLOCATE_TREE
            (TREE : in out TREE_REF_TYPE) is
-- Opposite of ALLOCATE_TREE
    procedure UNCHECKED_DEALLOCATE_TREE is new
        UNCHECKED_DEALLOCATION (TREE_TYPE, TREE_REF_TYPE);
begin
    if TREE = null then
        raise TREE_CREATION_ERROR;
    else
        UNCHECKED_DEALLOCATE_TREE (TREE);
    end if;
end DEALLOCATE_TREE;


procedure ALLOCATE_NODE
            (NODE_REF : out NODE_REF_TYPE) is
-- Creates a node, this may use recycled nodes, if this routine
-- and DEALLOCATE_NODE are altered
begin
    NODE_REF := new NODE_TYPE;
end;


procedure DEALLOCATE_NODE
            (NODE_REF : in out NODE_REF_TYPE) is
-- Opposite of ALLOCATE_NODE
    procedure UNCHECKED_DEALLOCATE_NODE is new
        UNCHECKED_DEALLOCATION (NODE_TYPE, NODE_REF_TYPE);
begin
    UNCHECKED_DEALLOCATE_NODE (NODE_REF);
end;


procedure INCREMENT_TREE_VERSION
            (TREE : in TREE_REF_TYPE) is
```

-- This routine isolates the adjustment of the version associated
-- with the tree being altered
```
begin
   if TREE.VERSION /= VERSION_TYPE' LAST then
      TREE.VERSION := VERSION_TYPE' SUCC (TREE.VERSION)
   else
      TREE.VERSION := VERSION_TYPE' FIRST;
   end if;
end INCREMENT_TREE_VERSION;


procedure DELETE_BRANCH
          (NODE_REF : in out NODE_REF_TYPE) is
begin
   if NODE_REF /= null then
      for CHILD in FIRST_CHILD .. LAST_CHILD loop
         DELETE_BRANCH (NODE_REF.CHILDREN_REF(CHILD))
      end loop;
      DEALLOCATE_NODE (NODE_REF);
   end if;
end DELETE_BRANCH;


procedure CREATE_TREE (TREE : in out TREE_REF_TYPE) is
begin
   if TREE /= null then
      raise TREE_CREATION_ERROR;
   else
      ALLOCATE_TREE (TREE);
   end if;
end CREATE_TREE;


procedure DESTROY_TREE (TREE : in out TREE_REF_TYPE)
begin
   if TREE = null then
      raise TREE_CREATION_ERROR;
   else
      DELETE_BRANCH (TREE.ROOT);
   end if;
   DEALLOCATE_TREE (TREE);
end DESTROY_TREE;
```

3.6 - Trees

```ada
procedure DEALLOCATE (TREE : in out TREE_REF_TYPE) is
begin
   DESTROY_TREE (TREE);
end DEALLOCATE;


procedure DUPLICATE_TREE
              (POSITION : in      POSITION_TYPE;
               TO_TREE  : in out TREE_REF_TYPE) is

   procedure DUPLICATE_NODE
              (FROM_NODE       : in      NODE_REF_TYPE;
               TO_NODE         : in out NODE_REF_TYPE;
               TO_NODE_PARENT  : in      NODE_REF_TYPE) is
      TEMP_NODE : NODE_REF_TYPE;
   begin
      if FROM_NODE = null then
         return;
      else
         ALLOCATE_NODE (TO_NODE);
         TO_NODE.DATA       := FROM_NODE.DATA;
         TO_NODE.PARENT_REF := TO_NODE_PARENT;
         for CHILD in FIRST_CHILD .. LAST_CHILD loop
            DUPLICATE_NODE
            (FROM_NODE.CHILDREN_REF (CHILD),
             TO_NODE.CHILDREN_REF (CHILD), TO_NODE);
         end loop;
      end if;
   end DUPLICATE_NODE;

begin
   CHECK_POSITION (POSITION);
   if TO_TREE /= null then
      raise DEST_TREE_CREATED_ERROR;
   else
      ALLOCATE_TREE  (TO_TREE);
      DUPLICATE_NODE (POSITION.NODE_REF,
                      TO_TREE.ROOT, null);
      TO_TREE.VERSION := VERSION_TYPE' FIRST;
   end if;
end DUPLICATE_TREE;
```

```
procedure INSERT_NODE (POSITION : in out POSITION_TYPE
                       CHILD    : in      CHILD_TYPE;
                       DATA     : in      DATA_TYPE) is
   NODE : NODE_REF_TYPE := POSITION.NODE_REF;
begin
   CHECK_POSITION (POSITION);
   if NODE = null then
      -- Trying to insert a node at the empty root location
      ALLOCATE_NODE (POSITION.TREE_COPY.ROOT);
      POSITION.TREE_COPY.ROOT.DATA := DATA;
      INCREMENT_TREE_VERSION (POSITION.TREE_COPY);
      POSITION.NODE_REF := POSITION.TREE_COPY.ROOT;
   else
      if CHILD = SELF then
         raise INVALID_CHILD_ERROR;
      elsif NODE.CHILDREN_REF(CHILD) /= null then
         raise NODE_ALREADY_EXISTS_ERROR;
      end if;
      ALLOCATE_NODE (NODE.CHILDREN_REF(CHILD));
      NODE.CHILDREN_REF(CHILD).PARENT_REF := NODE;
      NODE.CHILDREN_REF(CHILD).DATA       := DATA;
      INCREMENT_TREE_VERSION (POSITION.TREE_COPY);
   end if;
end INSERT_NODE;


procedure DELETE_NODE
                  (POSITION : in POSITION_TYPE;
                   CHILD    : in CHILD_TYPE := SELF)
   NODE        : NODE_REF_TYPE;
   VALID_TREE  : BOOLEAN := TRUE;

   function CHILDREN_EXIST
           (NODE : NODE_REF_TYPE) return BOOLEAN is
   begin
      for CHILD in FIRST_CHILD .. LAST_CHILD loop
         if NODE.CHILDREN_REF(CHILD) /= null then
            return TRUE;
         end if;
      end loop;
      return FALSE;
   end CHILDREN_EXIST;
```

3.6 - Trees 127

```
begin  -- procedure DELETE_NODE
   CHECK_POSITION (POSITION);
   NODE := POSITION.NODE_REF;
   if NODE = null then
      raise NODE_DOES_NOT_EXIST_ERROR;
   end if;
   if CHILD = SELF then
      -- attempt to delete the node at position pointer
      if CHILDREN_EXIST (NODE) then
         raise CHILDREN_EXIST_ERROR;
      else
         -- The node must be deallocated using the parent's pointer,
         -- to ensure that it is set to null. The parent's pointer for
         -- the root is special, so handle that case first
         if NODE.PARENT_REF = null then
            DEALLOCATE_NODE (POSITION.TREE_COPY.ROOT);
         else -- Locate the relevant parent's pointer, and deallocate
            VALID_TREE := FALSE;
            for CHILD in FIRST_CHILD .. LAST_CHILD loop
               if NODE.PARENT_REF.
                  CHILDREN_REF(CHILD) = NODE then
                  DEALLOCATE_NODE (NODE.PARENT_REF.
                     CHILDREN_REF(CHILD));
                  VALID_TREE := TRUE;
                  exit;
               end if;
            end loop;
         end if;
      end if;
   else
      -- Delete node at position pointer's child
      if NODE.CHILDREN_REF(CHILD) = null then
         raise NODE_DOES_NOT_EXIST_ERROR;
      end if;
      -- Check that the node to be deleted does not have children
      if CHILDREN_EXIST (NODE.CHILDREN_REF(CHILD)) then
         raise CHILDREN_EXIST_ERROR;
      else
         DEALLOCATE_NODE (NODE.CHILDREN_REF(CHILD));
      end if;
   end if;
   INCREMENT_TREE_VERSION (POSITION.TREE_COPY);
end DELETE_NODE;
```

```
procedure EXTRACT_TREE
        (POSITION : in      POSITION_TYPE;
         CHILD    : in      CHILD_TYPE := SELF;
         TO_TREE  : in out  TREE_REF_TYPE) is
   NODE : NODE_REF_TYPE := POSITION.NODE_REF;
begin
   -- Check versions, validity of tree and that the destination
   -- tree has not already been created
   CHECK_POSITION (POSITION);
   if TO_TREE /= null then
      raise DEST_TREE_CREATED_ERROR;
   end if;
   -- Extracting from an empty root is legal, but handled as a special case.
   if NODE = null then
      -- Extracting from the root of an empty tree
      ALLOCATE_TREE (TO_TREE);
   elsif CHILD = SELF then
      -- Extracting the node itself, not its child
      ALLOCATE_TREE (TO_TREE);
      TO_TREE.ROOT := NODE;
      -- If not the root, then clear the parent's pointer
      if NODE.PARENT_REF /= null then
         -- Must find which child of the parent this node is
         for CH in FIRST_CHILD .. LAST_CHILD loop
            if NODE.PARENT_REF.CHILDREN_REF(CH)
                  = NODE then
               -- It is child CH, so clear it down to null
               NODE.PARENT_REF.CHILDREN_REF(CH) := nul
            end if;
         end loop;
      else
         -- otherwise, clear the root pointer in the tree object
         POSITION.TREE_COPY.ROOT := null;
      end if;
      -- Set the destination's tree's root node parent pointer to null
      TO_TREE.ROOT.PARENT_REF := null;
   else
      -- Proper extraction of the branch given by the child of the position
      -- pointer. Set node to point to the relevant child, and make sure
      -- it exists. If so, create the tree and set the root node's parent
      -- pointer, and clear down the relevant 'from tree' child pointer.
      -- This also works for an empty child
      NODE := NODE.CHILDREN_REF(CHILD);
```

```
      ALLOCATE_TREE (TO_TREE);
      TO_TREE.ROOT := NODE;
      -- Parent pointer not to be cleared for an empty child
      if NODE /= null then
         NODE.PARENT_REF := null;
      end if;
      POSITION.NODE_REF.CHILDREN_REF(CHILD) := null;
   end if;
   -- Extraction has been successful, adjust the version of the 'from tree'
   INCREMENT_TREE_VERSION (POSITION.TREE_COPY);
end EXTRACT_TREE;


procedure INSERT_TREE
         (POSITION  : in      POSITION_TYPE;
          CHILD     : in      CHILD_TYPE;
          FROM_TREE : in out  TREE_REF_TYPE) is
   NODE  : NODE_REF_TYPE := POSITION.NODE_REF;
begin
   CHECK_POSITION (POSITION);
   if FROM_TREE = null then
      raise POSITION_NOT_SET_ERROR;
   end if;
   if NODE = null then
      -- Attempting to insert into an empty tree
      POSITION.TREE_COPY.ROOT := FROM_TREE.ROOT;
   else
      if CHILD = SELF then
         raise INVALID_CHILD_ERROR;
      end if;
      if NODE.CHILDREN_REF(CHILD) /= null then
         raise NODE_ALREADY_EXISTS_ERROR;
      end if;
      if FROM_TREE.ROOT /= null then
         NODE.CHILDREN_REF(CHILD) := FROM_TREE.ROOT;
         NODE.CHILDREN_REF(CHILD).PARENT_REF := NODE;
      end if;
   end if;
   FROM_TREE.ROOT := null;
   INCREMENT_TREE_VERSION (POSITION.TREE_COPY);
   INCREMENT_TREE_VERSION (FROM_TREE);
end INSERT_TREE;
```

```ada
procedure READ_DATA (POSITION : in       POSITION_TYPE;
                     DATA     :     out DATA_TYPE) is
begin
   CHECK_POSITION (POSITION);
   if POSITION.NODE_REF = null then
      raise NODE_DOES_NOT_EXIST_ERROR;
   end if;
   DATA := POSITION.NODE_REF.DATA;
end READ_DATA;


procedure WRITE_DATA (POSITION : in POSITION_TYPE;
                      DATA     : in DATA_TYPE) is
begin
   CHECK_POSITION (POSITION);
   if POSITION.NODE_REF = null then
      raise NODE_DOES_NOT_EXIST_ERROR;
   end if;
   POSITION.NODE_REF.DATA := DATA;
end WRITE_DATA;


procedure SET_TO_ROOT
                   (TREE     : in      TREE_REF_TYPE;
                    POSITION :     out POSITION_TYPE) is
begin
   if TREE = null then
      raise TREE_CREATION_ERROR;
   end if;
   POSITION := (NODE_REF  => TREE.ROOT,
                TREE_COPY => TREE,
                VERSION   => TREE.VERSION);
end SET_TO_ROOT;


procedure GOTO_PARENT
         (POSITION : in out POSITION_TYPE) is
begin
   CHECK_POSITION (POSITION);
   if POSITION.NODE_REF = null then
      raise NODE_DOES_NOT_EXIST_ERROR;
   elsif POSITION.NODE_REF.PARENT_REF = null then
      raise AT_ROOT_ERROR;
```

3.6 - Trees

```
      end if;
      POSITION.NODE_REF := POSITION.NODE_REF.PARENT_REF;
   end GOTO_PARENT;


   procedure GOTO_CHILD  (POSITION : in out POSITION_TYPE;
                          CHILD    : in      CHILD_TYPE) is
   begin
      CHECK_POSITION (POSITION);
      if CHILD /= SELF then
         if POSITION.NODE_REF = null then
            raise NODE_DOES_NOT_EXIST_ERROR;
         elsif POSITION.NODE_REF.CHILDREN_REF(CHILD)
               = null then
            raise NODE_DOES_NOT_EXIST_ERROR;
         end if;
         POSITION.NODE_REF := POSITION.NODE_REF.
                              CHILDREN_REF(CHILD);
      end if;
   end GOTO_CHILD;


   function CHILD_EXISTS (POSITION : in POSITION_TYPE;
                          CHILD    : in CHILD_TYPE)
                                 return BOOLEAN is
   begin
      CHECK_POSITION (POSITION);
      if POSITION.NODE_REF = null then
         if CHILD = SELF then
            return FALSE;
         else
            raise NODE_DOES_NOT_EXIST_ERROR;
         end if;
      end if;
      if CHILD /= SELF then
         return POSITION.NODE_REF.CHILDREN_REF(CHILD)
                /= null;
      else
         return TRUE;
      end if;
   end CHILD_EXISTS;
```

```
   function TREE_HAS_BEEN_CREATED (TREE : in TREE_REF_TYPE)
                                     return BOOLEAN
begin
   return TREE /= null;
end TREE_HAS_BEEN_CREATED;


   function IS_OBSOLETE (POSITION : in  POSITION_TYPE)
                                     return BOOLEAN is
begin
   if POSITION.TREE_COPY = null then
      raise POSITION_NOT_SET_ERROR;
   else
      return POSITION.VERSION
             /= POSITION.TREE_COPY.VERSION;
   end if;
end IS_OBSOLETE;



   function POSITION_HAS_BEEN_SET
         (POSITION : in POSITION_TYPE) return BOOLEAN
begin
   return POSITION.TREE_COPY /= null;
end POSITION_HAS_BEEN_SET;



   procedure WHICH_TREE
            (POSITION : in      POSITION_TYPE;
             TO_TREE  : in out  TREE_REF_TYPE) is
begin
   if POSITION.TREE_COPY = null then
      raise POSITION_NOT_SET_ERROR;
   end if;

   if TO_TREE /= null then
      raise DEST_TREE_CREATED_ERROR ;
   end if;

   TO_TREE := POSITION.TREE_COPY;
end WHICH_TREE;
```

3.6 - Trees

```ada
   procedure VERSION_CHECK (TREE    : in out TREE_REF_TYPE;
                            ENABLED : in     BOOLEAN) is
   begin
      TREE.CHECKING_ENABLED := ENABLED;
   end VERSION_CHECK;


   function VERSION_CHECK_ENABLED (TREE : TREE_REF_TYPE)
                                         return BOOLEAN is
   begin
      return TREE.CHECKING_ENABLED;
   end VERSION_CHECK_ENABLED;

begin
   if DEGREE < 2 then
      raise CONSTRAINT_ERROR;
   end if;
end GENERIC_UNSORTED_TREE_PKG;
```

3.7 LISTS

Description

This package provides facilities to manipulate an ordered list of items according to the value of an unique key associated with each item. The list is implemented in the form of a balanced tree, giving fast retrieval of items.

It is a generic package which may be instantiated for any data and key type, together with a function to compare key values. The implementation technique used, however, ensures that the time to search for items is kept to a minimum.

The facilities provided by the package are split into five categories as follows:

List manipulation	-	to alter the content of the list.
Data value manipulation	-	to alter or read the data values associated with a particular key.
List traversal	-	to step through the list or refer to the first or last item.
Condition test	-	exception avoidance
Management facilities	-	memory management control

Dependencies

External : None
Internal : The routines make extensive cross calls in order to keep the replication of code to a minimum.

Minimum Implementable Package

The boolean functions may be removed. They are present to enable the user of the package to avoid raising exceptions but can only be guaranteed to work in an environment where the package is being used under a single task's thread of control.

3.7 - Lists

The procedures for merging, duplicating and extracting lists may be individually removed.

Component Specification

```ada
generic
   type DATA_TYPE is private;
   type KEY_TYPE  is private;
   with function "<" (LEFT,RIGHT:KEY_TYPE) return BOOLEAN;

package LIST_PKG is
   type LIST_REF_TYPE is private;


   -- List Manipulation subprograms

   procedure INITIALISE_LIST (LIST : in out LIST_REF_TYPE);

   procedure DESTROY_LIST    (LIST : in out LIST_REF_TYPE);

   procedure DUPLICATE_LIST
                   (FROM_LIST : in     LIST_REF_TYPE;
                    TO_LIST   : in out LIST_REF_TYPE);
   generic
      type SET_OF_KEYS_TYPE is private ;
      with function KEY_IS_VALID
              (TEST_KEY    : KEY_TYPE;
               SET_OF_KEYS : SET_OF_KEYS_TYPE) return BOOLEAN;
   procedure EXTRACT_LIST
            (FROM_LIST   : in out LIST_REF_TYPE;
             SET_OF_KEYS : in     SET_OF_KEYS_TYPE;
             TO_LIST     : in out LIST_REF_TYPE);

   procedure MERGE_LIST (FROM_LIST : in out LIST_REF_TYPE;
                         TO_LIST   : in out LIST_REF_TYPE);

   procedure INSERT_ITEM (LIST : in out LIST_REF_TYPE;
                          KEY  : in     KEY_TYPE;
                          DATA : in     DATA_TYPE);

   procedure DELETE_ITEM (LIST : in out LIST_REF_TYPE;
                          KEY  : in     KEY_TYPE);
```

-- *Data Value Manipulation subprograms*

```
procedure READ_DATA    (LIST : in      LIST_REF_TYPE;
                        KEY  : in      KEY_TYPE;
                        DATA :     out DATA_TYPE);

procedure WRITE_DATA   (LIST : in      LIST_REF_TYPE;
                        KEY  : in      KEY_TYPE;
                        DATA : in      DATA_TYPE);
```

-- *List Traversal subprograms*

```
procedure HIGHEST_KEY (LIST : in      LIST_REF_TYPE;
                       KEY  :     out KEY_TYPE;
                       DATA :     out DATA_TYPE);

procedure LOWEST_KEY  (LIST : in      LIST_REF_TYPE;
                       KEY  :     out KEY_TYPE;
                       DATA :     out DATA_TYPE);

procedure HIGHER_KEY  (LIST : in      LIST_REF_TYPE;
                       KEY  : in  out KEY_TYPE;
                       DATA :     out DATA_TYPE);

procedure LOWER_KEY   (LIST : in      LIST_REF_TYPE;
                       KEY  : in  out KEY_TYPE;
                       DATA :     out DATA_TYPE);
```

-- *Condition Test subprograms*

```
function LIST_HAS_BEEN_INITIALISED (LIST: LIST_REF_TYPE)
                                          return BOOLEAN;

function KEY_EXISTS (LIST : LIST_REF_TYPE;
                     KEY : KEY_TYPE) return BOOLEAN;

function IS_EMPTY   (LIST : LIST_REF_TYPE)
                                          return BOOLEAN ;
```

3.7 - Lists

-- Management Facility subprogram

```
procedure DEALLOCATE (LIST : in out LIST_REF_TYPE);
```

-- Exceptions

```
LIST_INITIALISATION_ERROR  : exception;
KEY_ALREADY_EXISTS_ERROR   : exception;
KEY_DOES_NOT_EXIST_ERROR   : exception;

private

    type BALANCED_TYPE is (LEFT_IS_LONGER,
                           LEFT_AND_RIGHT_EVEN,
                           RIGHT_IS_LONGER);
    type NODE_TYPE;
    type NODE_REF_TYPE is access NODE_TYPE;

    type NODE_TYPE is record
        KEY       : KEY_TYPE;         -- Unique search ID
        DATA      : DATA_TYPE;        -- The data
        LEFT_REF  : NODE_REF_TYPE;    -- Values less than node
        RIGHT_REF : NODE_REF_TYPE;    -- Values greater than node
        BALANCED  : BALANCED_TYPE;    -- Used to balance tree
    end record;

    type LIST_TYPE is record
        ROOT : NODE_REF_TYPE;
    end record;

    type LIST_REF_TYPE is access LIST_TYPE;

end LIST_PKG;
```

Pragmatics

This package presents its facilities in a manner similar to those provided in the Trees component (3.6). The classes of facilities are the same, as are the operations that can be performed. The difference lies in the methods used to reference items within the list. Instead of referring to positions within a tree, the user makes use of keys with unique values. These keys are used as a basis for searching the list each time it is accessed.

In the same manner as with the tree objects in the tree manipulation package, the list objects in this package have to be initialised before they can be used. This is achieved by calling the INITIALISE_LIST procedure. This allocates the necessary memory from the heap to form a usable list. Prior to that call, the list object is an access type with a null value.

The following gives a detailed description of each of the subprograms provided in the package specification:

List Manipulation

INITIALISE_LIST
Called to initialise the list objects. Necessary before a list can be used for any of the other subprograms, except LIST_HAS_BEEN_INITIALISED and the destination lists for DUPLICATE_LIST and EXTRACT_LIST.

DESTROY_LIST
The opposite of INITIALISE_LIST, it removes all items on the list. To reuse the list object requires a call to the INITIALISE_LIST procedure.

DUPLICATE_LIST
Takes any initialised list and creates a duplicate. The destination list, TO_LIST, must not be initialised.

EXTRACT_LIST
This is a generic procedure whose purpose is to extract a controllable subset of the items contained in a list, and put them into a new list. The criteria against which each item in the list is tested, are specified in a generic function (KEY_IS_VALID) supplied as one of the generic parameters. An additional generic parameter of arbitrary complexity (as it is a private data type) is supplied at run time to provide flexibility. This allows, for example, the procedure to be instantiated to filter items between two run time supplied keys, to select all items whose keys are above or below a run time supplied value, or even to extract items according to data values. An example of an instantiation of this procedure is shown in the example section for this component. The destination list, TO_LIST, must not be initialised.

MERGE_LIST
This routine merges two lists, called the FROM_LIST and the TO_LIST. Any items in the FROM_LIST for which there are no matching keys in the TO_LIST are transferred into the TO_LIST. Those items in the FROM_LIST for which there are duplicate keys in the TO_LIST are left behind in the FROM_LIST. The destination list, TO_LIST, must have been initialised.

INSERT_ITEM
This routine inserts a single item into the list. The value of the data and its associated key must be supplied. An exception is raised if an item already exists in the list, due to the constraint that keys within a list are unique.

DELETE_ITEM
This routine removes an item from the list whose key exactly matches that supplied as the parameter. If no such item exists, an exception is raised.

Data Value Manipulation

READ_DATA
This routine searches for the item in the list whose key matches the key supplied in the parameter. If a match is found, then the item's data value is returned. If no such match is found, an exception is raised.

WRITE_DATA
This routine searches for an item in the list whose key matches the key supplied in the parameter. If a match is found, the routine overwrites that item's data with the value supplied in a second parameter. If no such match is found, an exception is raised.

List Traversal

HIGHEST_KEY
This routine returns the key and data value of the item whose key is highest, according to the actual generic function '<' supplied during the package's instantiation. The item remains in the list. If there are no items, and hence no highest item, an exception is raised.

LOWEST_KEY
Similar to HIGHEST_KEY, this returns the key and associated data value for the item with the lowest key. Again, for empty lists an exception is raised.

HIGHER_KEY
This procedure returns the key and data value of the item whose key value is the next higher to the key passed as a parameter. No item needs to exist in the list to match the key value passed. If no items have a higher key, then an exception is raised.

LOWER_KEY
Similar to HIGHER_KEY but the routine returns information on the item with the next lower key.

Condition Tests

LIST_HAS_BEEN_INITIALISED
This boolean function is provided to allow users to avoid LIST_INITIALISATION_ERROR.

KEY_EXISTS
This boolean function checks whether a particular key value is already present in the list.

IS_EMPTY
This boolean function checks for an empty list.

Management Facilities

DEALLOCATE
This routine is used to ensure that all the memory allocated to a list is recycled back into the heap, by forcing UNCHECKED_DEALLOCATE to be invoked, in accordance with Appendix F. The routine is superfluous with the current implementation, as the DELETE_ITEM procedure calls the necessary routines as standard. However, if an internal memory recycling technique is introduced (see Options) then this routine will be required.

3.7 - Lists

Restrictions on use

The generic formal parameter DATA_TYPE is private. The package implementation imposes the restriction that the generic actual parameter must be a constrained data type. Similarly, the generic formal parameter KEY_TYPE is private and must again be a constrained type.

The generic formal function "<" is used in the package body to compare value of keys in order to decide where to place an item in the binary tree structure. As such, the actual function must be well behaved, such that for any two keys, A and B, then A is either less than, equal to, or greater than B. Additionally the function must operate in a linear, non-cyclic fashion, thus for A less than B, and B less then C, then it must be that A is less than C. When instantiated with an actual function which is not well behaved as above, use of the List package is erroneous (see Implementation Points).

Due to the above restriction, it is erroneous to instantiate the List package with an access type for the key type (see Implementation Points).

Exceptions

The generic package declares only three exceptions. A description of the meaning of each of the exceptions is given below, followed by a table which shows which exceptions may be raised by each subprogram. The table refers to the exceptions by number as indicated below:

1   LIST_INITIALISATION_ERROR
    Raised if an uninitialised list is used when an initialised one is required, or vice versa.

2   KEY_ALREADY_EXISTS_ERROR
    Raised when attempting to insert an item whose key value is already present in the tree. It is not raised when merging lists.

3   KEY_DOES_NOT_EXIST_ERROR
    Raised when deleting an item whose key value is not present, or when attempting to locate a key in an empty list.

3.7 - Lists

	Exception Numbers		
Subprogram Name	1	2	3
INITIALISE_LIST	X		
DESTROY_LIST	X		
DUPLICATE_LIST	X		
EXTRACT_LIST	X		
MERGE_LIST	X		
INSERT_ITEM	X	X	
DELETE_ITEM	X		X
READ_DATA	X		X
WRITE_DATA	X		X
HIGHEST_KEY	X		X
LOWEST_KEY	X		X
HIGHER_KEY	X		X
LOWER_KEY	X		X
LIST_HAS_BEEN_INITIALISED			
KEY_EXISTS	X		
IS_EMPTY	X		
DEALLOCATE	X		

A STORAGE_ERROR exception may be raised by the underlying RTS if new items are being created and there is insufficient heap available.

Options

This implementation allocates memory dynamically using Ada access types. The memory occupied is freed by using the predefined package UNCHECKED_DEALLOCATION. This memory becomes available for general use by other packages. In some compilation systems, allocating and freeing memory may be a slow operation, particularly if multitasking is being used. In these circumstances, it may be better for the package to manage its own own dynamic memory. This can be done by modifying the ALLOCATE_NODE and DEALLOCATE_NODE procedures to maintain an internal list of free node objects, and modifying the LIST_TYPE to include a list of free node objects. The Flexible Queues component (3.5) contained in this book uses this implementation technique.

The list manipulation routines DUPLICATE_LIST and EXTRACT_LIST assume that the destination lists have not been initialised. This could be altered to assume that the lists have been initialised, or to allow both initialised and uninitialised lists. If initialised lists with items already present are to be supported, then the internals of the routines will have to be altered.

As there is no overlap between the two 'key' exceptions regarding the subprograms which can raise them, they could be combined to form a single KEY_ERROR.

In the implementation described, there is a single generic operator "<". It is used, together with the default "=", to maintain the ordering of the keys. This causes problems if it is desirable for the package to hold items keyed through access types, as the default "=" operator will not be able to maintain a correct key ordering. In this case, a further generic operator, EQ (not "=" as this is not permitted for private types) should be included into the generic specification, and should be used within the package body when comparing key values.

Example of use

The example chosen illustrates the use of a number of facilities provided by the package. It shows a list being built up from a succession of operations invoked through TEXT_IO. The user adds and deletes items until he requests to exit the loop. On exiting, the code calculates the second lowest key value, and also extracts a list containing all the items whose key lies between certain values.

Some aspects of this example are worth highlighting.

- In the case statement, the acceptability of each key is tested by two methods. The 'I' and 'R' options use exceptions raised by INSERT_ITEM and READ_DATA respectively. In the 'D' option, the KEY_EXISTS function is used, avoiding the possibility of exceptions being raised.

- The EXTRACT_LIST generic procedure is instantiated to allow the extraction of items between two key values. To instantiate requires that BETWEEN_TYPE is declared, and a boolean function, ACCEPT_KEY, is written that allows the comparison of a key against the run time supplied pair of keys. The instantiated procedure is used twice towards the end of the example, to extract every item whose key lie between 100 and 200 for the first call, and between 1000 and 2450 for the second call. A merge of the resulting lists produces a superset list for output.

- Each of the three lists produced within the example is deallocated, in accordance with Pragmatics.

```ada
with LIST_PKG;
with TEXT_IO;  use TEXT_IO;
procedure LIST_EXAMPLE is
   package IIO is new INTEGER_IO (INTEGER);
   subtype KEY_TYPE is INTEGER;
   type VALUE_TYPE is ...

   package LIST_PKG is new LIST_PKG
           (VALUE_TYPE, KEY_TYPE, "<");
   use LIST_PKG;

   procedure GET      (VALUE  :      out VALUE_TYPE) is ...
   procedure GET      (KEY    :      out KEY_TYPE) is ...
   procedure PUT_BOTH (KEY    : in       KEY_TYPE;
                       VALUE  : in       VALUE_TYPE) is ...
   procedure PUT      (LIST   : in       LIST_REF_TYPE) is 

begin
   declare
      KEY    : KEY_TYPE;
      VALUE  : VALUE_TYPE;
      BETWEEN_LIST_1, BETWEEN_LIST_2, LIST : LIST_REF_TYP
      SELECTION : CHARACTER;

      type BETWEEN_TYPE is
         record
            LOWER, UPPER : INTEGER;
         end record;

      function ACCEPT_KEY
              (KEY      : KEY_TYPE;
               KEY_PAIR : BETWEEN_TYPE) return BOOLEAN 
```

3.7 - Lists

```ada
   begin
      return KEY_PAIR.LOWER < KEY and
             KEY_PAIR.UPPER > KEY;
   end ACCEPT_KEY;

   procedure EXTRACT_BETWEEN is new EXTRACT_LIST
                           (BETWEEN_TYPE, ACCEPT_KEY);
begin
   INITIALISE_LIST (LIST);
   -- Enter a number of items into the list
   loop
      PUT (LIST);
      PUT ("E=>Exit, I=>Insert, D=>Delete, R=>Read -");
      GET (SELECTION);
      case SELECTION is
         when 'E'|'e' => exit;
         when 'I'|'i' =>  -- Insert an item
            GET (KEY); GET (VALUE);
            begin
               INSERT_ITEM (LIST, KEY, VALUE);
            exception
               when KEY_ALREADY_EXISTS_ERROR =>
                  PUT_LINE ("Key Already Exists");
            end;
         when 'D'|'d' =>  -- Delete an item
            GET (KEY);
            if KEY_EXISTS (LIST, KEY) then
               DELETE_ITEM (LIST, KEY);
            else
               PUT_LINE ("Key does not exist");
            end if;
         when 'R'|'r' =>  -- Read a value
            GET (KEY);
            begin
               READ_DATA (LIST, KEY, VALUE);
               PUT_BOTH (KEY, VALUE); NEW_LINE (2);
            exception
               when KEY_DOES_NOT_EXIST_ERROR =>
                  PUT_LINE ("Key does not exist");
            end;
         when others => PUT_LINE ("Invalid option");
      end case;
   end loop;
```

```
        -- Read the second lowest key and value
        LOWEST_KEY   (LIST, KEY, VALUE);
        HIGHER_KEY   (LIST, KEY, VALUE);
        PUT_LINE ("Second lowest key is:");
        PUT_BOTH (KEY, VALUE); NEW_LINE (2);

        -- Extract a tree only with key values between 100->200 or 1000->2450
        EXTRACT_BETWEEN (LIST, (100,200),   BETWEEN_LIST_1);
        EXTRACT_BETWEEN (LIST, (1000,2450), BETWEEN_LIST_2);
        MERGE_LIST (FROM_LIST => BETWEEN_LIST_1,
                    TO_LIST   => BETWEEN_LIST_2);
        PUT ("Extracted list with all items where: ");
        PUT_LINE ("100 < key < 200 or 1000 < key < 2450");
        PUT (BETWEEN_LIST_2); NEW_LINE (2);

        -- Tidy up the RAM
        DEALLOCATE (LIST);
        DEALLOCATE (BETWEEN_LIST_1);
        DEALLOCATE (BETWEEN_LIST_2);
    end;
end LIST_EXAMPLE ;
```

Implementation points

The Use of a Tree Structure

The items in a list object are held and maintained in the form of an ordered binary tree. Some examples of binary tree structures can be seen in the three diagrams below. Each node in the tree contain a data and key pair, with the value of the key being shown in the diagram. In an ordered tree, key values are assigned to nodes such that for any particular node all keys down the left branch are less than the node's key, and all keys down the right branch are greater than the node's key. Each of the tree structures illustrated in diagrams (a), (b) and (c) are ordered binary trees.

3.7 - Lists

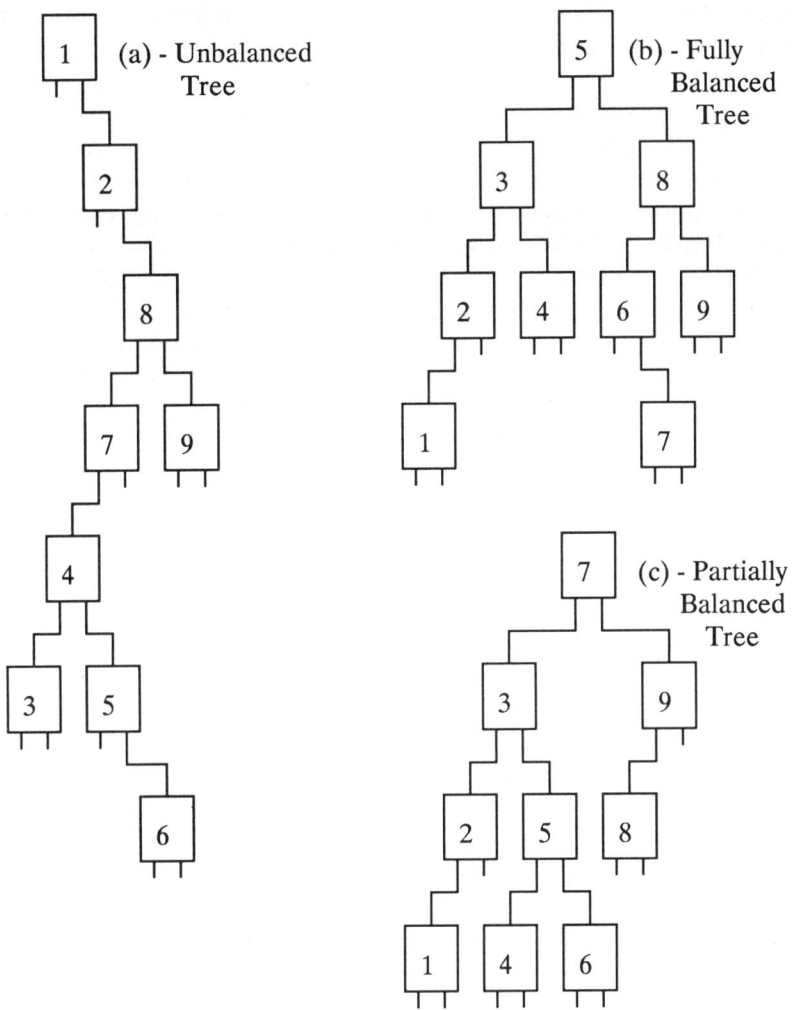

Operations, such as searching for values, can be very efficient using a tree structure compared to, say, a linear list. Searching a tree starts at the top node, called the root, and progresses down branches until a node at the bottom of the tree, called a 'leaf node', is reached. The number of nodes visited in scanning from the root to the leaf node, is called the path length.

To minimise the performance cost of operations on a tree, it is important to limit this path length. If a tree's structure is manipulated (adding or deleting nodes) then the structure changes. Over a number of such operations, a tree can become 'unbalanced', as illustrated in diagram (a). In such cases, whilst some search operations will be swift (such as for key 2 or 8) others will be quite long (key value 6 being the worst case).

Ideally, a tree's structure should be such that the longest path from root to leaf is kept to a minimum. This is achieved be keeping an even distribution of nodes. Such a fully balanced tree ensures that the maximum path length from the root node to any leaf node is no more than 1 longer than the minimum. Such a tree is illustrated in diagram (b).

In practice, it is very difficult to maintain a tree in a fully balanced state following insertions or deletions. A compromise is the 'partially balanced' tree. This is the structure that is within the List Package. In such a tree, for every node in the tree, the maximum path length down the left branch differs by no more than one from the maximum path length down the right branch. This is less restrictive than the fully balanced constraint, but still maintains a good level of performance. Such a tree is illustrated in diagram (c).

Destroy and Deallocate
Although the DESTROY_LIST and DEALLOCATE_LIST procedures have the same effect, they are both provided because they have different purposes; DESTROY_LIST corresponding to the opposite of INITIALISE_LIST, and DEALLOCATE_LIST is responsible for freeing all the memory used by the list data structure.

The DESTROY_LIST and DEALLOCATE_LIST procedures might well be different if the general implementation were different (for example if the package managed its own memory as described in the Options section above).

The Generic Formal Parameters
The keys are used in conjunction with the generic formal parameter "<" and the implicit function "=" to maintain the items in an ordered list. It is a nonobvious, but very important constraint, that the "<" formal parameter is satisfied with an actual parameter such that any pair of keys must satisfy one and only one of the following three conditions:
(i)   "<" (KEY_1, KEY_2) = TRUE;
(ii)   "=" (KEY_1, KEY_2) = TRUE;
(iii)   ("=" (KEY_1, KEY_2) or "<" (KEY_1, KEY_2)) = FALSE

This is necessary due to the internal structure of the list i.e. that of a binary tree. Each node holds an item with a particular key value. Items with a lesser key value are stored down the left branch, and those with a greater value, down the right branch. The supplied operator "<", together with the implicit "=" operator, is used to compare key values to determine where to place an item, or search for items. If the supplied operator does not adhere to the tests above, then the location of a key (at a node, down the left or right branch) is not uniquely defined. This invalidates the logic of the implementation, and hence is a firm constraint on the operator. An example of a function which does not satisfy those tests is "< =". Code which instantiates this package with the "< =" operator is erroneous.

This package must not be used to store items keyed by an access type. This is because the implementation uses the predefined "=" operator as well as the user supplied "<". Whilst the user may define the "<" to apply some logic to the object referenced by the access type, the default "=" will test the access type objects themselves. Thus the constraint discussed in the preceding paragraph will be violated as the "=" test would be based upon different information (values of the access types themselves, a meaningless concept) to the "<" operator (based upon what ever the user chooses). See Options.

Efficiency

This package can be used to contain a list of any items, for any purpose. However its implementation, that of a balanced tree, is quite large regarding the quantity of source code.

The benefits of using any form of binary tree structure are its efficiency for searches and manipulation, being on average $\log_2(n)$ (where n is the number of items in the list). However, if a tree becomes unbalanced, then performance can move towards the worst case situation of n. This package uses and maintains a partially balanced tree, and is able to maintain the $\log_2(n)$ type performance. Thus this package is particularly efficient, in comparison to a simple binary tree, in situations where a simple tree may become unbalanced. This is often the case if the items being added or removed from the tree are not random according to their key value. Manipulation of the tree in a systematic way, e.g. appending larger successive key values, will cause such unbalancing in simple tree implementation.

The general relationship between the run time performance of the facilities provided in the package, against the number of items in the list (termed n) is as follows:

INITIALISE_LIST	constant
DESTROY_LIST	log (n!)
DEALLOCATE_LIST	log (n!)
DUPLICATE_LIST	log (n * n!)
EXTRACT_LIST	log (n1 * n2!)
	n1 items in source list
	n2 items to be copied
MERGE_LIST	log (n1!*n1!*(n1+n2)!/n2!)
	n1 is source list length
	n2 is destination list length
INSERT_ITEM	log (n)
DELETE_ITEM	log (n)
READ_DATA	log (n)
WRITE_DATA	log (n)
HIGHEST_KEY	log (n)
LOWEST_KEY	log (n)
HIGHER_KEY	log (n)
LOWER_KEY	log (n)
LIST_HAS_BEEN_INITIALISED	constant
KEY_EXISTS	log (n)
IS_EMPTY	constant

Package Body

```
with UNCHECKED_DEALLOCATION;
package body LIST_PKG is

   procedure ALLOCATE_NODE
             (NODE_REF : out NODE_REF_TYPE) is
   begin
      NODE_REF := new NODE_TYPE;
   end ALLOCATE_NODE;


   procedure ALLOCATE_LIST (LIST : out LIST_REF_TYPE) is
   begin
      LIST := new LIST_TYPE;
   end ALLOCATE_LIST;
```

3.7 - Lists

```ada
procedure DEALLOCATE_NODE
  (NODE_REF : in out NODE_REF_TYPE) is
   procedure NODE_DEALLOCATION is new
      UNCHECKED_DEALLOCATION (NODE_TYPE,NODE_REF_TYPE);
begin
   NODE_DEALLOCATION (NODE_REF);
end DEALLOCATE_NODE;


procedure DEALLOCATE_LIST
         (LIST : in out LIST_REF_TYPE) is
   procedure LIST_DEALLOCATION is new
      UNCHECKED_DEALLOCATION (LIST_TYPE,LIST_REF_TYPE);
begin
   if LIST = null then
      raise LIST_INITIALISATION_ERROR;
   else
      LIST_DEALLOCATION (LIST);
   end if;
end DEALLOCATE_LIST;


procedure SINGLE_LEFT_ROTATION
  (NODE_REF: in out NODE_REF_TYPE) is
   TEMP_NODE_REF : NODE_REF_TYPE;
begin
   TEMP_NODE_REF            := NODE_REF.LEFT_REF;
   NODE_REF.LEFT_REF        := TEMP_NODE_REF.RIGHT_REF;
   TEMP_NODE_REF.RIGHT_REF  := NODE_REF;
   NODE_REF.BALANCED        := LEFT_AND_RIGHT_EVEN;
   NODE_REF                 := TEMP_NODE_REF;
end SINGLE_LEFT_ROTATION;


procedure DOUBLE_LEFT_ROTATION
                 (NODE_REF : in out NODE_REF_TYPE) is
   TEMP_NODE_1_REF : NODE_REF_TYPE;
   TEMP_NODE_2_REF : NODE_REF_TYPE;
begin
   TEMP_NODE_1_REF := NODE_REF.LEFT_REF;
   TEMP_NODE_2_REF := TEMP_NODE_1_REF.RIGHT_REF;
   TEMP_NODE_1_REF.RIGHT_REF :=
                     TEMP_NODE_2_REF.LEFT_REF;
```

3.7 - Lists

```
      TEMP_NODE_2_REF.LEFT_REF  := TEMP_NODE_1_REF;
      NODE_REF.LEFT_REF         :=
                                   TEMP_NODE_2_REF.RIGHT_REF;
      TEMP_NODE_2_REF.RIGHT_REF := NODE_REF;
      if TEMP_NODE_2_REF.BALANCED = LEFT_IS_LONGER then
         NODE_REF.BALANCED := RIGHT_IS_LONGER;
      else
         NODE_REF.BALANCED := LEFT_AND_RIGHT_EVEN;
      end if;
      if TEMP_NODE_2_REF.BALANCED = RIGHT_IS_LONGER then
         TEMP_NODE_1_REF.BALANCED := LEFT_IS_LONGER;
      else
         TEMP_NODE_1_REF.BALANCED := LEFT_AND_RIGHT_EVEN;
      end if;
      NODE_REF := TEMP_NODE_2_REF;
   end DOUBLE_LEFT_ROTATION;


   procedure SINGLE_RIGHT_ROTATION
                   (NODE_REF : in out NODE_REF_TYPE) is
      TEMP_NODE_REF : NODE_REF_TYPE;
   begin
      TEMP_NODE_REF           := NODE_REF.RIGHT_REF;
      NODE_REF.RIGHT_REF      := TEMP_NODE_REF.LEFT_REF;
      TEMP_NODE_REF.LEFT_REF  := NODE_REF;
      NODE_REF.BALANCED       := LEFT_AND_RIGHT_EVEN;
      NODE_REF                := TEMP_NODE_REF;
   end SINGLE_RIGHT_ROTATION;


   procedure DOUBLE_RIGHT_ROTATION
                   (NODE_REF : in out NODE_REF_TYPE) is
      TEMP_NODE_1_REF : NODE_REF_TYPE;
      TEMP_NODE_2_REF : NODE_REF_TYPE;
   begin
      TEMP_NODE_1_REF           := NODE_REF.RIGHT_REF;
      TEMP_NODE_2_REF           := TEMP_NODE_1_REF.LEFT_REF;
      TEMP_NODE_1_REF.LEFT_REF  := TEMP_NODE_2_REF.RIGHT_REF;
      TEMP_NODE_2_REF.RIGHT_REF := TEMP_NODE_1_REF;
      NODE_REF.RIGHT_REF        := TEMP_NODE_2_REF.LEFT_REF;
      TEMP_NODE_2_REF.LEFT_REF  := NODE_REF;
      if TEMP_NODE_2_REF.BALANCED = RIGHT_IS_LONGER then
         NODE_REF.BALANCED := LEFT_IS_LONGER;
```

3.7 - Lists

```ada
      else
         NODE_REF.BALANCED := LEFT_AND_RIGHT_EVEN;
      end if;
      if TEMP_NODE_2_REF.BALANCED = LEFT_IS_LONGER then
         TEMP_NODE_1_REF.BALANCED := RIGHT_IS_LONGER;
      else
         TEMP_NODE_1_REF.BALANCED := LEFT_AND_RIGHT_EVEN;
      end if;
      NODE_REF := TEMP_NODE_2_REF;
   end DOUBLE_RIGHT_ROTATION;


   procedure INSERT_NODE (NODE_REF : in out NODE_REF_TYPE;
                          KEY      : in     KEY_TYPE;
                          DATA     : in     DATA_TYPE;
                   HEIGHT_INCREASED : in out BOOLEAN) is
   begin
      if NODE_REF = null then
         -- KEY value not located, create one and initialise
         ALLOCATE_NODE (NODE_REF);
         HEIGHT_INCREASED  := TRUE;
         NODE_REF.KEY      := KEY;
         NODE_REF.DATA     := DATA;
         NODE_REF.BALANCED := LEFT_AND_RIGHT_EVEN;
      elsif KEY < NODE_REF.KEY then
         -- The KEY for the item to be inserted is less than
         -- this node's key so insert item into the left branch
         INSERT_NODE
           (NODE_REF.LEFT_REF,KEY,DATA,HEIGHT_INCREASED);

         -- The purpose of the following section of code is to maintain
         -- the partially balanced nature of the tree.  This is achieved
         -- by rotating the items around a node depending upon which
         -- branch has grown.  This technique reflects that used
         -- in [WIRTH 76]

         if HEIGHT_INCREASED then
            -- The left branch has grown, check the old balance
            -- prior to this insertion
            case NODE_REF.BALANCED is
            when RIGHT_IS_LONGER      => -- set lengths even
               NODE_REF.BALANCED := LEFT_AND_RIGHT_EVEN;
               HEIGHT_INCREASED  := FALSE;
```

```
            when LEFT_AND_RIGHT_EVEN => -- left is now longer
                NODE_REF.BALANCED := LEFT_IS_LONGER;
            when LEFT_IS_LONGER       => -- Left is too long
                -- Balance must be restored
                -- How depends upon which branch has grown
                if NODE_REF.LEFT_REF.BALANCED =
                 LEFT_IS_LONGER then
                    SINGLE_LEFT_ROTATION (NODE_REF);
                else
                    DOUBLE_LEFT_ROTATION (NODE_REF);
                end if;
                -- Now balanced, set the indicator and
                -- clear the increase in height flag
                NODE_REF.BALANCED := LEFT_AND_RIGHT_EVEN;
                HEIGHT_INCREASED  := FALSE;
            end case;
        end if;

    elsif NODE_REF.KEY < KEY then
        -- The KEY for the item to be inserted is greater than
        -- this node's key, insert the item into right branch
        INSERT_NODE
          (NODE_REF.RIGHT_REF,KEY,DATA,HEIGHT_INCREASED)
        if HEIGHT_INCREASED then
            -- The right branch has grown, check the old balance before inse
            case NODE_REF.BALANCED is
            when LEFT_IS_LONGER       => -- set the lengths even
                NODE_REF.BALANCED := LEFT_AND_RIGHT_EVEN;
                HEIGHT_INCREASED  := FALSE;
            when LEFT_AND_RIGHT_EVEN => -- right is now longer
                NODE_REF.BALANCED := RIGHT_IS_LONGER;
            when RIGHT_IS_LONGER     => -- right is too long
                -- Balance must be restored
                -- How depends upon which branch has grown
                if NODE_REF.RIGHT_REF.BALANCED =
                 RIGHT_IS_LONGER then
                    SINGLE_RIGHT_ROTATION (NODE_REF);
                else
                    DOUBLE_RIGHT_ROTATION (NODE_REF);
                end if;
                -- Now balanced, set the indicator, and
                -- clear the increase in height flag
                NODE_REF.BALANCED := LEFT_AND_RIGHT_EVEN;
```

3.7 - Lists

```
                    HEIGHT_INCREASED    := FALSE;
            end case;
        end if;
    else
        -- A match to the key has been found - raise exception
        raise KEY_ALREADY_EXISTS_ERROR;
    end if;
end INSERT_NODE;


procedure INSERT_ITEM (LIST : in out LIST_REF_TYPE;
                       KEY  : in      KEY_TYPE;
                       DATA : in      DATA_TYPE) is
    HEIGHT_INCREASED : BOOLEAN := FALSE;
begin
    if LIST = null then
        raise LIST_INITIALISATION_ERROR;
    else
        INSERT_NODE (LIST.ROOT,KEY,DATA,HEIGHT_INCREASED);
    end if;
end INSERT_ITEM;


procedure BALANCE_LEFT (NODE_REF : in out NODE_REF_TYPE;
                HEIGHT_DECREASED : in out BOOLEAN) is
-- Invoked when the left branch has shrunk.
-- Check former balance and act accordingly
    TEMP_NODE_REF   : NODE_REF_TYPE;
    TEMP_NODE_2_REF : NODE_REF_TYPE;
begin
    case NODE_REF.BALANCED is
    when LEFT_IS_LONGER         =>
        NODE_REF.BALANCED := LEFT_AND_RIGHT_EVEN;
    when LEFT_AND_RIGHT_EVEN =>
        NODE_REF.BALANCED := RIGHT_IS_LONGER;
        HEIGHT_DECREASED  := FALSE;
    when RIGHT_IS_LONGER =>
        TEMP_NODE_REF    := NODE_REF.RIGHT_REF;
        if TEMP_NODE_REF.BALANCED /= LEFT_IS_LONGER then
            -- Perform a single right rotate
            NODE_REF.RIGHT_REF     := TEMP_NODE_REF.LEFT_REF;
            TEMP_NODE_REF.LEFT_REF := NODE_REF;
            if TEMP_NODE_REF.BALANCED = LEFT_AND_RIGHT_EVEN
```

```
                    then
                        NODE_REF.BALANCED          := RIGHT_IS_LONGER
                        TEMP_NODE_REF.BALANCED     := LEFT_IS_LONGER;
                        HEIGHT_DECREASED           := FALSE;
                    else
                        NODE_REF.BALANCED := LEFT_AND_RIGHT_EVEN;
                        TEMP_NODE_REF.BALANCED :=
                                                LEFT_AND_RIGHT_EVEN;
                    end if;
                    NODE_REF := TEMP_NODE_REF;
                else
                    -- Perform a double right rotation
                    TEMP_NODE_2_REF    := TEMP_NODE_REF.LEFT_REF
                    TEMP_NODE_REF.LEFT_REF :=
                                      TEMP_NODE_2_REF.RIGHT_R
                    TEMP_NODE_2_REF.RIGHT_REF:= TEMP_NODE_REF;
                    NODE_REF.RIGHT_REF := TEMP_NODE_2_REF.LEFT_R
                    TEMP_NODE_2_REF.LEFT_REF := NODE_REF;
                    if TEMP_NODE_2_REF.BALANCED=RIGHT_IS_LONGER
                    then
                        NODE_REF.BALANCED := LEFT_IS_LONGER;
                    else
                        NODE_REF.BALANCED := LEFT_AND_RIGHT_EVEN;
                    end if;
                    if TEMP_NODE_2_REF.BALANCED = LEFT_IS_LONGER
                    then
                        TEMP_NODE_REF.BALANCED := RIGHT_IS_LONGER
                    else
                        TEMP_NODE_REF.BALANCED :=
                                                LEFT_AND_RIGHT_EVE
                    end if;
                    NODE_REF                   := TEMP_NODE_2_REF;
                    TEMP_NODE_2_REF.BALANCED:= LEFT_AND_RIGHT_EVI
                end if;
        end case;
end BALANCE_LEFT;


procedure BALANCE_RIGHT
                    (NODE_REF : in out NODE_REF_TYPE;
               HEIGHT_DECREASED : in out BOOLEAN) is
-- Invoked when the right branch has shrunk.
-- Check former balance and act accordingly
```

3.7 - Lists

```
      TEMP_NODE_REF    : NODE_REF_TYPE;
      TEMP_NODE_2_REF  : NODE_REF_TYPE;
begin
   case NODE_REF.BALANCED is
   when RIGHT_IS_LONGER      =>
      NODE_REF.BALANCED := LEFT_AND_RIGHT_EVEN;
   when LEFT_AND_RIGHT_EVEN =>
      NODE_REF.BALANCED := LEFT_IS_LONGER;
      HEIGHT_DECREASED  := FALSE;
   when LEFT_IS_LONGER       =>
      TEMP_NODE_REF     := NODE_REF.LEFT_REF;
      if TEMP_NODE_REF.BALANCED /= RIGHT_IS_LONGER then
         -- Perform a single right rotate
         NODE_REF.LEFT_REF    := TEMP_NODE_REF.RIGHT_REF;
         TEMP_NODE_REF.RIGHT_REF := NODE_REF;
         if TEMP_NODE_REF.BALANCED = LEFT_AND_RIGHT_EVEN
         then
            NODE_REF.BALANCED      := LEFT_IS_LONGER;
            TEMP_NODE_REF.BALANCED := RIGHT_IS_LONGER;
            HEIGHT_DECREASED       := FALSE;
         else
            NODE_REF.BALANCED := LEFT_AND_RIGHT_EVEN;
            TEMP_NODE_REF.BALANCED :=
                                   LEFT_AND_RIGHT_EVEN;
         end if;
         NODE_REF := TEMP_NODE_REF;
      else
         -- Perform a double right rotation
         TEMP_NODE_2_REF     := TEMP_NODE_REF.RIGHT_REF;
         TEMP_NODE_REF.RIGHT_REF :=
                              TEMP_NODE_2_REF.LEFT_REF;
         TEMP_NODE_2_REF.LEFT_REF:= TEMP_NODE_REF;
         NODE_REF.LEFT_REF := TEMP_NODE_2_REF.RIGHT_REF;
         TEMP_NODE_2_REF.RIGHT_REF := NODE_REF;
         if TEMP_NODE_2_REF.BALANCED=LEFT_IS_LONGER then
            NODE_REF.BALANCED := RIGHT_IS_LONGER;
         else
            NODE_REF.BALANCED := LEFT_AND_RIGHT_EVEN;
         end if;
         if TEMP_NODE_2_REF.BALANCED = RIGHT_IS_LONGER
         then
            TEMP_NODE_REF.BALANCED := LEFT_IS_LONGER;
         else
```

```
                    TEMP_NODE_REF.BALANCED :=
                                             LEFT_AND_RIGHT_EVE
            end if;
            NODE_REF                   := TEMP_NODE_2_REF;
            TEMP_NODE_2_REF.BALANCED :=
                                             LEFT_AND_RIGHT_EVE
        end if;
    end case;
end BALANCE_RIGHT;


procedure DELETE_NODE (NODE_REF : in out NODE_REF_TYPE
                       KEY : in KEY_TYPE;
                       HEIGHT_DECREASED : in out BOOLEAN) is
    TEMP_NODE_REF : NODE_REF_TYPE;

    procedure DEL (DEL_NODE_REF : in out NODE_REF_TYPE;
                   HEIGHT_DECREASED : in out BOOLEAN) is
    begin
        -- Find the highest value down the branch
        if DEL_NODE_REF.RIGHT_REF /= null then
            DEL (DEL_NODE_REF.RIGHT_REF,HEIGHT_DECREASED)
            if HEIGHT_DECREASED then
                BALANCE_RIGHT (DEL_NODE_REF,
                               HEIGHT_DECREASED);
            end if;
        else
            -- Then copy its values up to the 'deleted' node
            TEMP_NODE_REF.KEY  := DEL_NODE_REF.KEY;
            TEMP_NODE_REF.DATA := DEL_NODE_REF.DATA;
            -- and shift the pointers, so that this node will be picked up
            -- as the TEMP_NODE being deleted
            TEMP_NODE_REF      := DEL_NODE_REF;
            -- and shift the left item up a layer
            DEL_NODE_REF       := DEL_NODE_REF.LEFT_REF;
            HEIGHT_DECREASED := TRUE;
        end if;
    end DEL;

begin
    if NODE_REF = null then
        -- The key value has not been found, raise the exception
        raise KEY_DOES_NOT_EXIST_ERROR;
```

```
      elsif KEY < NODE_REF.KEY then
         DELETE_NODE (NODE_REF.LEFT_REF, KEY,
                     HEIGHT_DECREASED);
         if HEIGHT_DECREASED then
            BALANCE_LEFT (NODE_REF, HEIGHT_DECREASED);
         end if;
      elsif NODE_REF.KEY < KEY then
         DELETE_NODE (NODE_REF.RIGHT_REF, KEY,
                     HEIGHT_DECREASED);
         if HEIGHT_DECREASED then
            BALANCE_RIGHT (NODE_REF, HEIGHT_DECREASED);
         end if;
      else  -- Key has been found
         TEMP_NODE_REF    := NODE_REF;
         if TEMP_NODE_REF.RIGHT_REF = null then
            NODE_REF         := TEMP_NODE_REF.LEFT_REF;
            HEIGHT_DECREASED := TRUE;
         elsif TEMP_NODE_REF.LEFT_REF = null then
            NODE_REF         := TEMP_NODE_REF.RIGHT_REF;
            HEIGHT_DECREASED := TRUE;
         else
            DEL (TEMP_NODE_REF.LEFT_REF,HEIGHT_DECREASED);
            if HEIGHT_DECREASED then
               BALANCE_LEFT(NODE_REF,HEIGHT_DECREASED);
            end if;
         end if;
         DEALLOCATE_NODE (TEMP_NODE_REF);
      end if;
end DELETE_NODE;


procedure DELETE_ITEM (LIST : in out LIST_REF_TYPE;
                       KEY  : in      KEY_TYPE) is
   HEIGHT_DECREASED : BOOLEAN := FALSE;
begin
   if LIST = null then
      raise LIST_INITIALISATION_ERROR;
   else
      DELETE_NODE (LIST.ROOT,KEY,HEIGHT_DECREASED);
   end if;
end DELETE_ITEM;
```

3.7 - Lists

```ada
procedure DEALLOCATE (LIST : in out LIST_REF_TYPE) is
begin
   DESTROY_LIST (LIST);
end DEALLOCATE;


procedure INITIALISE_LIST
                     (LIST : in out LIST_REF_TYPE) is
begin
   if LIST /= null then
      raise LIST_INITIALISATION_ERROR;
   else
      ALLOCATE_LIST(LIST);
   end if;
end INITIALISE_LIST;


procedure DESTROY_LIST (LIST : in out LIST_REF_TYPE) is
begin
   if LIST = null then
      raise LIST_INITIALISATION_ERROR;
   end if;
   while LIST.ROOT /= null
   loop
       DELETE_ITEM (LIST,LIST.ROOT.KEY);
   end loop;
   DEALLOCATE_LIST (LIST);
end DESTROY_LIST;


procedure DUPLICATE_LIST
                 (FROM_LIST : in    LIST_REF_TYPE;
                  TO_LIST   : in out LIST_REF_TYPE)
   KEY  : KEY_TYPE;
   DATA : DATA_TYPE;
begin
   if FROM_LIST = null or TO_LIST /= null then
      raise LIST_INITIALISATION_ERROR;
   end if;
   INITIALISE_LIST (TO_LIST);
   LOWEST_KEY (FROM_LIST, KEY, DATA);
   loop
      begin
```

3.7 - Lists

```
                  INSERT_ITEM (TO_LIST   , KEY, DATA);
                  HIGHER_KEY  (FROM_LIST, KEY, DATA);
         end;
      end loop;
   exception
      when KEY_DOES_NOT_EXIST_ERROR =>
         -- From LOWEST_KEY or HIGHER_KEY
         -- End of FROM_LIST reached, so exit.
         null;
   end DUPLICATE_LIST;



   procedure EXTRACT_LIST
                       (FROM_LIST   : in out LIST_REF_TYPE;
                        SET_OF_KEYS : in     SET_OF_KEYS_TYPE;
                        TO_LIST     : in out LIST_REF_TYPE) is
      ITEM_KEY  : KEY_TYPE;
      ITEM_DATA : DATA_TYPE;
   begin
      if FROM_LIST = null or TO_LIST /= null then
         raise LIST_INITIALISATION_ERROR;
      end if;
      INITIALISE_LIST (TO_LIST);
      LOWEST_KEY (FROM_LIST, ITEM_KEY, ITEM_DATA);
      loop
         if KEY_IS_VALID(ITEM_KEY,SET_OF_KEYS) then
             INSERT_ITEM (TO_LIST, ITEM_KEY, ITEM_DATA);
             DELETE_ITEM (FROM_LIST, ITEM_KEY);
         end if;
         HIGHER_KEY  (FROM_LIST, ITEM_KEY, ITEM_DATA);
      end loop;
   exception
      when KEY_DOES_NOT_EXIST_ERROR =>
         null;
   end EXTRACT_LIST;



   procedure MERGE_LIST
                       (FROM_LIST : in out LIST_REF_TYPE;
                        TO_LIST   : in out LIST_REF_TYPE) is
      ITEM_KEY  : KEY_TYPE;
      ITEM_DATA : DATA_TYPE;
   begin
```

```
         if FROM_LIST = null or TO_LIST = null then
            raise LIST_INITIALISATION_ERROR;
         end if;
         LOWEST_KEY (FROM_LIST, ITEM_KEY, ITEM_DATA);
         loop
            begin
               INSERT_ITEM (TO_LIST  , ITEM_KEY, ITEM_DATA);
               DELETE_ITEM (FROM_LIST, ITEM_KEY);
            exception
               when KEY_ALREADY_EXISTS_ERROR =>
                  -- From INSERT_ITEM call
                  -- Insert not performed, ignore exception
                  null;
            end;
            HIGHER_KEY (FROM_LIST, ITEM_KEY, ITEM_DATA);
         end loop;
      exception
         when KEY_DOES_NOT_EXIST_ERROR =>
            -- From LOWEST_KEY or HIGHER_KEY
            -- End of FROM_LIST reached, terminate the routine
            null;
      end MERGE_LIST;



      procedure READ_DATA (LIST : in      LIST_REF_TYPE;
                           KEY  : in      KEY_TYPE;
                           DATA :     out DATA_TYPE) is
         NODE_REF : NODE_REF_TYPE;
      begin
         if LIST = null then
            raise LIST_INITIALISATION_ERROR;
         end if;
         NODE_REF := LIST.ROOT;
         if NODE_REF = null then
            raise KEY_DOES_NOT_EXIST_ERROR;
         end if;
         while NODE_REF.KEY /= KEY
         loop
            if NODE_REF.KEY < KEY then
               NODE_REF := NODE_REF.RIGHT_REF;
            else
               NODE_REF := NODE_REF.LEFT_REF;
            end if;
```

3.7 - Lists

```
      if NODE_REF = null then
         raise KEY_DOES_NOT_EXIST_ERROR;
      end if;
   end loop;
   DATA := NODE_REF.DATA;
end READ_DATA;


procedure WRITE_DATA (LIST : in     LIST_REF_TYPE;
                      KEY  : in     KEY_TYPE;
                      DATA : in     DATA_TYPE) is
   NODE_REF : NODE_REF_TYPE;
begin
   if LIST = null then
      raise LIST_INITIALISATION_ERROR;
   end if;
   NODE_REF := LIST.ROOT;
   if NODE_REF = null then
      raise KEY_DOES_NOT_EXIST_ERROR;
   end if;
   while NODE_REF.KEY /= KEY
   loop
      if NODE_REF.KEY < KEY then
         NODE_REF := NODE_REF.RIGHT_REF;
      else
         NODE_REF := NODE_REF.LEFT_REF;
      end if;
      if NODE_REF = null then
         raise KEY_DOES_NOT_EXIST_ERROR;
      end if;
   end loop;
   NODE_REF.DATA := DATA;
end WRITE_DATA;


procedure HIGHEST_KEY (LIST : in     LIST_REF_TYPE;
                       KEY  :    out KEY_TYPE;
                       DATA :    out DATA_TYPE) is
   NODE_REF: NODE_REF_TYPE;
begin
   if LIST = null then
      raise LIST_INITIALISATION_ERROR;
   end if;
```

```
      if LIST.ROOT = null then
         raise KEY_DOES_NOT_EXIST_ERROR;
      end if;
      NODE_REF := LIST.ROOT;
      while NODE_REF.RIGHT_REF /= null
      loop
         NODE_REF := NODE_REF.RIGHT_REF;
      end loop;
      KEY  := NODE_REF.KEY;
      DATA := NODE_REF.DATA;
   end HIGHEST_KEY;


   procedure LOWEST_KEY (LIST : in      LIST_REF_TYPE;
                         KEY  :     out KEY_TYPE;
                         DATA :     out DATA_TYPE) is
      NODE_REF : NODE_REF_TYPE;
   begin
      if LIST = null then
         raise LIST_INITIALISATION_ERROR;
      end if;
      if LIST.ROOT = null then
         raise KEY_DOES_NOT_EXIST_ERROR;
      end if;
      NODE_REF := LIST.ROOT;
      while NODE_REF.LEFT_REF /= null
      loop
         NODE_REF := NODE_REF.LEFT_REF;
      end loop;
      KEY  := NODE_REF.KEY;
      DATA := NODE_REF.DATA;
   end LOWEST_KEY;


   procedure HIGHER_KEY (LIST : in      LIST_REF_TYPE;
                         KEY  : in  out KEY_TYPE;
                         DATA :     out DATA_TYPE) is
      type RESULT_TYPE is (HIGHER_NODE_FOUND,
                           KEY_ONLY_FOUND,
                           KEY_NOT_FOUND);

      function FIND_HIGHER_NODE
               (NODE_REF : in NODE_REF_TYPE)
```

3.7 - Lists

```
            return RESULT_TYPE is
   RESULT      : RESULT_TYPE;
   CHASE_NODE : NODE_REF_TYPE;
begin
   if NODE_REF = null then
      return KEY_NOT_FOUND ;
   end if;
   -- Locate the node containing the relevant key item.
   if KEY < NODE_REF.KEY then
      RESULT := FIND_HIGHER_NODE(NODE_REF.LEFT_REF);
      case RESULT is
         when HIGHER_NODE_FOUND =>
            -- Search complete, return from nested calls
            return HIGHER_NODE_FOUND;
         when KEY_ONLY_FOUND | KEY_NOT_FOUND =>
            -- As this was returned from a left branch, this node's
            -- key is the next highest.  Copy the values into the
            -- results variables and start return from nested calls
            KEY  := NODE_REF.KEY;
            DATA := NODE_REF.DATA;
            return HIGHER_NODE_FOUND;
      end case;
   elsif NODE_REF.KEY < KEY then
      RESULT := FIND_HIGHER_NODE
                              (NODE_REF.RIGHT_REF);
      case RESULT is
         when HIGHER_NODE_FOUND =>
            -- Search complete, return from nested calls
            return HIGHER_NODE_FOUND;
         when KEY_ONLY_FOUND | KEY_NOT_FOUND =>
            -- As this was returned from a right branch, this node's
            -- key is less than the required value, so keep returning
            -- from the nested calls until the return is from a left branch
            return KEY_ONLY_FOUND ;
      end case;
   else -- Found matching key
      if NODE_REF.RIGHT_REF = null then
         return KEY_ONLY_FOUND;
      else -- there is a greater key below this node
         -- Find the right branch's left most node
         CHASE_NODE := NODE_REF.RIGHT_REF;
         while CHASE_NODE.LEFT_REF /= null
         loop
```

```
                    CHASE_NODE := CHASE_NODE.LEFT_REF;
              end loop;
              KEY  := CHASE_NODE.KEY;
              DATA := CHASE_NODE.DATA;
              return HIGHER_NODE_FOUND;
         end if;
      end if;
   end;

   begin  -- HIGHER_KEY
      if LIST = null then
         raise LIST_INITIALISATION_ERROR;
      end if;
      if FIND_HIGHER_NODE (LIST.ROOT) /= HIGHER_NODE_FOUN
      then
         raise KEY_DOES_NOT_EXIST_ERROR;
      end if;
   end HIGHER_KEY;



   procedure LOWER_KEY (LIST : in      LIST_REF_TYPE;
                        KEY  : in out  KEY_TYPE;
                        DATA :    out DATA_TYPE) is
      type RESULT_TYPE is (LOWER_NODE_FOUND,
                           KEY_ONLY_FOUND,
                           KEY_NOT_FOUND);

      function FIND_LOWER_NODE
               (NODE_REF : in NODE_REF_TYPE)
                return RESULT_TYPE is
         RESULT     : RESULT_TYPE;
         CHASE_NODE : NODE_REF_TYPE;
      begin
         if NODE_REF = null then
            return KEY_NOT_FOUND ;
         end if;
         -- Locate the node containing the relevant key item
         if NODE_REF.KEY < KEY then
            RESULT := FIND_LOWER_NODE(NODE_REF.RIGHT_REF)
            case RESULT is
               when LOWER_NODE_FOUND =>
                  -- Search complete, return from nested calls
                  return LOWER_NODE_FOUND;
```

3.7 - Lists

```
                    when KEY_ONLY_FOUND | KEY_NOT_FOUND =>
                        -- As this was returned from a right branch, this node's
                        -- key is the next lowest.  Copy the values into the
                        -- results variables and start return up the nested calls
                        KEY  := NODE_REF.KEY;
                        DATA := NODE_REF.DATA;
                        return LOWER_NODE_FOUND;
                end case;
            elsif KEY < NODE_REF.KEY then
                RESULT := FIND_LOWER_NODE (NODE_REF.LEFT_REF);
                case RESULT is
                    when LOWER_NODE_FOUND =>
                        -- Search complete, return from nested calls
                        return LOWER_NODE_FOUND;
                    when KEY_ONLY_FOUND | KEY_NOT_FOUND =>
                        -- As this was returned from a right branch, this node's
                        -- key is less than the required value, so keep returning
                        -- from the nested calls until the return is from a left branch
                        return KEY_ONLY_FOUND ;
                end case;
            else  -- Found matching key
                if NODE_REF.LEFT_REF = null then
                    return KEY_ONLY_FOUND;
                else  -- There is a greater key below this node
                    -- Find the left branch's right most node
                    CHASE_NODE := NODE_REF.LEFT_REF;
                    while CHASE_NODE.RIGHT_REF /= null
                    loop
                        CHASE_NODE := CHASE_NODE.RIGHT_REF;
                    end loop;
                    KEY  := CHASE_NODE.KEY;
                    DATA := CHASE_NODE.DATA;
                    return LOWER_NODE_FOUND;
                end if;
            end if;
        end;

begin
    if LIST = null then
        raise LIST_INITIALISATION_ERROR;
    end if;
    if FIND_LOWER_NODE (LIST.ROOT) /= LOWER_NODE_FOUND
    then
```

3.7 - Lists

```ada
         raise KEY_DOES_NOT_EXIST_ERROR;
      end if;
   end LOWER_KEY;


   function LIST_HAS_BEEN_INITIALISED
            (LIST : LIST_REF_TYPE) return BOOLEAN is
   begin
      return LIST /= null;
   end LIST_HAS_BEEN_INITIALISED;


   function KEY_EXISTS (LIST : LIST_REF_TYPE;
                        KEY : KEY_TYPE) return BOOLEAN i
      NODE_REF : NODE_REF_TYPE;
   begin
      if LIST = null then
         raise LIST_INITIALISATION_ERROR;
      end if;
      NODE_REF := LIST.ROOT;
      loop
         if NODE_REF = null then
            return FALSE;
         elsif KEY < NODE_REF.KEY then
            NODE_REF := NODE_REF.LEFT_REF;
         elsif NODE_REF.KEY < KEY then
            NODE_REF := NODE_REF.RIGHT_REF;
         else
            return TRUE;
         end if;
      end loop;
   end KEY_EXISTS;


   function IS_EMPTY
            (LIST : LIST_REF_TYPE) return BOOLEAN is
   begin
      if LIST = null then
         raise LIST_INITIALISATION_ERROR;
      end if;
      return LIST.ROOT = null;
   end IS_EMPTY;
end LIST_PKG;
```

3.8 DYNAMIC TASKING

Tasking is a wide subject. Here three distinctions will be made about the use of tasks before introducing the components. The distinctions are those of:
    Static versus Dynamic
    Bounded versus Unbounded allocation
    Homogeneous versus Heterogeneous

Static tasks are implicitly initiated when control passes to the scope region in which they are declared. Little or no management of static tasks is required and they are not considered further.

Dynamic tasks are explicitly allocated by an assignment statement. More control may be exercised over when and how the tasks are run. Their advantages lie in being available when needed, and with multiple copies if required to cope with demand.

Bounded allocation occurs when there is a limit, other than available disk or main memory, on the number of concurrent tasks. Typically it arises when tasks are mapped to array elements. It is suitable in situations where the maximum number of required tasks is known beforehand, e.g. if a certain server task is initiated for each terminal, and the maximum number of on-line terminals is known at compilation time.

Unbounded allocation occurs when there is no clear limit to the number of tasks that may be initiated, leaving aside the effects of competing for general resources such as CPU time and available memory.

Homogeneous tasks occur where all tasks under consideration are of the same type.

Heterogeneous tasks occur where the tasks under consideration are of different types.

Description

Tasks are initiated, monitored and terminated dynamically. The documentation of this component is split into two parts. Homogeneous

3.8 - Dynamic Tasking

tasks (i.e. of the same type) are introduced first, and two models are exhibited:
i) a bounded model (tasks of the same type referenced by an array of pointers)
ii) an unbounded model (tasks of the same type referenced by pointers in a linked list).

In the second part, an unbounded heterogeneous model is presented.

Although in the format of a component, the contents of 3.8 are more of an example, because in practice some application-specific changes will have to be made before use (for guidance on how to use, see Pragmatics below).

Dependencies

None

Minimum Implementable Package

Either the homogeneous or the heterogeneous models will suit the particular problem domain. Similarly only one of the bounded or unbounded models is likely to be appropriate at each instantiation. Unused models may be safely omitted.

As regards the facilities within each model, clearly only initiation and some method of cessation of the tasks are essential. Monitoring is not always necessary. See under Pragmatics for further information.

Note: Tasks do not necessarily cease when their "parent" attempts to exit the block in which the tasks are declared.

3.8.1   HOMOGENEOUS TASKING

Package Specification

```
generic
   type TSK_ID_TYPE is private;
package TSK_PKG is

   task type TSK_TYPE is            --{ Start Category 1 Area }--
      entry INITIALISE (TSK_ID : TSK_ID_TYPE);
      entry DO_SOME_WORK;
      -- This entry is a dummy operation representing the various
      -- functions the task will be required to perform
      entry FINISH;
   end TSK_TYPE;
   type TSK_REF_TYPE is access TSK_TYPE;
                                    --{ End Category 1 Area }--
end TSK_PKG;



with TSK_PKG;
generic
   MAX_TSK_INX : positive;      -- Maximum no of concurrent tasks
   type TSK_ID_TYPE is private;
package BOUNDED_PKG is
   -- This package is solely concerned with tasks whose pointers
   -- reside in an array

   package TC is new TSK_PKG (TSK_ID_TYPE);
   use TC;

   TERMINATION_DELAY  : constant := 5.0;  -- Seconds
   TSK_ID_ERROR       : exception;
   NO_FREE_TSK_ERROR  : exception;
   procedure INITIATE_TSK  (TSK_ID : TSK_ID_TYPE);
      -- Initiates a task
      -- Raises NO_FREE_TSK_ERROR if all tasks are already running
   procedure TERMINATE_TSK (TSK_ID : TSK_ID_TYPE);
      -- Terminates a task
      -- Raises TSK_ID_ERROR if TSK_ID cannot be found
```

3.8.1 - Homogeneous Tasking

```ada
        -- N.B. If the task is unable to rendezvous within
        -- TERMINATION_DELAY (to order it to finish),
        -- then it will be aborted
    function CALLABLE    (TSK_ID : TSK_ID_TYPE)
                         return BOOLEAN;
        -- Returns indication of TSK_ID'CALLABLE
        -- Raises TSK_ID_ERROR if TSK_ID cannot be found
    function TERMINATED (TSK_ID : TSK_ID_TYPE)
                         return BOOLEAN;
        -- Returns indication of TSK_ID'TERMINATED
        -- Raises TSK_ID_ERROR if TSK_ID cannot be found
    function TSK_REF     (TSK_ID : TSK_ID_TYPE)
                         return TSK_REF_TYPE;
        -- Returns pointer to task
        -- Raises TSK_ID_ERROR if TSK_ID cannot be found
end BOUNDED_PKG;



with TSK_PKG;
generic
    type TSK_ID_TYPE is private;
package UNBOUNDED_PKG is
    -- This package is solely concerned with tasks whose pointers reside
    -- in an linked list (and there is therefore no program limitation
    -- on their number)

    package TC is new TSK_PKG (TSK_ID_TYPE);
    use TC;

    TERMINATION_DELAY : constant := 5.0;  -- Seconds
    TSK_ID_ERROR      : exception;
    procedure INITIATE_TSK  (TSK_ID : TSK_ID_TYPE);
        -- Initiates a task
    procedure TERMINATE_TSK (TSK_ID : TSK_ID_TYPE);
        -- Terminates a task
        -- Raises TSK_ID_ERROR if TSK_ID cannot be found
        -- N.B. If the task is unable to rendezvous within
        -- TERMINATION_DELAY (to order it to finish),
        -- then it will be aborted
    function CALLABLE    (TSK_ID : TSK_ID_TYPE)
                         return BOOLEAN;
        -- Returns indication of TSK_ID'CALLABLE
```

```
            -- Raises TSK_ID_ERROR if TSK_ID cannot be found
    function TERMINATED (TSK_ID : TSK_ID_TYPE)
                              return BOOLEAN;
            -- Returns indication of TSK_ID'TERMINATED
            -- Raises TSK_ID_ERROR if TSK_ID cannot be found
    function TSK_REF      (TSK_ID : TSK_ID_TYPE)
                              return TSK_REF_TYPE;
            -- Returns pointer to task
            -- Raises TSK_ID_ERROR if TSK_ID cannot be found
end UNBOUNDED_PKG;
```

Pragmatics

Three package specifications have been provided above:

TSK_PKG : a small package specification with a minimal interface, which would likely be greatly expanded in actual use.

BOUNDED_PKG : the specification for the bounded model.

UNBOUNDED_PKG : the specification for the unbounded model.

The last two packages are independent and either may be omitted if not required.

What the user must do, as a minimum, is as follows:
(a) in TSK_PKG, expand the specification and body of TSK_TYPE. The two areas requiring attention are bracketed thus:
    --{ Start Category 1 Area }--
    ...
    --{ End   Category 1 Area }--
The two entries INITIALISE and FINISH are the bare minimum, though normally, because of the need to communicate, there will be more (represented here by DO_SOME_WORK);
(b) instantiate either BOUNDED_PKG or UNBOUNDED_PKG before use (see example). TSK_PKG is already instantiated in the declaration of BOUNDED_PKG and UNBOUNDED_PKG.

It is also highly desirable for the user to:
(c) change the name of the task to something more meaningful;
(d) change the TERMINATION_DELAY as described below;

3.8.1 - Homogeneous Tasking

(e) consider the inclusion of the "or terminate" alternative as described below under Implementation Points.

In order to control tasks, each must be given an identifier. The initiator (in these examples) decides on a value of TSK_ID_TYPE (preferably not already in use by any existing task) to pass, and that will be used to identify the task from then on. In the bounded model, there is no point in allowing MAX_TSK_INX to be greater than the number of legal values in TSK_ID_TYPE. INITIATE_TSK does not check for duplicate values of TSK_ID_TYPE, but such checks can easily be incorporated inside or outside the package. If there are duplicate values of TSK_ID, TSK_REF will return a pointer to the first one it finds, and similarly TERMINATE_TSK will terminate the same first one.

The function TSK_REF is provided to facilitate calls to task entries. The syntax is of the form:

```
X.TSK_REF (TSK_ID).all.DO_SOME_WORK
```

where X represents the name of the instantiated BOUNDED_PKG or UNBOUNDED_PKG. Note that the "all" refers, not to any possible duplication of the value of TSK_ID, but to the task pointed to by the result of calling TSK_REF.

The bounded model is useful where there is a natural or desirable limit on the number of tasks to be initiated. Otherwise the unbounded model is the most appropriate.

In the bounded model, the value supplied for MAX_TSK_INX indicates the maximum number of tasks which can co-exist.

The unbounded model is unconstrained by the number of tasks but of course is still constrained by the available memory. When this constraint is exceeded, the run time system will raise STORAGE_ERROR.

The task body TSK_TYPE will naturally be considerably amplified in a real application. This package is more of an example than a component, since:
- the task type TSK_TYPE should be declared separately, i.e. not in the same compilation unit as here;
- more facilities are provided here than are ever likely to be needed all together.

Not all compilers elegantly support the separate compilation of TSK_TYPE from the generic specification. However this does not affect the need for recompilation due to changes at a higher level of the program.

It is wise for tasks to have exception handlers, as otherwise exceptions are liable to propagate and (in the worst case) cause other tasks to deadlock or terminate.

Once this package has been instantiated in a block or subprogram, the latter cannot be exited until any initiated tasks have terminated. It is advantageous to have a program structure, as here, where the task and task access type are declared at the same level. Where the task access type is declared at a higher level than the task object (i.e. TSK_REF_TYPE has a wider scope than BOUNDED_PKG or UNBOUNDED_PKG), problems may occur, e.g. if an object of the access type is still in scope when the task object is not, then attempted entries will have TASKING_ERROR raised (see ALRM 9.4).

While this component was not designed for tasks that activate more tasks, it is possible to use it for that purpose. Designers should pay careful attention to the rules for dependent tasks in the ALRM 9.3 and 9.4.

Note that there is a distinction in the ALRM between a task that has completed its execution (i.e. completed its executable statements) and one that is terminated (i.e. completed its execution and all dependent tasks are terminated; or, when conditions are such that the "terminate" alternative in a "select" statement is selected -- see ALRM 9.4). Because the tasks in this component do not have dependents, completion and termination take place at the same time.

Restrictions on use

Implementors should bear in mind the effects of address space, available memory, and CPU performance on tasking.

Exceptions

TSK_ID_ERROR is raised in all subroutines except INITIATE_TSK when an invalid TSK_ID, i.e. one corresponding to an uninitiated or terminated task, is passed as a parameter (but see TASKING_ERROR below).

3.8.1 - Homogeneous Tasking

N.B. The language prescribes that CONSTRAINT_ERROR should be raised for all usages of the task attributes TERMINATED and CALLABLE on uninitiated tasks. After termination, no exception is raised. In this component, because of the possibility of re-initiating a task, no distinction is made between the uninitiated and the terminated: all give rise to the same exception with TERMINATED and CALLABLE.

TASKING_ERROR is raised in package BOUNDED_PKG, procedure TERMINATE_TSK, when the task has already terminated voluntarily. The other situations, i.e. when the task has not been initiated and when the task has been explicitly terminated, give rise to TSK_ID_ERROR. BOUNDED_PKG is unique in that it retains data on terminated tasks, and so can distinguish between tasks that have exited on TERMINATE_TSK and those that exited anyway. If that distinction is considered to hinder more than help, then an exception handler could be added to TERMINATE_TSK. This handler would only handle TASKING_ERROR, and would reset the appropriate entry in TSK_BUSY_AY and then raise TSK_ID_ERROR.

NO_FREE_TSK_ERROR is raised in package BOUNDED_PKG, procedure INITIATE_TSK, when the maximum number of permitted tasks (MAX_TSK_INX) is exceeded.

STORAGE_ERROR is raised in any procedure when an attempt is made to obtain more memory than is currently available (normally after very many tasks are created).

Options

Options of bounded and unbounded are provided.

The timeout period for task self-termination to occur, TERMINATION_DELAY, should be altered to suit the intended circumstances.

It is possible to guard against the use of non-unique values of TSK_ID_TYPE if required. The simplest way to accomplish this is for INITIATE_TSK to be altered to call TSK_REF upon entry. If no exception is raised, the TSK_ID already exists, and an error returned, possibly through the use of an exception being raised. If an exception is raised when

178   3.8.1 - Homogeneous Tasking

TSK_REF is called, the TSK_ID is unique, and, after trapping the exception within a handler inside INITIATE_TSK, normal processing can continue.

This component was written to be particularly flexible. Many other possible enhancements, too numerous to identify, could be made.

Example of Use

A monitor task which allocates a server task for each terminal as a user logs on. There are a limited number of such servers. It is assumed that TSK_PKG has already been expanded, and that each TSK_TYPE task is capable of servicing one terminal. The monitor task shown below is only concerned with initiating and terminating the TSK_TYPE tasks, although other monitoring uses could be found.

```
package MONITOR_PKG is
    type TERM_ID_TYPE is      -- i.e. terminal ids
        (ACCOUNTS, DESIGN, MANUFACTURING, RESEARCH, STORE
         TRANSPORT);
    task MONITOR is
        entry LOGON  (TERM_ID : TERM_ID_TYPE);
        -- LOGON may pass on NO_FREE_TSK_ERROR
        entry LOGOFF (TERM_ID : TERM_ID_TYPE);
        -- LOGOFF may pass on TSK_ID_ERROR
        entry MONITOR_FINISH;
    end MONITOR;
end MONITOR_PKG;


with BOUNDED_PKG;
package body MONITOR_PKG is

    task body MONITOR is
        MAX_TSKS  : constant := 4;  -- Insufficient machine
                                    -- resources for more than 4 tasks
        COUNT     : INTEGER := 0;   -- Count of live tasks
        FINISHING : BOOLEAN := FALSE;

        package DTB is new BOUNDED_PKG
                        (MAX_TSKS, TERM_ID_TYPE);

    begin   -- body of MONITOR
```

3.8.1 - Homogeneous Tasking

```ada
          while not FINISHING loop
             begin   -- block
                loop
                   select
                      accept LOGON (TERM_ID : TERM_ID_TYPE) do
                         DTB.INITIATE_TSK (TERM_ID);
                         -- INITIATE_TSK may raise an exception
                         -- Log start time for this session etc
                      end LOGON;
                      COUNT := COUNT + 1;
                   or
                      accept LOGOFF (TERM_ID : TERM_ID_TYPE) do
                         DTB.TERMINATE_TSK (TERM_ID);
                         -- TERMINATE_TSK may raise an exception
                         -- Log finish time for this session etc
                      end LOGOFF;
                      COUNT := COUNT - 1;
                   or
                      when COUNT = 0 =>
                         accept MONITOR_FINISH;
                            FINISHING := TRUE;
                            exit;
                   or
                      terminate;
                   end select;
                end loop;
             exception
                when DTB.NO_FREE_TSK_ERROR|DTB.TSK_ID_ERROR =>
                   null;  -- Let caller deal with exception
             end;  -- of block
          end loop;
       end MONITOR;
    end MONITOR_PKG;
```

Implementation points

Note that dynamic tasks only come into existence by the use of the allocator **new**. Hence the liberal use of access types, even in the bounded model.

It should be remembered that tasks do not necessarily cease when their "parent" attempts to exit the block in which the tasks are declared. The rules for task termination in the ALRM should be consulted. There is a question of whether to leave in the "or terminate" alternative in the body of TSK_PKG; if in doubt, it is generally best to include it, as a hung (i.e. deadlocked) system then becomes less likely. In the body of TSK_PKG, the terminate alternative is present as well as the FINISH entry which signals a task to exit.

The TERMINATE_TSK procedure contains a procedure RENDEZVOUS which actually communicates with the task that is to finish. It attempts to rendezvous with the designated task within a delay period of TERMINATION_DELAY. The user must ensure that a "rendezvousing" task will complete its execution immediately afterwards (as in the body of TSK_TYPE above). Failing a rendezvous within the stipulated time, the task is unconditionally aborted. Because an attempted rendezvous with a completed task raises TASKING_ERROR, an exception handler for that exception causes RENDEZVOUS to be exited immediately in the event that the task has already terminated (for whatever reason).

TERMINATION_DELAY is the fixed period in which a task must rendezvous to be told to terminate, failing which it is aborted. It is a matter for judgement as to whether to abort slow tasks. If this facility is included, some experimentation may be necessary to find a suitable value of TERMINATION_DELAY for each application on a given processor.

Task IDs are actually stored in the body of the component. It is usually necessary to record externally relevant mappings or other data. E.g. in the example shown above, it may be necessary to keep a record of which terminals have servers allocated.

The unbounded model makes use of a single linked list. The first element in the list is pointed to by LIST_START. The last element is pointed to by LIST_END, in order to facilitate adding to the list.

In the bounded model, array elements are not reused because the corresponding element in TSK_BUSY_AY is not reset. This arrangement may be changed to permit reuse, by including an assignment of that array in procedure TERMINATE_TSK. It should be noted that there normally needs to be some minimum period before such reuse, in order to allow the RTS time to complete any necessary housekeeping associated with the termination. Experimentation should determine the appropriate period; a more satisfactory solution may well be to invoke an operating system inquiry function to ensure that the RTS believes that the previous task has terminated.

3.8.1 - Homogeneous Tasking

In the unbounded model, it would be tidier if the procedure TERMINATE_TSK could make use of the function TSK_REF. However, the pointers (access types) for all tasks are in a single linked list and, in order to remove a terminated task from the linked list, the previous pointer must be available. TSK_REF does not supply the previous pointer. Rewriting the package UNBOUNDED_PKG to use a double linked list would enable TSK_REF to be used.

Efficiency

The efficiency of the package has a minor dependence on the number of tasks declared or initiated. Essentially a search of an array or a linked list must take place in several procedures and functions, to find a given identifier, and that clearly depends on the number of identifiers.

To be specific, all the visible procedures and functions have TSK_ID as a parameter, requiring (except in INITIATE_TSK) a search for that value. They will therefore perform proportionally to the number of array elements (in BOUNDED_PKG) or the number of tasks initiated (in UNBOUNDED_PKG).

It should also be borne in mind that, depending on the implementation of the RTS in use, the overhead in servicing a rendezvous may be partially dependent on the number of tasks waiting on it.

Package Body

```
package body TSK_PKG is

      task body TSK_TYPE is          --{ Start Category 1 Area }--
         -- This task body is a dummy, shown for completeness. In practice
         -- it would be much larger and separately compiled much later

         MY_TSK_ID : TSK_ID_TYPE;
      begin
         accept INITIALISE (TSK_ID : TSK_ID_TYPE) do
            MY_TSK_ID := TSK_ID;
         end INITIALISE;
         loop
            select
```

3.8.1 - Homogeneous Tasking

```ada
         accept DO_SOME_WORK;
         -- This entry is a dummy operation representing the
         -- functions the task will be required to perform
      or
         accept FINISH;
         exit;
      or
         terminate;
      end select;
   end loop;
end TSK_TYPE;                        --{ End Category 1 Area }--
end TSK_PKG;



package body BOUNDED_PKG is
   -- This package is solely concerned with tasks whose pointers
   -- reside in an array

   subtype TSK_INX_TYPE is positive
                              range 1 .. MAX_TSK_INX;
   TSK_AY       : array (TSK_INX_TYPE) of TSK_REF_TYPE
   TSK_ID_AY    : array (TSK_INX_TYPE) of TSK_ID_TYPE;
   TSK_BUSY_AY  : array (TSK_INX_TYPE) of BOOLEAN :=
                              (others => FALSE);
                              -- TRUE  means Initiated
                              -- FALSE means Not initiated

   function NEXT_FREE_TSK return TSK_INX_TYPE is
   begin
      for T in TSK_INX_TYPE loop
         if not TSK_BUSY_AY (T) then
            return T;
         end if;
      end loop;
      raise NO_FREE_TSK_ERROR;
   end NEXT_FREE_TSK;

   function INX_OF (TSK_ID : TSK_ID_TYPE)
      return TSK_INX_TYPE is
   begin
      for T in TSK_INX_TYPE loop
         if TSK_BUSY_AY (T) then
```

3.8.1 - Homogeneous Tasking

```ada
         if TSK_ID_AY (T) = TSK_ID then
            return T;
         end if;
      end if;
   end loop;
   raise TSK_ID_ERROR;
end INX_OF;

function TSK_REF (TSK_ID : TSK_ID_TYPE)
   return TSK_REF_TYPE is
begin
   return TSK_AY (INX_OF (TSK_ID));
end TSK_REF;

procedure INITIATE_TSK (TSK_ID : TSK_ID_TYPE) is
   TSK_INX : TSK_INX_TYPE;
begin
   TSK_INX                   := NEXT_FREE_TSK;
   TSK_AY (TSK_INX)          := new TSK_TYPE;
   TSK_ID_AY (TSK_INX)       := TSK_ID;
   TSK_BUSY_AY (TSK_INX)     := TRUE;
   TSK_AY (TSK_INX).INITIALISE (TSK_ID);
end INITIATE_TSK;

procedure TERMINATE_TSK (TSK_ID : TSK_ID_TYPE) is
   TSK_INX : TSK_INX_TYPE;
begin
   TSK_INX := INX_OF (TSK_ID);
   select
      TSK_AY (TSK_INX).FINISH;
   or
      delay TERMINATION_DELAY;
      abort TSK_AY (TSK_INX).all;
   end select;
   TSK_BUSY_AY (TSK_INX) := FALSE;
end TERMINATE_TSK;

function  CALLABLE   (TSK_ID : TSK_ID_TYPE)
   return BOOLEAN is
begin
   return TSK_AY (INX_OF (TSK_ID)).all 'CALLABLE;
end CALLABLE;
```

```ada
      function TERMINATED (TSK_ID : TSK_ID_TYPE)
         return BOOLEAN is
      begin
         return TSK_AY (INX_OF (TSK_ID)).all 'TERMINATE
      end TERMINATED;
   end BOUNDED_PKG;



   package body UNBOUNDED_PKG is
      -- This package is solely concerned with tasks whose pointers
      -- reside in a linked list (and there is therefore no
      -- program limitation on their number)

      type LIST_ITEM_TYPE;
      type LINK_TYPE is access LIST_ITEM_TYPE;
      type LIST_ITEM_TYPE is record
         TSK    : TSK_REF_TYPE;
         TSK_ID : TSK_ID_TYPE;
         LINK   : LINK_TYPE;
      end record;

      LIST_START, LIST_END : LINK_TYPE;

      procedure INITIATE_TSK (TSK_ID : TSK_ID_TYPE) is
      begin
         if LIST_START = null then   -- list is empty
            LIST_START := new LIST_ITEM_TYPE'
                              (TSK    => new TSK_TYPE,
                               TSK_ID => TSK_ID,
                               LINK   => null);
            LIST_END := LIST_START;
         else
            LIST_END.LINK := new LIST_ITEM_TYPE'
                              (TSK    => new TSK_TYPE,
                               TSK_ID => TSK_ID,
                               LINK   => null);
            LIST_END := LIST_END.LINK;
         end if;
         LIST_END.TSK.all.INITIALISE (TSK_ID);
      end INITIATE_TSK;
```

3.8.1 - Homogeneous Tasking

```
procedure TERMINATE_TSK (TSK_ID : TSK_ID_TYPE) is
-- Terminates a task
L, M : LINK_TYPE;
procedure RENDEZVOUS (TSK : TSK_REF_TYPE) is
begin
   select
      TSK.FINISH;
   or
      delay TERMINATION_DELAY;
      abort TSK.all;
   end select;
exception
   when TASKING_ERROR => raise TSK_ID_ERROR;
end RENDEZVOUS;

begin      -- TERMINATE_TSK
   L := LIST_START;
   if L = null then
      raise TSK_ID_ERROR;
   end if;
   if L.TSK_ID = TSK_ID then
      LIST_START := LIST_START.LINK;
      if LIST_START = null then
         LIST_END := null;
      end if;
      RENDEZVOUS (L.TSK);
      return;
   end if;
   M := LIST_START;
   L := M.LINK;
   while L /= null loop
      if L.TSK_ID = TSK_ID then
         M.LINK := L.LINK;
         if M.LINK = null then
            LIST_END := M;
         end if;
         RENDEZVOUS (L.TSK);
         return;
      else
         M := L;
         L := L.LINK;
      end if;
   end loop;
```

```
      raise TSK_ID_ERROR;
   end TERMINATE_TSK;


   function  TSK_REF (TSK_ID : TSK_ID_TYPE)
      return TSK_REF_TYPE is
      L, M : LINK_TYPE;
   begin
      L := LIST_START;
      if L = null then
         raise TSK_ID_ERROR;
      end if;
      if L.TSK_ID = TSK_ID then
         return L.TSK;
      end if;
      M := LIST_START;
      L := M.LINK;
      while L /= null loop
         if L.TSK_ID = TSK_ID then
            return L.TSK;
         else
            M := L;
            L := L.LINK;
         end if;
      end loop;
      raise TSK_ID_ERROR;
   end TSK_REF;


   function  CALLABLE   (TSK_ID : TSK_ID_TYPE)
      return BOOLEAN is
   begin
      return TSK_REF (TSK_ID).all'CALLABLE;
   end CALLABLE;


   function  TERMINATED (TSK_ID : TSK_ID_TYPE)
      return BOOLEAN is
   begin
      return TSK_REF (TSK_ID).all'TERMINATED;
   end TERMINATED;
end UNBOUNDED_PKG;
```

3.8.2   HETEROGENEOUS TASKING

Package Specification

```ada
generic
   type TSK_ID_TYPE is private;

package HETEROGENEOUS_TSK_PKG is

   task type RED_TSK_TYPE is        --{ Start Category 1 Area }--
      entry INITIALISE (TSK_ID : TSK_ID_TYPE);
      entry DO_SOME_WORK;
      -- This entry is a dummy operation representing the various
      -- functions the task will be required to perform
      entry FINISH;
   end RED_TSK_TYPE;
   task type YELLOW_TSK_TYPE is
      entry INITIALISE (TSK_ID : TSK_ID_TYPE);
      entry DO_SOME_WORK;       -- This entry is a dummy operation
      entry FINISH;
   end YELLOW_TSK_TYPE;
   task type GREEN_TSK_TYPE is
      entry INITIALISE (TSK_ID : TSK_ID_TYPE);
      entry DO_SOME_WORK;       -- This entry is a dummy operation
      entry FINISH;
   end GREEN_TSK_TYPE;           --{ End Category 1 Area }--

                                 --{ Start Category 2 Area }--
   type VAR_TSK_TYPE is (RED, YELLOW, GREEN);
   type TSK_TYPE (VAR : VAR_TSK_TYPE) is record
      case VAR is
         when RED    => RT : RED_TSK_TYPE;
         when YELLOW => YT : YELLOW_TSK_TYPE;
         when GREEN  => GT : GREEN_TSK_TYPE;
      end case;
   end record;                   --{ End Category 2 Area }--
   type TSK_REF_TYPE is access TSK_TYPE;

end HETEROGENEOUS_TSK_PKG;
```

3.8.2 - Heterogeneous Tasking

```ada
with HETEROGENEOUS_TSK_PKG;

generic
   type TSK_ID_TYPE is private;

package HETEROGENEOUS_PKG is

   package VTP is new HETEROGENEOUS_TSK_PKG
                           (TSK_ID_TYPE);
   use VTP;
   TERMINATION_DELAY : constant := 5.0;  -- Seconds
   TSK_ID_ERROR      : exception;

   procedure INITIATE_TSK  (TSK_ID : TSK_ID_TYPE;
                            VAR    : VAR_TSK_TYPE);
      -- Initiates a task of type VAR
   procedure TERMINATE_TSK (TSK_ID : TSK_ID_TYPE);
      -- Terminates a task
      -- Raises TSK_ID_ERROR if TSK_ID cannot be found
      -- N.B. If the task is unable to rendezvous within
      -- TERMINATION_DELAY (to order it to finish),
      -- then it will be aborted
   function  CALLABLE    (TSK_ID : TSK_ID_TYPE)
                           return BOOLEAN;
      -- Returns indication of TSK_ID'CALLABLE
      -- Raises TSK_ID_ERROR if TSK_ID cannot be found
   function  TERMINATED  (TSK_ID : TSK_ID_TYPE)
                           return BOOLEAN;
      -- Returns indication of TSK_ID'TERMINATED
      -- Raises TSK_ID_ERROR if TSK_ID cannot be found
   function  TSK_REF     (TSK_ID : TSK_ID_TYPE)
                           return TSK_REF_TYPE;
      -- Returns pointer to task
      -- Raises TSK_ID_ERROR if TSK_ID cannot be found
   function  TSK_VAR     (TSK_ID : TSK_ID_TYPE)
                           return VAR_TSK_TYPE;
      -- Returns task type (red, yellow, etc)
      -- Raises TSK_ID_ERROR if TSK_ID cannot be found
end HETEROGENEOUS_PKG;
```

3.8.2 - Heterogeneous Tasking

Pragmatics

Two package specifications have been provided above:

HETEROGENEOUS_TSK_PKG:
A small package specification with a minimal interface, which should be greatly expanded in actual use. Three different task types (RED_TSK_TYPE, YELLOW_TSK_TYPE, and GREEN_TSK_TYPE) have been used as an illustration.

HETEROGENEOUS_PKG:
The specification for the unbounded heterogeneous model.

What the user must do, as a minimum, is as follows:
(a) As in section 1, fill in the specifications and bodies, in this case of all the required task types. Clearly more or less than three types may be needed. The areas affected in the source code are highlighted as Category 1 Areas, just as in the homogeneous model.
(b) Ensure that VAR_TSK_TYPE in the package specification contains one value for each task type. The area needing attention here is highlighted as a Category 2 Area in the source.
(c) Expand the variant record TSK_TYPE such that any selection of the discriminant VAR will select the corresponding task type. This is also a Category 2 Area.
(d) Expand the case statements in INITIATE_TSK, TERMINATE_TSK, CALLABLE and TERMINATED so that the corresponding entry of the correct task type is selected by VAR. These case statements are highlighted as Category 3 Areas in the source.
(e) Instantiate HETEROGENEOUS_PKG, which instantiates HETEROGENEOUS_TSK_PKG automatically.

The highly desirable things to do are as in the pragmatics for homogeneous tasks.

The heterogeneous case is clearly more complicated than the homogeneous in that the task type now has to be catered for. Here the variable identifying the task type is an enumeration type with three values (RED, YELLOW and GREEN), but clearly any discrete type will do. As before, each task is provided with a unique identifier of TSK_ID_TYPE.

Also as before, the function TSK_REF is provided to allow access to task entries. The syntax is of the form:

```
X.TSK_REF (TSK_ID).YT.DO_SOME_WORK
```

where X represents the name of the instantiated HETEROGENEOUS_PKG and YT is the task component of TSK_TYPE corresponding to the task's type. The latter may always be found, if not already known, by an invocation of TSK_VAR.

Only an unbounded model has been provided because the bounded model would be awkward to manage in the heterogeneous case and would be unlikely to be required. As before, however, there are practical limits to the number of tasks, depending on the implementation and the application.

For other pragmatics related to dynamic tasking, please refer to the section for homogeneous tasks. For an alternative implementation of heterogeneous tasks, please refer to Implementation Points below.

Restrictions on Use

As for homogenous tasks

Exceptions

TSK_ID_ERROR is raised in all subroutines, except INITIATE_TSK, when an invalid TSK_ID, i.e. one corresponding to an uninitiated or terminated task, is passed as a parameter.

N.B. The language prescribes that CONSTRAINT_ERROR should be raised for all usages of the task attributes TERMINATED and CALLABLE on uninitiated tasks. After termination, no exception is raised. In this component, because of the possibility of re-initiating a task, no distinction is made between the uninitiated and the terminated: all give rise to the same exception with TERMINATED and CALLABLE.

STORAGE_ERROR is raised in any procedure when an attempt is made to obtain more memory than is currently available (normally after very many tasks are created).

3.8.2 - Heterogeneous Tasking

Options

As for the options for homogeneous tasks, except that an unbounded option only is provided.

Example of Use

A despatcher for peripheral device drivers. First, a general package of types, DEVICE_PKG, is declared:

```
package DEVICE_PKG is
   type DEVICE_CODE_TYPE is new INTEGER range 1 .. 255;
   -- values above are for example only
   type DEVICE_TYPE is (MAG_TAPE, PRINTER, PLOTTER,
                        FLOPPY_DISK);
   type MAG_TAPE_TYPE is (NRZ, PE, GCR);
   type DEVICE_INFO_REC (DEV : DEVICE_TYPE) is
      record
          DEVNO : DEVICE_CODE_TYPE;
          case DEV is
             when MAG_TAPE =>
                MTYPE            : MAG_TAPE_TYPE;
                MIN_BLOCKSIZE    : POSITIVE;
                MAX_BLOCKSIZE    : POSITIVE;
                -- etc
             when others =>
                -- etc
          end case;
       end record;
   type TERM_ID_TYPE is new INTEGER range 1 .. 100;
end DEVICE_PKG;
```

Next, the Category 1 and 2 areas of the specification of HETEROGENEOUS_TSK_PKG are declared (the body follows from the spec and so is not shown):

```
with DEVICE_PKG; use DEVICE_PKG;
generic
   type TSK_ID_TYPE is private;
package HETEROGENEOUS_TSK_PKG is
   task type MAG_TAPE_TYPE is        --{ Start Category 1 Area }--
```

3.8.2 - Heterogeneous Tasking

```ada
        entry INITIALISE (TSK_ID  : TSK_ID_TYPE;
                          DEVINFO : DEVICE_INFO_REC);
        entry READ    (S : out STRING);
        entry WRITE   (S : STRING);
        entry REWIND;
        entry FINISH;
     end MAG_TAPE_TYPE;
     task type PRINTER_TYPE is
        -- etc
     end PRINTER_TYPE;
     task type PLOTTER_TYPE is
        -- etc
     end PLOTTER_TYPE;
     task type FLOPPY_DISK_TYPE is
        -- etc
     end FLOPPY_DISK_TYPE;               --{ End Category 1 Area }--

                                         --{ Start Category 2 Area }--
     type TSK_TYPE (VAR : DEVICE_TYPE) is record
        case VAR is
           when PRINTER     => PT  : PRINTER_TYPE;
           when PLOTTER     => PLT : PLOTTER_TYPE;
           when MAG_TAPE    => MT  : MAG_TAPE_TYPE;
           when FLOPPY_DISK => FT  : FLOPPY_DISK_TYPE;
        end case;
     end record;                         --{ End Category 2 Area }--
     type TSK_REF_TYPE is access TSK_TYPE;

end HETEROGENEOUS_TSK_PKG;
```

The specification of HETEROGENEOUS_PKG is unchanged, save for:

```ada
with HETEROGENEOUS_TSK_PKG, DEVICE_PKG;
use  DEVICE_PKG;
generic   -- etc
```

The package body HETEROGENEOUS_PKG is also unchanged except for the Category 3 areas, of which one, in INITIATE_TSK, is given as an example:

3.8.2 - Heterogeneous Tasking

```
        case VAR is             --{ Start of Category 3 Area }--
           when PRINTER      => LIST_END.TSK.PT.INITIALISE
                                  (TSK_ID, DEVINFO);
           when PLOTTER      => LIST_END.TSK.PLT.INITIALISE
                                  (TSK_ID, DEVINFO);
           when MAG_TAPE     => LIST_END.TSK.MT.INITIALISE
                                  (TSK_ID, DEVINFO);
           when FLOPPY_DISK  => LIST_END.TSK.MT.INITIALISE
                                  (TSK_ID, DEVINFO);
        end case;               --{ End of Category 3 Area }--
```

We now declare the code that is going to make use of the dynamic tasking component.

```
with DEVICE_PKG; use DEVICE_PKG;
with HETEROGENEOUS_TSK_PKG;
with HETEROGENEOUS_PKG;

package DESPATCHER_PKG is

    -- The body of this package will instantiate HETEROGENEOUS_PKG with
    -- DETAILED_DEVICE_TYPE as TSK_ID_TYPE

    type DETAILED_DEVICE_TYPE is
         (LINEPRINTER, LASERPRINTER, CYL_PLOTTER,
          MAG_TAPE_NRZ, MAG_TAPE_PE, MAG_TAPE_GCR,
          FLOPPY_DISK_3_HALF_IN);

    task DESPATCHER is

         entry ASSIGN (TERM_ID : TERM_ID_TYPE;
                       DDEV    : DETAILED_DEVICE_TYPE);
         -- ASSIGN checks that the device is not already assigned, creates a
         -- device information record, records the device as assigned to the
         -- terminal, deduces the device type (and therefore task type) VAR
         -- from a table, and initiates the appropriate task using a call such
         -- as: INITIATE_TSK (DDEV, DEVINFO, VAR); the caller is
         -- then able to call directly the entries of the device-handling task
         -- using DDEV as task id
```

3.8.2 - Heterogeneous Tasking

```
            entry DEASSIGN (TERM_ID : TERM_ID_TYPE;
                            DDEV     : DETAILED_DEVICE_TYPE);
            -- DEASSIGN is the reverse of ASSIGN. It checks that the device is
            -- currently assigned to that terminal, records it as unassigned, and
            -- issues a task termination such as: TERMINATE_TSK (DDEV);

            entry DESPATCHER_FINISH;

        end DESPATCHER;

end DESPATCHER_PKG;
```

Implementation Points

The difficulty in implementing dynamic heterogeneous tasking lies in the fact that the type of an access variable depends on the type that it points to. This inevitably results in case statements and variant records, and an interface less clean than would be wished; except for one other possibility. The entry points of a task do not all have to be in the same select statement; sets of entry points corresponding to the different types could be grouped in different select statements within general-purpose tasks.

Which set of entry points to select would probably be determined by a case statement depending on the task type. Then the unbounded model of the homogeneous tasks could be used, with the modification that the INITIALISE entry would have to pass to each task its type as well as its TSK_ID.

Such general-purpose tasks would be very big as regards size of code, and would be very unlikely to be suitable in real-time systems. In non-real-time systems with virtual memory, they may be worth consideration.

Otherwise, the implementation points are as for the unbounded model in the homogeneous tasks.

Efficiency

As for the unbounded model described under homogeneous tasks.

Package Body

```ada
package body HETEROGENEOUS_TSK_PKG is

   task body RED_TSK_TYPE is          --{ Start Category 1 Area }--
      MY_TSK_ID : TSK_ID_TYPE;
   begin
      accept INITIALISE (TSK_ID : TSK_ID_TYPE) do
         MY_TSK_ID := TSK_ID;
      end INITIALISE;
      loop
         select
            accept DO_SOME_WORK;
         or
            accept FINISH;
            exit;
         or
            terminate;
         end select;
      end loop;
   end RED_TSK_TYPE;

   task body YELLOW_TSK_TYPE is
      MY_TSK_ID : TSK_ID_TYPE;
   begin
      accept INITIALISE (TSK_ID : TSK_ID_TYPE) do
         MY_TSK_ID := TSK_ID;
      end INITIALISE;
      loop
         select
            accept DO_SOME_WORK;
         or
            accept FINISH;
            exit;
         or
            terminate;
         end select;
      end loop;
   end YELLOW_TSK_TYPE;

   task body GREEN_TSK_TYPE is
      MY_TSK_ID : TSK_ID_TYPE;
   begin
```

3.8.2 - Heterogeneous Tasking

```ada
            accept INITIALISE (TSK_ID : TSK_ID_TYPE) do
               MY_TSK_ID := TSK_ID;
            end INITIALISE;
            loop
               select
                  accept DO_SOME_WORK;
               or
                  accept FINISH;
                  exit;
               or
                  terminate;
               end select;
            end loop;
      end GREEN_TSK_TYPE;                    --{ End Category 1 Area }--

   end HETEROGENEOUS_TSK_PKG;



   package body HETEROGENEOUS_PKG is

      type LIST_ITEM_TYPE;
      type LINK_TYPE is access LIST_ITEM_TYPE;
      type LIST_ITEM_TYPE is record
         TSK    : TSK_REF_TYPE;
         TSK_ID : TSK_ID_TYPE;
         VAR    : VAR_TSK_TYPE;
         LINK   : LINK_TYPE;
      end record;

      LIST_START, LIST_END : LINK_TYPE;

      procedure INITIATE_TSK  (TSK_ID : TSK_ID_TYPE;
                               VAR    : VAR_TSK_TYPE) is
      begin
         if LIST_START = null then   -- list is empty
            LIST_START := new LIST_ITEM_TYPE'
                              (TSK     => new TSK_TYPE (VAR)
                               TSK_ID  => TSK_ID,
                               VAR     => VAR,
                               LINK    => null);
            LIST_END := LIST_START;
         else
```

3.8.2 - Heterogeneous Tasking

```ada
            LIST_END.LINK := new LIST_ITEM_TYPE'
                              (TSK    => new TSK_TYPE (VAR),
                               TSK_ID => TSK_ID,
                               VAR    => VAR,
                               LINK   => null);
            LIST_END := LIST_END.LINK;
         end if;
         case VAR is            --{ Start Category 3 Area }--
            when RED    =>
               LIST_END.TSK.RT.INITIALISE (TSK_ID);
            when YELLOW =>
               LIST_END.TSK.YT.INITIALISE (TSK_ID);
            when GREEN  =>
               LIST_END.TSK.GT.INITIALISE (TSK_ID);
         end case;              --{ End Category 3 Area }--
      end INITIATE_TSK;

      procedure TERMINATE_TSK (TSK_ID : TSK_ID_TYPE) is
         -- Terminates a task

         L, M : LINK_TYPE;

         procedure RENDEZVOUS (TSK : TSK_REF_TYPE) is
            VAR : VAR_TSK_TYPE := TSK.VAR;
         begin
            case VAR is         --{ Start Category 3 Area }--
               when RED =>
                  select
                     TSK.RT.FINISH;
                  or
                     delay TERMINATION_DELAY;
                     abort TSK.RT;
                  end select;
               when YELLOW =>
                  select
                     TSK.YT.FINISH;
                  or
                     delay TERMINATION_DELAY;
                     abort TSK.YT;
                  end select;
               when GREEN =>
                  select
                     TSK.GT.FINISH;
```

3.8.2 - Heterogeneous Tasking

```
              or
                 delay TERMINATION_DELAY;
                 abort TSK.GT;
              end select;
         end case;                      --{ End Category 3 Area }--
      exception
         when TASKING_ERROR => raise TSK_ID_ERROR;
      end RENDEZVOUS;

   begin   -- TERMINATE_TSK
      L := LIST_START;
      if L = null then
         raise TSK_ID_ERROR;
      end if;

      if L.TSK_ID = TSK_ID then
         LIST_START := LIST_START.LINK;
         if LIST_START = null then
            LIST_END := null;
         end if;
         RENDEZVOUS (L.TSK);
         return;
      end if;

      M := LIST_START;
      L := M.LINK;

      while L /= null loop
         if L.TSK_ID = TSK_ID then
            M.LINK := L.LINK;
            if M.LINK = null then
               LIST_END := M;
            end if;
            RENDEZVOUS (L.TSK);
            return;
         else
            M := L;
            L := L.LINK;
         end if;
      end loop;
      raise TSK_ID_ERROR;
   end TERMINATE_TSK;
```

3.8.2 - Heterogeneous Tasking

```ada
function TSK_REF (TSK_ID : TSK_ID_TYPE)
                 return TSK_REF_TYPE is
   L, M : LINK_TYPE;
begin
   L := LIST_START;
   if L = null then
      raise TSK_ID_ERROR;
   end if;

   if L.TSK_ID = TSK_ID then
      return L.TSK;
   end if;

   M := LIST_START;
   L := M.LINK;
   while L /= null loop
      if L.TSK_ID = TSK_ID then
         return L.TSK;
      else
         M := L;
         L := L.LINK;
      end if;
   end loop;
   raise TSK_ID_ERROR;
end TSK_REF;


function CALLABLE (TSK_ID : TSK_ID_TYPE)
                   return BOOLEAN is
   VAR : VAR_TSK_TYPE := TSK_VAR (TSK_ID);
begin
   case VAR is              --{ Start Category 3 Area }--
      when RED    =>
         return TSK_REF (TSK_ID).RT 'CALLABLE;
      when YELLOW =>
         return TSK_REF (TSK_ID).YT 'CALLABLE;
      when GREEN  =>
         return TSK_REF (TSK_ID).GT 'CALLABLE;
   end case;                --{ End Category 3 Area }--
end CALLABLE;
```

```
      function   TERMINATED (TSK_ID : TSK_ID_TYPE)
                            return BOOLEAN is
         VAR : VAR_TSK_TYPE := TSK_VAR (TSK_ID);
      begin
         case VAR is              --{ Start Category 3 Area }--
            when RED    =>
               return TSK_REF (TSK_ID).RT 'TERMINATED;
            when YELLOW =>
               return TSK_REF (TSK_ID).YT 'TERMINATED;
            when GREEN  =>
               return TSK_REF (TSK_ID).GT 'TERMINATED;
         end case;                --{ End Category 3 Area }--
      end TERMINATED;

      function  TSK_VAR (TSK_ID : TSK_ID_TYPE)
                         return VAR_TSK_TYPE is
      begin
         return TSK_REF (TSK_ID).VAR;
      end TSK_VAR;

   end HETEROGENEOUS_PKG;
```

3.9 SETS

Description

This package provides facilities to manipulate sets of objects. The usual operations from set theory (union, intersection, membership tests, etc) are included. Those familiar with Pascal should note that the Pascal set features and manipulations are provided, except for set constructors that create an explicit set.

It should be noted that in a set a given element may either be present or absent, but that is the limit to its freedom. The Set should be distinguished from another abstract data type, not provided here, called a Bag. In a bag, none or several instances of a given element may be present at any given moment.

Dependencies

External : None.
Internal : The functions "<", "<=" and ">=" all depend on ">".

Minimum Implementable Package

Subject to the internal dependencies mentioned above, the functions and procedures stand on their own, and can therefore be arranged in any suitable selection.

Package Specification

```
generic
   type ELEMENT_TYPE is (<>);
package SETS_PKG is
   type SET_TYPE is private;
   EMPTY_SET : constant SET_TYPE;
   function "+" (LEFT,RIGHT : SET_TYPE) return SET_TYPE;
   function "-" (LEFT,RIGHT : SET_TYPE) return SET_TYPE;
```

3.9 - Sets

```ada
function "*" (LEFT,RIGHT : SET_TYPE) return SET_TYPE;

-- Equality and inequality are automatically provided by the language definition

function "+" (LEFT  : ELEMENT_TYPE;
              RIGHT : SET_TYPE)         return SET_TYPE;
function "+" (LEFT  : SET_TYPE;
              RIGHT : ELEMENT_TYPE)     return SET_TYPE;
function "+" (LEFT,RIGHT : ELEMENT_TYPE)
                                        return SET_TYPE;
function "-" (LEFT  : SET_TYPE;
              RIGHT : ELEMENT_TYPE)     return SET_TYPE;
-- The way to delete an element from a set

function "not" (RIGHT : SET_TYPE)       return SET_TYPE;
-- This function negates every element in the set

function ">"  (LEFT,RIGHT : SET_TYPE) return BOOLEAN;
function "<"  (LEFT,RIGHT : SET_TYPE) return BOOLEAN;
function ">=" (LEFT,RIGHT : SET_TYPE) return BOOLEAN;
function "<=" (LEFT,RIGHT : SET_TYPE) return BOOLEAN;
function RANGE_OF (LEFT,RIGHT: ELEMENT_TYPE)
                                        return SET_TYPE;
-- Returns set with all elements in that range set to present. The word
-- 'range' is reserved in Ada, so it could not be used

function MEMBER_OF (ELEMENT : ELEMENT_TYPE;
                    SET     : SET_TYPE) return BOOLEAN;

private

    type SET_AY_TYPE is array (ELEMENT_TYPE) of BOOLEAN;
    pragma PACK (SET_AY_TYPE);
    type SET_TYPE is
       record
           SET_AY : SET_AY_TYPE := (others => FALSE);
       end record;

    EMPTY_SET : constant SET_TYPE :=
                (SET_AY => (others => FALSE));
end SETS_PKG;
```

Pragmatics

This package must be instantiated with an element type. Any type that is an integer type or an enumeration type, or derived from them, is acceptable. The types that are not permitted are float and fixed (see Restrictions on Use).

The set operations that are provided here are:

Intersection :
The '*' function. This is the same as the logical "And" function on sets in standard Pascal.

Union :
The '+' function. This is the same as the logical "Or" function on sets in standard Pascal.

Difference :
The '-' function. The difference between two sets is a set containing all the items from the first set that are not in the second. Similarly the difference between a set and an element is the set without that element (see below under Deleting).

Adding an element to a set :
The '+' function. A way of creating a set with a single element is to add that element to the empty set.

Deleting an element from a set :
The '-' function.

Adding elements from a range to a set :
The RANGE_OF function. This creates a set with each element contained within the limits specified by the parameters present, inclusive of the range delimiters. Specifying a null range causes the EMPTY_SET to be returned. It cannot be used to add items to an already existing set.

Negation :
Negating a set returns a set where all formerly present elements are absent, and vice versa. It can be seen that for any set S, where the negated set is represented by notS, the following are identities:

    S or notS =   {All elements present}
    S and notS =   {Empty-set}

3.9 - Sets

Membership test :
The boolean MEMBER_OF function. Checks whether a particular item is present in a set.

Equality :
A = B gives the result of true if A and B are sets created from the same instantiation of SETS_PKG, and all the elements of A are in B, and of B are in A.

Inclusion :
If A and B are sets created from the same instantiation of SETS, then
    A > B and
    B < A
are both true if B is a proper subset of A (i.e. all elements of B are in A, and A has more elements). Furthermore,
    A > = B and
    B < = A
will be true if either of the above conditions, equality or inclusion, holds.

Initial assignment :
Sets are created empty. If necessary, they may be re-initialised to the constant EMPTY_SET. A set with a single element present may be created by union of the element and the EMPTY_SET.

Note that the operations provided above use the mathematical notation. There are exactly equivalent operations using logical notation, as follows:

	Mathematical	Logical
Intersection	*	and
Union	+	or
Negation		not
Difference	-	not-implies

Exactly the same functions may be defined using the logical notation, e.g.
function "or" (LEFT,RIGHT : SET_TYPE) **return** SET_TYPE
etc.

Possible Ambiguous Case
It is possible for an ambiguous case to arise where the operators defined for set operations are also valid for other operators on the element type. For instance, consider the following example (that will not compile) of a set of integers.

```
declare
   subtype REDUCED_RANGE_INTEGER is INTEGER range 1..100
   package INTEGER_SET_PKG is new SETS_PKG
                                    (REDUCED_RANGE_INTEGER
   use INTEGER_SET_PKG;
   S1, S2       : SET_TYPE;
   E1, E2, E3   : INTEGER;
begin
   E3 := E1 +   E2;
   S1 := S1 +   E1 + E2;
   S2 := S2 +   (E1 + E2);  -- Ambiguous case
end;
```

The "+" operation on two integers is defined both arithmetically (yielding integer result) and in terms of this package (yielding a set result). The first assignment, of E3, is clearly the result of an arithmetical operation. The expression to the right of S1 is evaluated left to right so that two set additions are compiled. It is the last assignment that is ambiguous; the compiler is given no clue as to what is required by the programmer.

It is always possible to write statements unambiguously, possibly necessitating intermediate variable assignments.

An alternative is to redefine the operations in equivalent logical terms as indicated above. The disadvantage is that, if instantiated for boolean element types, there will be new ambiguous cases.

A third alternative is not to **use** the instantiation, and only express as, e.g. S2 := S2 + INTEGER_SET_PKG."+"(E1, E2);

Restrictions on Use

This implementation is dependent upon the use of an object declared to be an array of booleans, with one element per potential set element. Clearly this implementation cannot be used if there is an infinite number of potential set members, such as would be the case for unbounded or contiguous (i.e. non-discrete) types.

For contiguous but bounded sets, (e.g. -10.0 .. 10.0, in floating point) it may be possible to map the items onto integers (e.g. -10,000 .. 10,000). This might be used for sets of floating-point numbers, where some resolution unit may be used (i.e. 0.001 in the example). Such a mapping would have to be chosen with care to ensure portability due to restricted ranges of integer types available.

For unbounded sets, or contiguous sets which require precise representation (or at least more precise than any of the available integer types can provide), then an implementation is needed which only uses RAM for each item contained in the set, rather then for each item that can potentially be contained in the set. This could be achieved using a linked list approach, possibly using the List component (3.7).

The above argument should also be used for bounded sets, but where the memory required to create the boolean array is unacceptably large. This might well be the case for sets of INTEGERs or even more so for LONG_INTEGERs, both of which are discrete and bounded, but would use very large amounts of memory.

If a set of fixed point numbers is required, then they too should be mapped onto a suitable set of integers.

Exceptions

None.

Options

None.

Example of Use

A function NEXT_FLOOR in an elevator control program determines which floor is the next one for the elevator to stop at. The floors requested are held in a set. The function picks the first floor requested in the current direction; if there are none, then the first one in the opposite direction; failing that, it returns to the bottom floor.

```
with SETS_PKG;
    .
    .
    TOP_FLOOR     : constant := 10;  -- say
    BOTTOM_FLOOR  : constant := 1;
```

```ada
subtype FLOOR_TYPE is integer
                    range BOTTOM_FLOOR .. TOP_FLOOR;
package FLOOR_SET_PKG is new SETS_PKG (FLOOR_TYPE);
type DIRECTION_TYPE is (UP, DOWN);

-- Parameters to NEXT_FLOOR :
-- FS              : set of requested floors
-- CURR_FLOOR      : floor which elevator is about to depart
-- DIR             : direction last moved
function NEXT_FLOOR
     (FS              : FLOOR_SET_PKG.SET_TYPE;
      CURR_FLOOR      : FLOOR_TYPE;
      DIR             : DIRECTION_TYPE) return FLOOR_TYPE
   use FLOOR_SET_PKG;
   S : FLOOR_SET_PKG.SET_TYPE := FS - CURR_FLOOR;

   function NEXT_FLOOR_IN_DIRECTION
      (D : DIRECTION_TYPE;
       S : FLOOR_SET_PKG.SET_TYPE) return FLOOR_TYPE
   begin
      if D = UP then
         if S - RANGE_OF(FLOOR_TYPE'FIRST, CURR_FLOOR)
            FLOOR_SET_PKG.EMPTY_SET then
            return NEXT_FLOOR_IN_DIRECTION (DOWN, S);
         end if;
         for F in CURR_FLOOR+1 .. FLOOR_TYPE'LAST loop
            if MEMBER_OF (F, S) then
               return F;
            end if;
         end loop;
      else  -- Down
         if S - RANGE_OF (CURR_FLOOR, FLOOR_TYPE'LAST)
            FLOOR_SET_PKG.EMPTY_SET then
            return NEXT_FLOOR_IN_DIRECTION (UP, S);
         end if;
         for F in reverse
             FLOOR_TYPE'FIRST .. CURR_FLOOR-1 loop
            if MEMBER_OF (F, S) then
               return F;
            end if;
         end loop;
      end if;
```

3.9 - Sets

```
        end NEXT_FLOOR_IN_DIRECTION;

begin    -- NEXT_FLOOR
    if S = FLOOR_SET_PKG.EMPTY_SET then
        return FLOOR_TYPE'FIRST;   -- No floors requested
    end if;
    return NEXT_FLOOR_IN_DIRECTION (DIR, S);
end NEXT_FLOOR;
```

Implementation Points

A record structure is used for SET_TYPE in the private part of the package spec in order to be able to guarantee that every set is empty on its creation.

Pragma PACK is used (after the declaration of SET_AY_TYPE) to enable the most efficient packing available on the target machine. On some machines this pragma has no effect.

Efficiency

The internal representation of a set is that of an array of booleans, one per potential set member. The performance of each of the subprograms is dependent upon the size of this array, and hence the maximum number of items in the set. The exception is MEMBER_OF whose performance is unrelated to size.

Package Body

```
package body SETS_PKG is

    function "+" (LEFT,RIGHT : SET_TYPE) return SET_TYPE is
        SET : SET_TYPE;
    begin
        for ELEMENT in ELEMENT_TYPE loop
            SET.SET_AY (ELEMENT) := LEFT.SET_AY (ELEMENT) or
                                    RIGHT.SET_AY (ELEMENT);
        end loop;
        return SET;
    end "+";
```

```
function "-" (LEFT,RIGHT : SET_TYPE) return SET_TYPE i
   SET : SET_TYPE;
begin
   for ELEMENT in ELEMENT_TYPE loop
      SET.SET_AY (ELEMENT) := LEFT.SET_AY (ELEMENT) an
                                  not RIGHT.SET_AY (ELEMENT
   end loop;
   return SET;
end "-";


function "*" (LEFT,RIGHT : SET_TYPE) return SET_TYPE i
   SET : SET_TYPE;
begin
   for ELEMENT in ELEMENT_TYPE loop
      SET.SET_AY (ELEMENT) := LEFT.SET_AY (ELEMENT) an
                                  RIGHT.SET_AY (ELEMENT);
   end loop;
   return SET;
end "*";


function "+" (LEFT  : ELEMENT_TYPE;
              RIGHT : SET_TYPE) return SET_TYPE is
   SET : SET_TYPE := RIGHT;
begin
   SET.SET_AY (LEFT) := TRUE;
   return SET;
end "+";


function "+" (LEFT  : SET_TYPE;
              RIGHT : ELEMENT_TYPE) return SET_TYPE is
   SET : SET_TYPE := LEFT;
begin
   SET.SET_AY (RIGHT) := TRUE;
   return SET;
end "+";


function "+" (LEFT,RIGHT : ELEMENT_TYPE)
                                       return SET_TYPE i
   SET : SET_TYPE := EMPTY_SET;
```

3.9 - Sets

```ada
begin
   SET.SET_AY (LEFT ) := TRUE;
   SET.SET_AY (RIGHT) := TRUE;
   return SET;
end "+";


function "-" (LEFT  : SET_TYPE;
              RIGHT : ELEMENT_TYPE) return SET_TYPE is
   SET : SET_TYPE := LEFT;
begin
   SET.SET_AY (RIGHT) := FALSE;
   return SET;
end "-";


function "not" (RIGHT : SET_TYPE) return SET_TYPE is
-- This function negates every element in the set
   SET : SET_TYPE;
begin
   SET.SET_AY := not RIGHT.SET_AY;
   return SET;
end "not";


function ">"  (LEFT,RIGHT : SET_TYPE) return BOOLEAN is
   LEFT_TOTAL, RIGHT_TOTAL : NATURAL := 0;
begin
   for ELEMENT in ELEMENT_TYPE loop
      if RIGHT.SET_AY (ELEMENT) and not
         LEFT.SET_AY (ELEMENT) then
         return FALSE;
      end if;
      if LEFT.SET_AY (ELEMENT) then
         LEFT_TOTAL := LEFT_TOTAL + 1;
      end if;
      if RIGHT.SET_AY (ELEMENT) then
         RIGHT_TOTAL := RIGHT_TOTAL + 1;
      end if;
   end loop;
   return (LEFT_TOTAL > RIGHT_TOTAL);
end ">";
```

```
function "<"  (LEFT,RIGHT : SET_TYPE) return BOOLEAN i
begin
   return RIGHT > LEFT;
end "<";


function ">="  (LEFT,RIGHT : SET_TYPE) return BOOLEAN i
begin
   return LEFT > RIGHT or LEFT = RIGHT;
end ">=";


function "<="  (LEFT,RIGHT : SET_TYPE) return BOOLEAN i
begin
   return RIGHT >= LEFT;
end "<=";


function RANGE_OF (LEFT,RIGHT : ELEMENT_TYPE)
                                          return SET_TYPE
   SET : SET_TYPE := EMPTY_SET;
begin
   for ELEMENT in LEFT .. RIGHT loop
      SET.SET_AY (ELEMENT) := TRUE;
   end loop;
   return SET;
end RANGE_OF;


function MEMBER_OF (ELEMENT: ELEMENT_TYPE;
                    SET    : SET_TYPE) return BOOLEAN
begin
   return SET.SET_AY (ELEMENT);
end MEMBER_OF;

end SETS_PKG;
```

3.10 PERMUTATIONS

Description

Sometimes is is necessary to obtain all possible permutations of a set of objects, for example for generating test conditions, cryptoanalysis or even for anagrams.

This package provides a generic facility to generate all permutations of a set of discrete values.

A permutation is a complete arrangement of a set of distinct values in some order. For example, "14235" is a permutation of the set '1'..'5'; "43521" is another.

Dependencies

None.

Component Specification

```
generic

   type INDEX_TYPE is (<>);
   type PERM_TYPE  is array (INDEX_TYPE) of INDEX_TYPE;

package PERMUTATION_PKG is

   procedure NEXT_PERMUTATION  (RIGHT : in out PERM_TYPE
   procedure PREV_PERMUTATION  (RIGHT : in out PERM_TYPE
   procedure FIRST_PERMUTATION (RIGHT :    out PERM_TYPE
   procedure LAST_PERMUTATION  (RIGHT :    out PERM_TYPE

end PERMUTATION_PKG;
```

3.10 - Permutations

Pragmatics

The NEXT_PERMUTATION procedure generates the next permutation in "lexicographic" order, as defined in the ALRM, section 4.5.2. The PREV_PERMUTATION procedure generates the previous permutation. For example, the next permutation of "14235" is "14253".

It is necessary to supply both the INDEX_TYPE and PERM_TYPE as parameters to the instantiation, rather than the PERM_TYPE only. This is a quirk of the Ada language, but has no particular significance.

Note that the index type and component type of PERM_TYPE must be the same. Thus this generic cannot be used to permute the characters 'A' .. 'F' indexed by 1..6. This avoids the risk of the index type and component type being of different lengths; it would be meaningless to try to permute 'A' .. 'F' indexed by 1..9.

However, the user of this package can employ the 'POS and 'VAL attributes to convert to or from integer values, as in the example below.

String literals can be used for CHARACTER permutations, as shown in the example below. However, objects of the type used to satisfy the formal generic parameter PERM_TYPE cannot be used as parameters to the TEXT_IO package. This is because although, like type STRING, PERM_TYPE would be an array of CHARACTER, its index would be CHARACTER, not INTEGER as in STRING's case.

Although the set of values to be permuted is fixed when the generic is instantiated, the range can be determined dynamically. For example, the numbers 1..N, where N is a run time variable, can be permuted.

If the package is instantiated for an ITEM_TYPE with only a single value, then some compilers may issue warnings that CONSTRAINT_ERROR will be raised. It occurs because the package body has code which attempts to perform calculations using SUCC and PRED attributes. This is correct, and in accordance with the behaviour documented in the exceptions section.

Instantiating generic units can be slow on some compilers. If so, you should instantiate PERMUTATION_PKG as a library package, and use the instantiation, rather than instantiating PERMUTATION_PKG locally.

3.10 - Permutations

Restrictions on use

The INDEX_TYPE generic parameter must be discrete, that is either enumeration types or integers. For certain objects, such as test conditions, it will be necessary to construct an external mapping to a convenient discrete type.

The use of an instantiation of this package for null ranges of ITEM_TYPE is erroneous and the results undefined. If the package is instantiated for an ITEM_TYPE with a null range, then the procedures will return values which are uninitialised. The use of such values is erroneous.

Exceptions

CONSTRAINT_ERROR is raised explicitly if NEXT_PERMUTATION is called on the last permutation; also if PREV_PERMUTATION is called on the first permutation.

In addition a compiler may issue a warning that a CONSTRAINT_ERROR will be raised within the package body, if the package is instantiated for a type with only a single value, due to some static expressions (e.g. in LAST_PERMUTATION) which will not be invoked at run time. As such, these warnings should be ignored.

Calling NEXT_PERMUTATION or PREV_PERMUTATION with an unassigned RIGHT value is erroneous. Its effect is undefined and may result in an exception being raised.

Options

Instantiations of the package which are erroneous due to the use of null range PERM_TYPEs could be trapped by the addition of an executable part to the package. As in the case for instantiations for PERM_TYPEs with only a single value, when an instantiation for null range is compiled, warnings regarding CONSTRAINT_ERRORs may be issued (see Pragmatics). Warnings, if issued, may be disregarded, or simply not seen. If code were inserted into the executable part of the package body that explicitly raised an exception when PERM_TYPE was found to be a null range, then this could be trapped at elaboration time. This approach may be useful, but is not a recommended means of avoiding erroneous code.

3.10 - Permutations

Example of use

```ada
with PERMUTATION_PKG;

procedure PERMUTATION_PKG_EXAMPLE is
   type LETTER_TYPE is new CHARACTER range 'A' .. 'D';
   type LETTER_PERM_TYPE is array (LETTER_TYPE)
                                   of LETTER_TYPE;
   package PERM is new PERMUTATION_PKG (LETTER_TYPE,
                                        LETTER_PERM_TYPE);
   P: LETTER_PERM_TYPE :=   "BDCA";
   -- note the use of a string literal assignment

begin
   PERM.NEXT_PERMUTATION(P);
   -- P = "CABD" and P('C') = 'B'
end PERMUTATION_PKG_EXAMPLE;
```

Implementation points

The implementations of NEXT_PERMUTATION and PREV_PERMUTATION differ only by two comparison tests, and therefore lend themselves to be implemented as instantiations of a generic procedure declared locally within the package body. The algorithm for both is as follows:

1. There is only one permutation of length 1, so eliminate this case first as an exception.

2. Search back from the end of the permutation for the start of the slice of the permutation array that is to be changed. If none, this is the last (or first) permutation, so treat as an exception.

3. Search forward again to find the last component in the slice of the permutation array.

4. Reverse the order of these components in the slice to give the next (previous) permutation by interchanging them a pair at a time. If there is an odd number of components, the middle one does not need to be interchanged.

Efficiency

The performance of each function is proportional to the number of elements in the ITEM_TYPE.

Package Body

```
package body PERMUTATION_PKG is

   generic -- Local to the body, to reduce code size
      with function COMPARE (LEFT,RIGHT : INDEX_TYPE)
                                              return BOOLEAN
   procedure NEXTDOOR_PERM (RIGHT : in out PERM_TYPE);

   procedure NEXTDOOR_PERM (RIGHT : in out PERM_TYPE) is
      START, FINISH, SWAP_TEMP : INDEX_TYPE;
   begin
      if RIGHT'LENGTH < 2 then
         raise CONSTRAINT_ERROR;
      end if;

      for J in reverse
      RIGHT'FIRST .. INDEX_TYPE'PRED (RIGHT'LAST) loop
         if COMPARE (RIGHT(J), RIGHT(INDEX_TYPE'SUCC(J))
         then
            START := J;
            exit;
         elsif J = RIGHT'FIRST then
            raise CONSTRAINT_ERROR;
         else
            null;
         end if;
      end loop;

      for J in INDEX_TYPE'SUCC(START) .. RIGHT'LAST loop
         if COMPARE (RIGHT(J), RIGHT(START)) then
            FINISH := INDEX_TYPE'PRED(J);
            exit;
         elsif J = RIGHT'LAST then
            FINISH := J;
         end if;
      end loop;
```

3.10 - Permutations

```
         SWAP_TEMP      := RIGHT (START);
         RIGHT (START)  := RIGHT (FINISH);
         RIGHT (FINISH) := SWAP_TEMP;
         START          := INDEX_TYPE'SUCC (START);
         FINISH         := RIGHT'LAST;

         while START < FINISH loop
            SWAP_TEMP      := RIGHT (START);
            RIGHT (START)  := RIGHT (FINISH);
            RIGHT (FINISH) := SWAP_TEMP;
            START          := INDEX_TYPE'SUCC (START);
            FINISH         := INDEX_TYPE'PRED (FINISH);
         end loop;
      end NEXTDOOR_PERM;


      procedure NEXT_PERM is new NEXTDOOR_PERM ("<");
      procedure PREV_PERM is new NEXTDOOR_PERM (">");


      procedure NEXT_PERMUTATION (RIGHT : in out PERM_TYPE) is
      begin
         NEXT_PERM (RIGHT);
      end NEXT_PERMUTATION;


      procedure PREV_PERMUTATION (RIGHT : in out PERM_TYPE) is
      begin
         PREV_PERM (RIGHT);
      end PREV_PERMUTATION;


      procedure FIRST_PERMUTATION (RIGHT: out PERM_TYPE) is
      begin
         for J in RIGHT'RANGE loop
            RIGHT(J) :=  J;
         end loop;
      end FIRST_PERMUTATION;


      procedure LAST_PERMUTATION (RIGHT: out PERM_TYPE) is
         J : INDEX_TYPE := INDEX_TYPE'LAST;
      begin
```

```
      for K in RIGHT'RANGE loop
         RIGHT(K) := J;
         if J /= INDEX_TYPE'FIRST then
            J := INDEX_TYPE'PRED(J);
         end if;
      end loop;
   end LAST_PERMUTATION;

end PERMUTATION_PKG;
```

3.11 CHECKSUM

Description

This package provides the ability to calculate a checksum for a file containing compilable Ada source code. In conjunction with an Ada compiler, the package is able to provide a high level of confidence that a file of Ada source code is unaltered from some baseline. This can be used in aid of configuration control over source code files, and has been used on the source code contained within this book (see appendix E).

A facility is provided whereby the compressed source code, produced as an intermediate step in the checksum calculation, can be output to a file.

Dependencies

External : TEXT_IO
Internal : None

Minimum Implementable Package

Of the facilities provided within the package, only the optional intermediate file generation may be removed.

Component Specification

```
package CHECKSUM_PKG is
   function CHECKSUM
     (SOURCE_CODE_FILE_NAME         : in STRING;
      MAX_LINE_LENGTH               : in POSITIVE:= 255;
      CREATE_COMPRESSED_CODE_FILE   : in BOOLEAN := FALSE;
      COMPRESSED_CODE_FILE_NAME     : in STRING  := "COMPOU‍
                                      return INTEGER;
   LINE_TOO_LONG_ERROR : exception;
end CHECKSUM_PKG;
```

Pragmatics

The compression procedure applies an elementary set of the Ada syntax rules in order to standardise the input file without affecting its functionality. A knowledge of the compression criteria allows the user to know what flexibility there is in entering the source code without affecting the result of the checksum.

The rules applied to reduce the code are as follows:

1. String and character literals may not be changed in any way. Therefore they are an exception to the rules following.

2   Source code is case independent.

3   Comments do not affect the code. A comment is terminated at the end of the line on which it starts.

4   Tab characters and space characters are interchangeable.

5   A new line may be started without affecting the code wherever a space character is permissible.

6   Multiple spaces are equivalent to a single space.

7   Spaces which immediately follow or precede any of the characters identified below do not affect the code.
    '+' '-' '*' '/' '<' '=' '>' '&' '|' '.' ':' '(' ')' ';' '!' '#'

8   The character '!' is equivalent to the character '|'.

9   The character ':' may be used instead of the character '#'.

N.B. *A character literal is recognised as a three character string, as follows: 'X', where X is any character. A character literal must not span lines.*

A string literal is recognised as a sequence of two or more characters, whose first and last characters must be a '"' (i.e. ASCII.QUOTATION). A string literal must not span lines.

Comments are recognised as two consecutive hyphens plus any text following on the same line, unless the hyphens are within a string literal.

The following Ada options are not recognised as equivalent when calculating the checksum:
- Use of '%' as an alternative to the '"' character as a string literal delimiter.
- Inconsistent use of the optional insertion of subprogram and package names after their last **end** statement.

The checksum algorithm used is a simple one, but can detect character transposition. The result is of type INTEGER.

A facility is provided, through the parameters, to allow the intermediate, standardised code to be copied to a file. Such is the nature of the standardisation that the resulting code will still compile, although it will be somewhat difficult to read (a sort of "ugly" printer facility!). The default is that this facility is not invoked.

Restrictions on use

The program will not perform reliably if it is asked to operate upon a file which does not contain compilable source code.

Exceptions

The following standard TEXT_IO exceptions may be raised when attempting to access the input file:
    STATUS_ERROR
    NAME_ERROR
    USE_ERROR
    DEVICE_ERROR
They may be raised for the standard reasons described in ALRM 14.4, when operating upon either the input file or the optional output file. The other TEXT_IO exceptions cannot be raised.

An exception, LINE_TOO_LONG_ERROR may also be raised. This will occur if the input file which is being processed contains any lines which are longer than the input buffer being used. The length of this buffer is set by the user of the function, with the value alterable at run time by a parameter which defaults to 255 characters.

When an exception is raised, any open files are closed (if possible) and the exception is propagated to the calling code.

Options

The algorithm used to calculate the checksum may be altered. The calculating procedure currently implemented requires to be fed a single character at a time. Any algorithm which operates in the same way may be substituted with ease, by altering the internal procedure INCREMENT_CHECKSUM.

Example of use

```
with CHECKSUM_PKG;
use  CHECKSUM_PKG;
with TEXT_IO; use TEXT_IO;

procedure CHECKSUM_EXAMPLE is
   INPUT_NAME, OUTPUT_NAME  : STRING(1..20);
   VALUE : INTEGER;
   INPUT_NAME_LEN, OUTPUT_NAME_LEN : INTEGER;
   package IIO is new INTEGER_IO (INTEGER);
begin
   ... get an input file name
   ... get an output file name for the condensed source code

   VALUE := CHECKSUM (INPUT_NAME (1..INPUT_NAME_LEN),
                      100, TRUE,
                      OUTPUT_NAME (1..OUTPUT_NAME_LEN));
   PUT ("The value of the checksum = "); IIO.PUT (VALUE);
end CHECKSUM_EXAMPLE;
```

Implementation points

The calculation of the checksum is performed on the reduced code constructed as a result of applying the rules described under Pragmatics. Some implementation details of the rules may be of interest:

Rule
- 2   All characters are converted to upper case.
- 4   Each tab is converted to a single space.
- 5   A new line is interpreted as a space character.
- 6   Multiple spaces (even if inserted by other rules) are reduced to single spaces.
- 7   Spaces either side of the listed operators are removed.

8   All '!'s are converted to '|'s.
9   All '#'s are converted to ':'s.

N.B.   The above are all applied to all characters except those in character or string literals.

The checksum calculation itself is a simple one. It is performed by the addition of the ASCII values of alternate characters, applying a modulo of 128 to the sum. The resulting two numbers (one for odd characters, one for even) are then combined as follows:
  The value obtained from the addition of the odd characters is multiplied by 256.
  To this is added the value obtained from the addition of the even characters. This value is returned as type INTEGER.

Although the calculation is simple, in conjunction with a clean compilation, it gives a high level of confidence that the two pieces of code are functionally equivalent. The checksum is intended to detect many problems, such as typing in the wrong variable name, or inverting an operator (e.g. '<' being typed as '>').

The package has been implemented using a state transition approach. The states identified are shown in the enumeration type declared in the body. As characters are processed, they are copied to an output buffer, and the state is updated according to the character type. Once a line is processed, it is then passed, one character at a time, to the checksum calculating routine.

A description of the states used by the implementation are:
  INITIALISE   Processing blank lines, looking for a line with at least 1 character in it.
  IN_STRING   Processing a string literal.
  POSS_LIT_1   Processing a possible character literal, as the opening prime has been found, but the closing prime has not yet been met.
  POSS_LIT_2   A state following on from POSS_LIT_1 which requires different processing.
  POSS_COMMENT   Looking for a second hyphen (having found one) which would identify the remaining text on the line as a comment.
  NORMAL   Processing characters when not in any of the above states.

3.11 - Checksum

DONE_LINE   Processing the line as a whole, therefore calculating the checksum etc.

The optional characters identified in ALRM 2.10 have been addressed. The optional use of the '%' to replace '"' has not been implemented as this would significantly increase the complexity of the code required to handle strings, and also because almost all keyboards have a '"' character on them.

Efficiency

The function performs a significant amount of I/O. Thus, on most computer systems, the efficiency of this package is much more likely to be limited by I/O rather than by the CPU utilisation. The efficiency of the procedure is therefore linearly dependent upon the length of the input file.

Package Body

```
with TEXT_IO;
use  TEXT_IO;

package body CHECKSUM_PKG is

   package IIO is new INTEGER_IO (INTEGER);

   function CHECKSUM
     (SOURCE_CODE_FILE_NAME        : in STRING;
      MAX_LINE_LENGTH              : in POSITIVE:= 255;
      CREATE_COMPRESSED_CODE_FILE  : in BOOLEAN := FALSE;
      COMPRESSED_CODE_FILE_NAME    : in STRING   := "COMPOUT")
                                    return INTEGER is

         INPUT, OUTPUT       : FILE_TYPE;
         IN_NDX, OUT_NDX     : INTEGER;
         IN_LENGTH           : INTEGER;
         EOF                 : BOOLEAN;
         IN_LINE, OUT_LINE   : STRING (1 .. MAX_LINE_LENGTH+1);

         type STATE_TYPE is (INITIALISE, NORMAL, IN_STRING,
                             POSS_LIT_1, POSS_LIT_2,
                             POSS_COMMENT, DONE_LINE);
         STATE : STATE_TYPE;
```

3.11 - Checksum

```ada
    type CHECK_TYPE is
      record
        CHECKSUM_1 : INTEGER := 0;
        CHECKSUM_2 : INTEGER := 0;
      end record;
CHECK_REC     : CHECK_TYPE;
EVEN_COUNTER : BOOLEAN := FALSE;

procedure INCREMENT_CHECKSUM
           (CHAR : in     CHARACTER;
            CHK  : in out CHECK_TYPE) is

  WRAP_VALUE : INTEGER := 128;
  CHAR_VALUE : INTEGER := CHARACTER'POS(CHAR);
begin
  if EVEN_COUNTER then
    if CHK.CHECKSUM_1 >=
       WRAP_VALUE - CHAR_VALUE then
       -- Perform the wrap round
       CHK.CHECKSUM_1 := CHK.CHECKSUM_1-WRAP_VALUE
    end if;
    CHK.CHECKSUM_1 := CHK.CHECKSUM_1 + CHAR_VALUE;
  else
    if CHK.CHECKSUM_2 >=
       WRAP_VALUE - CHAR_VALUE then
       -- Perform the wrap
       CHK.CHECKSUM_2 := CHK.CHECKSUM_2-WRAP_VALUE
    end if;
    CHK.CHECKSUM_2 := CHK.CHECKSUM_2 + CHAR_VALUE;
  end if;
  EVEN_COUNTER := not EVEN_COUNTER;
end INCREMENT_CHECKSUM;

procedure POSS_OVER_WRITE (CHAR  : in CHARACTER;
                           PARAM : in STATE_TYPE) is
begin
  if CHAR = ' ' then  -- Handle spaces carefully
    case OUT_LINE (OUT_NDX) is
      when '&' | '|' | '.' | ',' | ';' |
           ':' | '(' | ')' | '+' | '*' |
           '/' | '=' | '<' | '>' | '''  |
           '-' | ' ' =>
```

3.11 - Checksum

```
                    null;      -- Do not increment OUT_NDX or copy
                               -- across the character as 'operators'
                               -- do not require spaces after them
                               -- and single spaces are sufficient
               when others =>
                  OUT_NDX := OUT_NDX + 1;
                  OUT_LINE (OUT_NDX) := CHAR;
            end case;
         else
            if OUT_LINE (OUT_NDX) /= ' ' then
               OUT_NDX := OUT_NDX + 1;
            end if;
            OUT_LINE (OUT_NDX) := CHAR;
         end if;
         STATE := PARAM;
      end POSS_OVER_WRITE;


      function STANDARDISE (CHAR : CHARACTER)
         return CHARACTER is
      begin
         if CHARACTER'POS(CHAR) >= CHARACTER'POS('a') and
            CHARACTER'POS(CHAR) <= CHARACTER'POS('z') then
            return CHARACTER'VAL(CHARACTER'POS(CHAR)-32);
         else
            case CHAR is
               when '!'       => return '|';
               when '#'       => return ':';
               when ASCII.HT  => return ' ';
               when others    => return CHAR;   -- No change
            end case;
         end if;
      end STANDARDISE;

   begin   -- CHECKSUM

   -- Initialise
      OPEN (INPUT, IN_FILE, SOURCE_CODE_FILE_NAME);
      if CREATE_COMPRESSED_CODE_FILE then
         CREATE (OUTPUT, OUT_FILE,
                 COMPRESSED_CODE_FILE_NAME);
      end if;
```

3.11 - Checksum

```
         OUT_LINE(1) := ';';    -- This is a dummy, any non-space
                                -- character that requires no spaces
                                -- either side of it would do
OUT_NDX       := 1;
STATE:= INITIALISE;
loop

   case STATE is

      when INITIALISE =>
         loop
            EOF := END_OF_FILE (INPUT);
            exit when EOF;
            -- GET_LINE works past page boundaries,
            -- so no worry there
            GET_LINE (INPUT, IN_LINE, IN_LENGTH);
            if IN_LENGTH = MAX_LINE_LENGTH + 1 then
               raise LINE_TOO_LONG_ERROR;
            end if;
            exit when IN_LENGTH /= IN_LINE'FIRST -
         end loop;
         if EOF then
            CLOSE (INPUT);
            if CREATE_COMPRESSED_CODE_FILE then
               CLOSE (OUTPUT);
            end if;
            return CHECK_REC.CHECKSUM_1 +
                   (CHECK_REC.CHECKSUM_2 * 256);
         else
            OUT_LINE(1) := OUT_LINE(OUT_NDX);
            OUT_NDX     := 1;
            IN_LINE(1..IN_LENGTH + 1):= ' ' &
               IN_LINE(1..IN_LENGTH);
            IN_LENGTH := IN_LENGTH + 1;
            IN_NDX    := 0;
            STATE     := NORMAL;
         end if;

      when DONE_LINE =>
         if OUT_LINE (OUT_NDX) = ' ' then
            -- Strip trailing space
            OUT_NDX := OUT_NDX - 1;
         end if;
```

3.11 - Checksum

```ada
            if OUT_NDX > 1 then
               -- line composed of more than spaces and/or tabs
               if CREATE_COMPRESSED_CODE_FILE then
                  PUT_LINE (OUTPUT,
                            OUT_LINE (2 .. OUT_NDX));
               end if;
               for J in 2 .. OUT_NDX loop
                  INCREMENT_CHECKSUM (OUT_LINE(J),
                                      CHECK_REC);
               end loop;
            end if;
            STATE := INITIALISE;

         when NORMAL =>
            case IN_LINE (IN_NDX) is
               when ' ' | ASCII.HT =>
                  -- Convert tab to space if necessary
                  POSS_OVER_WRITE (' ', NORMAL);
               when '"' => -- Found the start of a string literal
                  POSS_OVER_WRITE ('"', IN_STRING);
               when ''' => -- Possible start of a character literal
                  POSS_OVER_WRITE (''', POSS_LIT_1);
               when '-' =>    -- Possible start of a comment
                  POSS_OVER_WRITE ('-', POSS_COMMENT);
               when '&' | '|' | '.' | ',' | ';' |
                    ':' | '(' | ')' | '+' | '*' |
                    '/' | '=' | '<' | '>' =>
                  POSS_OVER_WRITE (IN_LINE(IN_NDX),
                                   NORMAL);
               when '!' | '#' =>
                  POSS_OVER_WRITE
                     (STANDARDISE (IN_LINE(IN_NDX)),
                                   NORMAL);
               when others =>
                  OUT_NDX := OUT_NDX + 1;
                  OUT_LINE (OUT_NDX) :=
                     STANDARDISE (IN_LINE(IN_NDX));
                  STATE := NORMAL;
            end case;   -- for IN_LINE (IN_NDX)

         when IN_STRING =>
            OUT_NDX := OUT_NDX + 1;
            OUT_LINE (OUT_NDX) := IN_LINE (IN_NDX);
```

```
            if IN_LINE (IN_NDX) = '"' then
               STATE := NORMAL;
            end if;

         when POSS_LIT_1 =>
            -- No case conversion or substitution
            OUT_NDX := OUT_NDX + 1;
            OUT_LINE (OUT_NDX) := IN_LINE (IN_NDX);
            STATE := POSS_LIT_2;

         when POSS_LIT_2 =>
            case IN_LINE (IN_NDX) is
               when ''' =>   -- Found a valid character literal
                  OUT_NDX := OUT_NDX + 1;
                  OUT_LINE (OUT_NDX) := ''';
                  STATE      := NORMAL;
               when '"' =>
                  OUT_LINE (OUT_NDX) :=
                     STANDARDISE(OUT_LINE(OUT_NDX));
                  OUT_NDX := OUT_NDX + 1;
                  OUT_LINE (OUT_NDX) := '"';
                  STATE      := IN_STRING;
               when ' '|ASCII.HT =>
                  OUT_LINE (OUT_NDX) :=
                     STANDARDISE(OUT_LINE(OUT_NDX));
                  POSS_OVER_WRITE (' ', NORMAL);
               when '-' =>
                  if OUT_LINE (OUT_NDX) = '-' then
                     -- Found the start of a comment
                     OUT_NDX := OUT_NDX - 1;
                     STATE     := DONE_LINE;
                  else
                     OUT_LINE (OUT_NDX) :=
                        STANDARDISE (OUT_LINE (OUT_NDX)
                     POSS_OVER_WRITE ('-',POSS_COMMENT
                  end if;
               when others =>
                  OUT_LINE (OUT_NDX) :=
                     STANDARDISE (OUT_LINE (OUT_NDX));
                  POSS_OVER_WRITE
                     (STANDARDISE (IN_LINE (IN_NDX)),
                                   NORMAL);
            end case;   -- for IN_LINE (IN_NDX)
```

3.11 - Checksum

```ada
            when POSS_COMMENT =>
               case IN_LINE (IN_NDX) is
                  when '-' =>
                     -- remove first '-'
                     OUT_NDX := OUT_NDX - 1;
                     STATE   := DONE_LINE;
                  when '"' =>   -- Found the start of a string literal
                     OUT_NDX := OUT_NDX + 1;
                     OUT_LINE (OUT_NDX) := '"';
                     STATE   := IN_STRING;
                  when ''' =>   -- Possible start of a character literal
                     OUT_NDX := OUT_NDX + 1;
                     OUT_LINE (OUT_NDX) := ''';
                     STATE   := POSS_LIT_1;
                  when ' '|ASCII.HT =>
                     -- Space character not required on RHS of '-'
                     STATE := NORMAL;
                  when others =>
                     OUT_NDX := OUT_NDX + 1;
                     OUT_LINE (OUT_NDX) :=
                        STANDARDISE (IN_LINE (IN_NDX));
                     STATE   := NORMAL;
               end case; -- for IN_LINE (IN_NDX)
         end case; -- for STATE

         exit when EOF;

         IN_NDX := IN_NDX + 1;
         if STATE /= INITIALISE and IN_NDX > IN_LENGTH then
            if STATE = POSS_LIT_2 then
               -- Cancel preservation of the possible literal's case
               OUT_LINE (OUT_NDX) :=
                  STANDARDISE (OUT_LINE (OUT_NDX));
            end if;
            STATE := DONE_LINE;
         end if;
      end loop;

exception
   when LINE_TOO_LONG_ERROR => -- Tidy up the open files
      CLOSE (INPUT);
```

```
                    if CREATE_COMPRESSED_CODE_FILE then
                        CLOSE (OUTPUT);
                    end if;
                    raise;
                when others =>  -- Standard file exceptions
                    if IS_OPEN(INPUT) then
                        CLOSE (INPUT);
                    end if;
                    if IS_OPEN(OUTPUT) then
                        CLOSE (OUTPUT);
                    end if;

                    raise;

        end CHECKSUM;

end CHECKSUM_PKG;
```

4 HOW TO ESTABLISH A REUSABLE LIBRARY

4.1 Introduction

Little practical reuse of software is likely to be achieved until a reusable software source code library is created and administered. One of the questions that must first be answered is what is the intended scope of the library (i.e. is it to be project wide, division wide, or company wide?). Frequently, circumstances will determine the answer, with considerable impact on the benefits to be gained and the resources required for implementation.

4.2 Beginnings

The technology of software reuse is still a relatively young one, with management involvement essential in order to reap the benefits. It is not enough simply to appoint a software librarian, as there is a danger that less than the proper amount of software may be collected, and also that that which is collected may not be sufficiently utilised. A manager must be designated to carry the responsibility for the successful introduction of reuse, with enough time available after his other duties to ensure that other managers are aware and supportive of the initiative, and that sufficient resources (personnel, budget, time) are allocated to it. In the case of a project-wide library only, the responsibilities may be carried out at a lower level, so that the designated person is (say) a team leader rather than a full manager.

How does one begin to fill a library? Basically, there are three probable sources and usually some combination of the three is used.

One possible source is an existing in-house library, possibly from a completed project or from another department. The advantages of this are that it is immediately available and already has some relevance to the organisation. The disadvantages are that it may not be up-to-date, and there may be ownership problems (see later).

Alternatively commercially available component collections (such as the present work) may be used as a starting point. The advantages are immediate availability and known costs of acquisition. The disadvantages are that the resulting library may not necessarily reflect the fields of interest of the organisation.

The third option is to initiate a reuse policy during in-house software development (see section 4.5). The advantages are that components are likely to reflect current organisational practice and standards, and that the method provides a natural means for continuing to expand the library. The disadvantages include a greater need for management involvement and the possibility of apparent conflicts of interest with the developer (see below).

4.3 Adoption of Existing Component Collections

The adoption of existing in-house components is only superficially an attractive option, for the following reasons:

> Intellectual property rights may be an issue. Some software houses investigating the reuse of source code originally written for clients have found this to be an especially tricky problem.
>
> The components may not have been designed with reuse in mind, and so maybe insufficiently general to have a strong appeal. In some cases of hurriedly developed or poorly maintained code, the components may have undesirable properties such as side effects or an inability to work outside the parameters of the originally conceived system.
>
> The components may have to be checked in case any part of their working was in some way confidential. This is especially likely to be a problem where source code was written on behalf of a client.

4.4 Adaptation of Components

Modification is more common than adoption, so that a component can be repackaged, perhaps generalised, to meet the latest standards and be thoroughly tested and documented. However, there are still problems, including the IPR issue mentioned above. The question arises as to who performs the modification. If it is to be the original developer, his/her project must be willing to stand the extra delay. Decisions have to be made as to who funds the modification, and who the design authority is.

Standards for submission must be rigorously enforced. There is no chance, for example, that a component will be selected for reuse without high quality documentation. There must be a standard format for submission. Performance in terms of (typically) memory and CPU usage must be measured. In some cases a complexity metric may be needed. Nothing should be admitted to the library until it has passed a Q.A. review.

It is possible that a component may have optional parts. For example, [Firesmith 87] reports that some packages have been created with alternative bodies optimised for space and time.

One problem found in existing libraries is that of the long dependency chain, where a component depends on a package that depends on another and so on. A key area of judgement is to decide what the maximum chain length should be, and where and how to break chains.

It is essential to be objective about the anticipated gains from generalising components. To guide their staff, it would be a good idea if sites developed some kind of cost-benefit criterion, e.g. if the probability of reuse of a candidate component over the next three years is less than 80%, then don't generalise it.

4.5   Incentive to Be a Library Supplier

There must be an incentive to be a library supplier. Possibly there could be some reward, and certainly recognition, for those whose components are actually reused. At all events there must be a policy (whether project, division or organisation-wide) on contributing to the library.

There are a number of strategies for obtaining candidate components for reuse. At some sites there are formal reviews at the preliminary design stage to identify suitable candidates. At others it is left to individuals, sometimes with a reward system. Many professional software engineers are only too happy to see their work publicised amongst their peers.

4.6   Library Maintenance Policy

There must be an active and public maintenance policy, with an appropriate budget. All changes, whether to source code or documentation, must be made through a central authority. There should be regular reviews of the components, to weed out effective duplicates and components that have become obsolete.

4.7 Component Retrieval

When the number of components collected has reached a critical mass, an indexed catalogue should be published. It is likely that individual components will each appear under a number of classifications. Finding suitable components for reuse on a given project, particularly when it is not known if any are present or the form they may take, is an especially difficult task, so it is recommended that considerable care and effort be put into the cataloguing and indexing.

Once the catalogue has been published, software designers must be encouraged to peruse it regularly. There must be some incentive to reuse. There is frequently a resistance to anything from outside of the organisation (the "Not Invented Here" syndrome). The danger is also always present that a designer will prefer to specify something that is entirely within his/her own control. Hitachi uses monthly exercises for its staff which can only be completed on time by picking items from the reuse catalogue [Tajima 84].

The catalogue must be regularly updated, say once a month. New accessions and component updates must be highlighted.

4.8 The Role of the Librarian

At times of cost saving, there is a temptation for organisations to assign a non-technical person to the post of source code librarian. In fact a number of fine technical decisions are likely to have to be made and a technical person should therefore be appointed, preferably with several years of experience in the organisation. The position is probably most suitable for a promising senior programmer or junior team leader.

In most organisations the librarian's job will be a full-time one. His or her responsibilities include decisions on accessions; reviews of individual components for the catalogue; production and dissemination of the catalogue; reviews of the library to eliminate duplicates and to pursue a logical and coherent development of the organisation's field of interest; and the recording of usage of library components in order to notify existing users of updates. Quality reviews must be arranged for conduct by the Quality Assurance department. Configuration Management must be undertaken in conjunction with the organisation's existing department. The librarian will be responsible for keeping statistics, answering queries from potential users and for physical storage and backup.

The librarian must ensure that the manager responsible for reuse receives a regular report on the reuse levels actually achieved. This should draw attention to deficiencies, whether in lack of components for specific areas, lack of awareness of the library, lack of resources for its upkeep, etc.

Ultimately the justification for the reuse activity is to save on scarce resources such as time, money and personnel. The library has to be able to prove its worth.

5 TESTING OF COMPONENTS

5.1 Introduction

Any project manager will insist that the software used on his project is well tested, whether it is custom designed and coded, or obtained from a library.

If a project wishes to alter tested software, or to recompile it with a different compiler, it is essential to retest the altered software. If software is enhanced, then so too must be the test suite.

The components contained in this book have been thoroughly tested on at least two validated compilers. However, testing cannot guarantee a component's behaviour, at least not in today's world of non-formal software languages. It therefore remains essential that a project has definite and verifiable evidence of the correctness of its software.

To allow the components contained in this book to be used on a practical project, where software may need to be changed, a full suite of tests is available on discs (see introductory pages).

The remainder of this section describes the approach taken when developing the test suites, to give the reader the ability to install and maintain not only the component, but also the tests. Some examples have been included to demonstrate the techniques used.

5.2 Testing Overview

The testing of software forms one particular phase of the development process. Testing is intended to ensure that the developed software meets its requirements. It cannot tackle the problem of whether a requirement specification adequately meets the user's true needs. Comprehensive testing cannot in itself ensure product quality, but it is a prerequisite for quality.

When developing components in Ada, the functional characteristics can be captured, for the most part, in an Ada package specification, particularly when supplemented by descriptive text. The Ada package specification plus the text must be reviewed against the user requirement. In the case of the components contained in this book, the end user's requirements are not known. The Ada specifications and text were reviewed by the authors against a generalised user requirement. The result may fall short of, or exceed, an individual user's requirements, so the documentation for each component gives some guidance as to how components may be reduced or enhanced. It is important that users of library components, whether from this book or any other source, critically review a component to establish whether it sufficiently meets their particular requirements. If there is a close enough match, then the user may wish to alter the component to meet his particular requirements. In doing so, it is vital that the user changes not only the Ada specification and body, but also the associated text and test documentation. However, users of library components should be aware that some of the benefit of using ready tested and documented components is lost directly any of the component's code or documentation is altered.

The approach to testing employed was chosen with two objectives:
- To ensure the component operates in accordance with its specification
- To facilitate retesting in the event of changes to the component.

Whilst the former is a usual aim, ease of retesting is necessary for reusable components. It is expected that these components will be altered in some way by the user, and certainly run on compiler/target combinations on which they have not been tested by the authors. For these reasons, support for a largely automated means of retesting the components is important, although the reasons to retest in each case, change of code or change of compiler, are different.

These objectives have been met using a technique based upon black and white box testing coupled with a high degree of hard coded result checking.

5.2.1   Black Box Testing

Black box testing is aimed at ensuring that the component complies with its requirement specification. Such testing views the component as a black box. There is no visibility of the internals of the box, but its interface is entirely known.

Black box testing relies upon each component having an encapsulated interface, the Ada package specification. A good design principle employed heavily in component design is that of encapsulation, whereby the component interface is entirely captured though its Ada specification. Thus

5 - Testing of Components

the use of a technique such as access of shared data is not permitted, because it would hide an important data flow interface.

In order to black box test a package, it is only necessary methodically to test each of the facilities provided by the Ada specification, with particular emphasis on boundary and threshold conditions. All the results of black box tests are visible outside the component.

It is important to recognise what comprises the interface requirements against which the component will be tested. They are captured in the Ada specification together with the supporting text. As a minimum, each subprogram is methodically worked through, together with exceptions and generic formal parameters (if any). There may be requirements described in the text which cannot be captured in the Ada specification. For example whilst it is possible to specify in Ada the precision of a square root function (using **digits**) it is not possible to specify the accuracy. Such requirements must also be tested. The real time behaviour of a component, both in time and memory, is highly dependent upon the particular compiler and RTS, and the target hardware. Thus for a reusable component, those aspects are not usually recognised as requirements, except in very general terms (see Appendix A).

5.2.2 White Box Testing

White box testing is aimed at ensuring that all aspects of the design of the component are well exercised, rather than simply its external interface. To achieve this it is necessary to see into the component, to be aware of its design, hence the term White Box. Complete (exhaustive) white box testing can be prohibitively expensive in terms of time and money so it is often the case that only suspected "weak points" in the design are the focus of particularly intensive testing.

With white box testing it is often necessary to monitor the internal behaviour of a package as well as inspect objects declared within the package body in order to ensure that the design is operating correctly. Indeed it may be necessary for the sake of practicality to alter the values of internal objects, although this is a potentially dangerous practice.

Additional code may be inserted to aid white box testing. Such code may have to be inserted into the package specification if testing is to be carried out by using an external test harness. For example, in the Tree component (3.6) a PRINT_TREE procedure was inserted into the package specification as well as the body, to print out a tree's structure directly from the internal data structure and to validate all the access object values.

In order to keep the size of the published components down, the code which is specific to white box testing has been removed. Clearly, clean removal of the relevant code must be ensured, so regression testing using the black box tests is undertaken following removal of the "unnecessary" code. The disc version of the components also contains the code with the white box test code still in place, but commented for their clean removal.

5.3 Example Tests

The tests employed for a particular component are derived in a two stage process. The first stage is to identify the logical tests to be undertaken. A logical test specifies a particular aspect of behaviour without specifying how the test is to be carried out, i.e. the "what", not the "how".

Logical test identification is undertaken for both black and white box tests.

The DELETE_NODE routine of the Tree component (3.6) is used to illustrate the testing strategy. The procedure provides a capability to remove one of the nodes in an unsorted tree of nodes whose topological structure is visible to the user. The procedure's declaration is as follows:

```
procedure DELETE_NODE
            (POSITION : in    POSITION_TYPE;
             CHILD    : in    CHILD_TYPE := SELF);
```

The routine removes a node from trees. The routine can remove a specified child of a particular node, as indicated by the POSITION parameter; or it can remove the node itself, rather than the child by use of the default value of CHILD, being "remove self". In all cases, a node can only be removed if that node has no children.

From the specification of the procedure, and the text which accompanies it, logical tests are derived. Some structure has been imposed on the tests. Firstly, logical tests of the procedure's ability correctly to raise each valid exception are identified. Secondly, tests to confirm the precedence of exceptions are identified. Thirdly comes the testing of the normal working of the procedure. Finally, any "unusual" situations, for example black box boundary conditions, are considered. The twelve logical tests used to test the DELETE_NODE procedure are as follows:

5 - Testing of Components

DELETE_NODE
   Exception Generation (Simple)
   Routine may raise CONSTRAINT_ERROR,
   POSITION_NOT_SET_ERROR,
   OBSOLETE_POSITION_ERROR,
   CHILDREN_EXIST_ERROR,
   NODE_DOES_NOT_EXIST_ERROR

1 (T) child < 0 or > degree
   (R) Raise CONSTRAINT_ERROR
2 (T) uninitialised pointer
   (R) Raise POSITION_NOT_SET_ERROR
3 (T) altered tree
   (R) Raise OBSOLETE_POSITION_ERROR
4 (T) Delete a node when no node exists at the position
   (R) Raise NODE_DOES_NOT_EXIST_ERROR
5 (T) Delete a node which still has children
   (R) Raise CHILDREN_EXIST_ERROR

   Exception Generation (Precedence)

6 (T) child < 0 or > degree, uninitialised pointer
   (R) Raise CONSTRAINT_ERROR
7 (T) child <0 or > degree, altered tree
   (R) Raise CONSTRAINT_ERROR
8 (T) Altered tree, no node at position
   (R) Raise OBSOLETE_POSITION_ERROR
9 (T) Altered tree, node for deletion has children
   (R) Raise OBSOLETE_POSITION_ERROR

   Simple Invocations

10 (T) Delete a node using child set to SELF
   (R) Node removed
11 (T) Delete a node using child not set to SELF
   (R) Node removed

   Unusual Invocations

12 (T) Delete the root node
   (R) Root node removed

The suite of logical tests are written up and reviewed by someone other than the author of the component, in the same way as a component specification is reviewed. This use of a second party is extremely important, and at this stage, economical in terms of human resources. The author of a component is in some ways the person least suited to identify a full set of tests.

Not only has he been intimately involved in the component's construction and so will believe in its correctness, but also because he will have to undertake the running of the tests, he is liable to be reluctant to create too many! The former problem, a sort of tunnel vision, is the more serious, where the author is so familiar with his work that he may miss aspects that a newcomer may see. A common example is the way in which a component's author interprets a requirement. Having decided upon his interpretation he is unlikely to question it, whereas newcomers, with their tendency to ask embarrassingly obvious questions, can highlight ambiguities and other significant problems.

Having said that the author is least suited to identify the tests, the practicalities of staffing projects, as well as timescale problems usually constrain a project manager to use the author to undertake the test identification, coding up of the tests, and checking of the results. A reasonable compromise is to ensure that a second party at least reviews the set of tests that are proposed by the author.

Following successful review of the logical tests, at least by a second party, the tester must turn the set of logical tests into physical tests. As mentioned earlier, the technique for writing the actual tests should emphasise automatic retesting. Automated result checking is preferred, with visual checking only used where necessary. An ability to validate rerun tests by a byte-by-byte comparison of two files of test results is highly desirable.

As an example, the test code used to implement a number of logical tests is shown below.

The ... notation indicates that some code has been left out for brevity in this section.

5 - Testing of Components

-- *Test of Unsorted Tree Package - DELETE_NODE*

```
with TEXT_IO;   use TEXT_IO;
with IIO;       use IIO;
with GENERIC_UNSORTED_TREE_PKG;

-- Component number 6, test group 4.
procedure C06_G04 is
   -- Set up package to be tested
   type ACTUAL_DATA_TYPE is new INTEGER;
   INDENT : STRING (1..40) := (others=>'-');
   package DIO is new INTEGER_IO (ACTUAL_DATA_TYPE);
   procedure TEMP_PUT (ACTUAL_DATA : ACTUAL_DATA_TYPE) is
   begin
      DIO.PUT(ACTUAL_DATA);
   end ;
   package UNSORTED_TREE_PKG is new
    GENERIC_UNSORTED_TREE_PKG
           (DATA_TYPE => ACTUAL_DATA_TYPE,
            DEGREE    => 5,
            PUT       => TEMP_PUT);
   use UNSORTED_TREE_PKG;

   -- General Purpose Test routines
   procedure PASSED is
   ... PUTs a standard PASSED message
   procedure FAILED (REASON : POSITIVE) is
   ... PUTs a standard FAILED message, plus a 'reason'
   procedure VISUAL_CHECK is
   ... PUTs a standard warning to carry out a visual check
   procedure GAP is
   ... PUTs a gap in the output
   procedure STANDARD_TREE_1
           (TREE : in out TREE_REF_TYPE) is
   ... Sets up a specific complex tree for test purposes

begin
   begin
      PUT_LINE ("Exception generation");
      PUT_LINE ("6.1 - Use a child < 0 and > Degree");
      PUT_LINE ("     - Raise CONSTRAINT_ERROR");
      declare
         BYPASS : BOOLEAN:= FALSE;
```

```
            TREE_6_1 : TREE_REF_TYPE;
            POS_6_1  : POSITION_TYPE;
        begin
            STANDARD_TREE_1 (TREE_6_1);
            SET_TO_ROOT (TREE_6_1,POS_6_1);
            begin
                DELETE_NODE (POS_6_1,-1);
                FAILED (1);
                BYPASS := TRUE;
            exception
                when CONSTRAINT_ERROR =>  -- So far so good
                    null;
                when others =>
                    FAILED (2);
                    BYPASS := TRUE;
            end ;
            if not BYPASS then
                ... similar test for the case child = 6
            end if;
        end;

        ... Tests 6.2 -> 6.5

        PUT_LINE ("Exception Generation (Precedence)");
        PUT      ("6.6 - Use a child < 0 or > degree, ");
        PUT_LINE ("uninitialised position object");
        PUT_LINE ("     - raise CONSTRAINT_ERROR");
        declare
            BYPASS : BOOLEAN := FALSE;
            TREE_6_6 : TREE_REF_TYPE;
            POS_6_6  : POSITION_TYPE;
        begin
            begin
                DELETE_NODE (POS_6_6,-1);
                FAILED (1);
                BYPASS := TRUE;
            exception
                when CONSTRAINT_ERROR =>
                    null;
                when others =>
                    FAILED (2);
                    raise;
            end;
```

5 - Testing of Components

```
            if not BYPASS then
                ... similar test for child = 6
            end if;
        end;



    ... Tests 6.7 -> 6.9

        PUT_LINE ("Simple Invocation");
        PUT_LINE
        ("6.10 - Delete a node, using CHILD set to self");
        PUT_LINE ("     - Node removed");
        declare
            TREE_6_10 :   TREE_REF_TYPE;
            POS_6_10  :   POSITION_TYPE;
        begin
            STANDARD_TREE_1 (TREE_6_10);
            VISUAL_CHECK;
            PUT_LINE ("Start value of TREE_6_10 should be:");
            ... print out of expected tree

            PUT ("End value of tree should be the same,");
            PUT_LINE ("less the '13' node");
            PUT_LINE ("Start value of TREE_6_10 is :");
            PUT (TREE_6_10);
            SET_TO_ROOT (TREE_6_10,POS_6_10);
            GOTO_CHILD (POS_6_10,3);
            DELETE_NODE (POS_6_10,SELF);
            PUT_LINE ("End value of TREE_6_10 is :");
            PUT (TREE_6_10);
        exception
            when others =>
                FAILED (1);
                raise;
        end;

    ... Tests 6.11 -> 6.12

end C06_G04 ;
```

5.4 Summary

Comprehensive testing, coupled with a maintainable test suite is a prerequisite for library units of source code to be usable.

The components contained within this book have all been tested using two or more validated compilers. The complete test suites, together with the logic behind those tests, are available on floppy discs.

APPENDIX A   EFFICIENCY

This section discusses the topic of efficiency in general and the interpretation of the Efficiency section of each component

When considering designs for software, the first responsibility must be to ensure that a design correctly implements the functional aspects of the requirements.

For many systems the real time characteristics may also be important. In real-time systems, where the timeliness of the operations forms part of the correctness of the system, the calculation time is as important as the right answer. In most systems there is some performance requirement, often contractual, but even in these cases it is still a minority of the code that is critical for such purposes.

The components in chapter 3 will be targeted to many different systems using many different compilers. It is therefore impossible to arrive at useful performance figures. What can be provided, however, is a statement of how the performance varies with quantities of data.

The classic use of this type of information has been when considering sorting algorithms. It is generally well known that a simple bubble sort performs badly for large numbers of items. In fact, its performance degrades in proportion to the square of the number of items. In terms of a real performance calculation, the cost of performing the comparison of each item in the list may be significant. However, when considering the relative efficiency of different designs, the major factor to consider may be the relative efficiency of the algorithms for varying numbers of items. Thus the "order" of a design can be considered to be the relative behaviour of a design when varying one or more parameters.

Thus a bubble sort performs as $N**2$, whereas a binary insertion sort performs as $N*log(N)$, where N is the number of items in the list. Therefore, irrespective of the underlying implementation overheads, when N gets large, a binary sort is more (CPU) efficient than a bubble sort.

As processor efficiency tends to be the most closely scrutinised aspect of performance, each of the components contained in this book have a statement on processor efficiency. For each of the facilities provided by the component, an assessment of its CPU efficiency, in terms of its order is given, in the same way as a bubble sort's design has CPU performance

252 Efficiency

behaviour which goes as order N**2. These assessments can only be approximate, and in particular, the implications may be misleading for small values of N (what ever that may represent) where constant factors typically predominate.

For comparison purposes, the following relationships (for N > 2) may be useful:

N ** N	> N * N
N * N	> N * Log(N)
N * Log(N)	> Log(N!)
Log(N!)	> N
N	> Log(N) ** 2
Log(N) ** 2	> Log(N)

APPENDIX B   GENERICS

This section briefly describes the significance of generics and how to instantiate an example based on the types of generic used in the components

The generic construct is a key to reusability. It is a means of abstracting an algorithm and forming a template into which different data types may be inserted (within certain limits). One example might be the Flexible Queues component, where an abstract data type can be declared without reference to the type of data stored. Another example might be a sorting package where the emphasis is on data manipulation, not storage, but again the details of data composition are irrelevant.

All generics have to be instantiated before use, i.e. the compiler must be given notice of which data types the generics are to be invoked with. To illustrate instantiation an example of a generic specification is given below:

```
generic
    X : X_TYPE;
    type DISCRETE_TYPE is (<>);
    type SOME_TYPE is private;
    type DISCRETE_AY_TYPE is array (DISCRETE_TYPE)
                                of SOME_TYPE;
    with function SOME_FUNCTION (D : DISCRETE_TYPE)
                                return SOME_TYPE;
package EXAMPLE_GENERIC_PKG is
    function GENERIC_FUNCTION return SOME_TYPE;
end;
```

This example is more complex than any in the book, but the generic parameters are composed of all the different kinds found in the components.

The first generic parameter is of type X_TYPE and is effectively a constant declaration. The value X to be supplied on instantiation is available for use by the package. Either a constant or a variable of X_TYPE may be used as the instantiation parameter. If a variable, then the value at that time is saved and later changes to the variable's value will have no effect. Note that X_TYPE is the only type or value in this example that must be declared before the generic declaration, as all the others are formal parameters.

The second generic parameter is DISCRETE_TYPE. The "box" in the declaration means that it must be replaced on instantiation by an actual parameter which is a discrete type or subtype, i.e. either an integer or enumeration type. This actual parameter does not have to have been declared before the generic.

The third generic parameter, SOME_TYPE, can be replaced on instantiation by any non-limited type. In certain cases, and in particular with the components, the actual parameter should not be an unconstrained type.

The fourth generic parameter, DISCRETE_AY_TYPE, must be replaced on instantiation by a constrained array type indexed by the actual parameter used for DISCRETE_TYPE, composed of elements of the type of the actual parameter used for SOME_TYPE.

The fifth generic parameter is a function that must be replaced on instantiation by a function or entry with the same parameters and result type profile. The names of the formal parameters to the formal SOME_FUNCTION and to its actual replacement need not be the same.

Assuming that the specification and body of EXAMPLE_GENERIC_PKG have been compiled as part of another unit, the following might be a typical instantiation:

```
with EXAMPLE_GENERIC_PKG;
...
    XX : X_TYPE;   -- X_TYPE declared before EXAMPLE_GENERIC_PKG
    type CITY_TYPE is (LONDON, PARIS, NEW_YORK);
    type POP_TYPE is
       record
          POP_1992      : POSITIVE;
          POP_DENSITY : POSITIVE;
       end record;
    type POP_AY_TYPE is array (CITY_TYPE) of POP_TYPE;
    function POP_DETAILS (C : CITY_TYPE) return POP_TYPE;
    -- Now the instantiation
    package POPULATION_PKG is new EXAMPLE_GENERIC_PKG
        (XX, CITY_TYPE, POP_TYPE, POP_AY_TYPE, POP_DETAILS)
    use POPULATION_PKG;
```

Note that it is the generic specification that is **with**ed, the instantiation that is **used**.

APPENDIX C   PORTABILITY

This appendix contains some background to the issue of software portability. It provides some guidance on areas that should be considered by software engineers when designing code to be portable.

When creating components of software for reuse it is essential to consider the issue of portability.

The Ada language was designed to be portable; most of its features are machine independent and the standard does not allow language extensions by compiler vendors. All the optional or implementation-dependent features are collected into Appendix F of the ALRM. Since all Ada compilers have to be validated, this provision is policed and works well.

Ada was designed to tackle the problem of through life costs, one factor of which is the difficulty encountered when software must be ported, either with regard to the target machine, the host machine, or the compilation system. The rigorous definition of Ada, together with the validation process, is aimed, amongst other things, at allowing software engineers to write code which they can be confident will be portable.

With the best will in the world, portability, even in Ada, is not achieved without some knowledge about the strengths and weaknesses of Ada compilers in general.

There are a number of areas which can prove problematic when porting Ada code. Some issues to consider are given below.

Packages Supplied by Compiler Vendors

No matter how useful, if a software engineer uses a vendor supplied package, the code may not be portable. Whilst the use of such packages looks attractive in the short term, the designer must be confident that such packages can be replaced or themselves ported in order to avoid risks in porting the software later. The most significant area is probably where a software system has direct access to the RTS in order to bypass the Ada tasking model. Whatever the vendor package, the robustness of the system can only be preserved if such dependence is encapsulated in such a way that when porting, all the dependencies upon the vendor supplied package have been clearly isolated. The use of object oriented design techniques, which to some extent complement the Ada language, can help.

Declared Implementation Dependent areas

The ALRM makes explicit some areas where the compiler vendor has flexibility in implementation that is visible to the user.

The best known is probably the size of the default INTEGER type, where the highest and lowest values which can be stored are dependent upon the numbers of bits allocated, which is implementation dependent. Many other areas exist, from the flexibility of representation clauses, to the representation for variant records (which on some compilers can force internal fields of a record not to fall on word boundaries, hence slowing down the run time performance of a program quite considerably).

In systems where speed is important and software exists in a number of conceptual levels (e.g. database or communication software), it is common to design for as little data copying as possible, and use some form of pointer passing approach instead. Ada's rigorous typing rules, including those of access types, can get in the way, so it is then common to rely upon the internal representation of access types, and use SYSTEM.ADDRESS to perform shortcuts.

When faced with these types of issues, there is a trade-off. If portability is important, then either the code must avoid areas of poor portability, or the structure of the code should enable problematic areas to be isolated and altered. Support for modularity is one of the strengths of Ada, especially in packaging. Again the main means of tackling this area is to isolate the code which is dependent upon these facilities, inside a stable interface, hence decoupling the majority of the system from the implementation dependent area.

Use of Heap

Implementation of an efficient means of handling heap forms a significant part of the complexity of the run time system. Two main problems can occur when using heap, that of heap creep and heap fragmentation. The former is where heap is progressively allocated and not deallocated, becoming eventually exhausted. The latter is when heap is deallocated, but due to implementation limitations in the RTS, the resulting space is not easily able to be reused. This is similar in nature to the disc fragmentation problem often encountered in some computers. Whilst the former is basically an application design problem, some compilers cope better than others. The fragmentation problem is wholly a characteristic of the RTS and there is little the software engineer can do to cure it.

The only certain solution to heap problems is to avoid its use, at least in a dynamic sense. It is not possible to avoid its use altogether, as for example task stacks are normally allocated from the heap. However, software is likely to be more portable if the design of the software takes on board responsibility of recycling certain types of objects itself, rather than depending upon the memory management system of the RTS. Needless to say, though, this increases the complexity and cost of the software to be developed.

The Flexible Queues package illustrates this straightforwardly, where items holding queued objects are recycled within the Queue itself on an empty list. Such an approach is greedy on memory, which is never released to other users, but it is portable, and often more importantly, it is deterministic in its behaviour. An extension of this principle is to allocate from heap all the items which the software engineer feels appropriate, when the program first starts running. In this case, "no **new**s is good news".

Compilers will often cause the heap to be used for all manner of operations. If the software engineer is particularly concerned about heap, then it would be prudent to identify which Ada constructs call upon heap, and how well the recycling of memory is handled. For example it is often the case that heap is used to pass unconstrained types through parameters.

Use of I/O

Ada provides quite a comprehensive set of I/O facilities through TEXT_IO and associated packages. However, this is not sufficient to ensure portability. Often the operating system which underpins the Ada RTS will impose restrictions that vary from system to system. Issues such as the ability to read in single characters from a keyboard (without having to wait for an end of line character), whether Line Feed is necessary, printer or terminal control characters, how I/O from concurrent tasks is handled and a host of other areas, make this topic problematic regarding portability. Again the separation of the machine dependent code is the answer.

Tasking

Efficiency of implementation varies considerably in this area. Elegant solutions to certain problems often point towards the use of a large number of identical tasks. To rely upon such a design, even if the compiler being used supports tasking well, can prove awkward when porting. Limitations which are common include large values for the minimum task stack size (or too low a value for the maximum, e.g. 64Kbytes) and an inability to share code, each potentially leading to difficulties in RAM usage. The processor cost of task switching has long been of concern to the Ada community, and has exerted pressure on designers for many years. Keeping the count of Ada tasks small helps, as does keeping a careful control over the stack requirements for each task. Use of "high water" techniques (putting in a recognisable pattern of bits in the stack space before running the task) to see how much of the stack allocated is actually used, can also be illuminating if it is suspected that run time systems are being wasteful of stack space.

APPENDIX D   EXCEPTIONS

This section describes the rationale behind the way in which exceptions have been used in the components, and a recent ruling on the use of NUMERIC_ERROR.

Use of Exceptions

One of the design decisions to be undertaken on setting up a reusable library is whether abnormal conditions (e.g. attempt to pop off an empty stack) should be capable of being detected by functions (normally returning booleans), or be signalled by the raising of an exception. Occasionally in this book, both approaches are used, as for instance in the Trees component (3.6), there is a function called TREE_HAS_BEEN_CREATED as well as an exception called TREE_CREATED_ERROR.

The advantage of using exceptions are:

> An exception has to be handled and cannot be inadvertently ignored as can a boolean or other result;

> In a multitasking situation, a previous test, e.g. for non-emptiness of a stack, does not guarantee that any given condition will still hold at the time of the next operation, e.g. the stack may be emptied by another task before a pop.

For these reasons, a decision was made in favour of exceptions as being the most general solution. However care must be exercised - there are a number of points to note:

- Exceptions are notoriously liable to over use by junior software engineers, leading to "spaghetti" code. Exceptions should not be regarded as occurring frequently; if they do, then they should not be exceptions, for reasons both of design and runtime performance.

- Exception handlers should be in the immediate block or subprogram where they are likely to be raised. Otherwise (a) it may be difficult to know where a particular exception was raised in order to take appropriate action, and (b) due to changes in subprogram calling, it may happen that the exception is inadvertently handled by a handler other than the intended one.

- Where an exception must be propagated out of a block or subprogram, it must be made visible outside it.

- Exception handlers must be kept simple in order to avoid the danger of their inadvertently raising an exception.

- If an exception can be raised during a rendezvous (in an accept statement), it should be put in a block with an exception handler, otherwise the exception will also be propagated to the caller.

- If an exception is raised in a critical region, the handler should normally take the task out of criticality.

- Exceptions may not be generic parameters. The usual way round that is to provide a package of exceptions, much as IO_EXCEPTIONS is used by TEXT_IO. The disadvantage of this is that imported exceptions raised by different instantiations of a generic are indistinguishable.

Use of NUMERIC_ERROR

Uniformity Issue UI0052 [Wichmann 90] recommends that CONSTRAINT_ERROR should always be raised in places where NUMERIC_ERROR would otherwise be. The reason is that code generated by optimising compilers cannot reliably distinguish between situations where the two exceptions may be raised. In this book the old distinction between the two is kept, for the sake of those sites that have not yet adopted the recommendation. Those sites that have conformed with UI0052 may easily bring the components into line with a straightforward textual replacement of NUMERIC_ERROR by CONSTRAINT_ERROR. None of the components have separate exception handlers for the two situations, but the Flexible Queues component (3.5) uses exception handlers that handle both explicitly. The reference to NUMERIC_ERROR should be deleted from these handlers.

Inevitably the component test programs (available on disc) do have specific tests for NUMERIC_ERROR wherever it is likely to be raised. Again a textual substitution by CONSTRAINT_ERROR will bring into line.

APPENDIX E COMPONENT ENTRY CHECKS

This section, when used in conjunction with the Checksum component, provides information to allow users of components to be confident that they have entered them into their system correctly.

For users of this book who decide not to purchase the code on floppy disc, the components will have to be entered manually. Clearly this is an error prone business. Having obtained a clean compilation of the typed in component, there is still a significant risk that errors may remain.

Use of the Checksum component (3.11) allows cleanly compiled Ada code to be passed through an Ada specific calculation which provides a single resultant integer. The program is flexible in that certain adjustments are permissible without altering the value calculated. For example comments can be altered or removed, the character alignment and the layout of pages can be altered, and there is no differentiation between upper and lower case characters (except in character and string literals). A full description of the flexibility allowed in changing the code can be found in section 3.11.

This section contains the values which the checksum program calculates for each of the eleven components. Two figures are provided, one for the specification and one for the body. These have been calculated using the version of the code presented in the book, without any of the documented options used.

The figures should be compared to the results obtained on the code typed in. A difference in the checksum value is caused by a significant difference in the code, and must be investigated. If there is no difference in the checksum values, there can be high confidence that a true copy has been created.

3.1 Text Handler
    Package Name   : TEXT_HANDLER_PKG
    Specification : 15,124   Body : 11,834

3.2 Date-Time
    Package Name   : DATE_TIME_PKG
    Specification : 3,612   Body : 9,060

3.3 Universal Integer Arithmetic
Package Name   : UNIVERSAL_INTEGER_PKG
Specification : 25,202   Body   : 14,405

3.4 Universal Real Arithmetic
Package Name   : UNIVERSAL_REAL_PKG
Specification : 6,173   Body   : 15,442

3.5 Flexi-Queue
Package Name   : FQ_TYPES_PKG
Specification : 7,442   Body   : (none, types only)

Package Name   : FQ_PACKAGE
Specification : 20,588   Body   : 8,218

3.6 Trees
Package Name   : GENERIC_UNSORTED_TREES_PKG
Specification : 30,052   Body   : 3,407

3.7 Lists
Package Name   : LIST_PKG
Specification : 28,185   Body   : 23,888

3.8 Dynamic Tasking
Package Name   : TSK_PKG
Specification : 4,440   Body   : 1,649

Package Name   : BOUNDED_PKG
Specification : 6,154   Body   : 11,577

Package Name   : UNBOUNDED_PKG
Specification : 1,147   Body   : 12,102

Package Name   : HETEROGENEOUS_PKG
Specification : 4,373   Body   : 20,250

Package Name   : HETEROGENEOUS_TSK_PKG
Specification : 6,249   Body   : 17,925

3.9 Sets
Package Name   : SETS_PKG
Specification : 13,323   Body   : 887

3.10 Permutations
Package Name : PERMUTATIONS_PKG
Specification : 10,094   Body   : 21,613

3.11 Checksum
Package Name : CHECKSUM_PKG
Specification : 4,461   Body   : 4,723

APPENDIX F   STANDARDS

This section describes the standards which have been employed in creating the components

This appendix contains details of the coding standards employed for the code contained in this book. It is also applicable to the test code available on the floppy disc.

General:

1.   [Nissen 84] is used regarding style and portability unless overridden by any of other standards.

Naming:

2.   Standard suffices are used for certain classes of Ada identifiers as follows:

Types	_TYPE
Exceptions	_ERROR
Access objects	_REF
Access types	_REF_TYPE
Packages	_PKG

When using types exported from standard packages (STANDARD, CALENDAR etc), they are not retitled.

3.   The following abbreviations are used when it is desirable to keep the length of an identifier down:

LEN	Length
DEST	Destination
MAX	Maximum
MIN	Minimum
TSK	Task

4.   Boolean functions are identified such that it is meaningful to read the phrase 'If X then' where X is the function identifier.

Interfaces:

5. The "=" operator is not overloaded. If meaningful, a function called "EQ" is declared. Other operators such as "**" are not used with meanings that are not generally recognised.

6. For packages capable of locking up heap associated with an abstract data type, (by use of **new** invocations) a DEALLOCATE subprogram is provided to attempt to recycle the memory, using the UNCHECKED_DEALLOCATION function.

7. Conversion functions, if provided, are symmetric,
   eg. VALUE (IMAGE(A)) = A and
   IMAGE (VALUE(B)) = B

8. The mode used in the formal parameters for procedures is explicitly stated. For functions where **in** is the only option, the mode is not stated.

Layout:

9. Comments are used fairly heavily during development of components, but are edited back for the publication in the book. In particular comments in the specification are kept to a low level in order to focus on clearer information in the textual part of the component's description. (For most components the version of the code available in the floppy disk has more comments than that shown in the book.) Comments are placed on separate lines unless related to a subprogram's arguments or the alternative of a **case** statement. For the book version, comments are presented in italics.

10. Indentation is 3 characters per level. Line width is no more than 64 characters. All reserved words are in lower case (and bold in the book version), with all others in upper case.

11. No use is made of the following character substitutions permissible in the ALRM:
    ```
    !   for    |
    :   for    #
    %   for    "
    ```

APPENDIX G   GLOSSARY

This appendix contains an expansion of abbreviations and an explanation of terms used within this book.

The following descriptions should not be regarded as definitive, but rather an explanation of their use. Terms which are described in the Ada Language Reference Manual (ALRM) are not reproduced here.

Accuracy
How close a calculated value is to the theoretically correct value.

Ada Tasking Model
The way in which Ada treats concurrency. A significant characteristic of this is the use of rendezvous in which tasks communicate synchronously.

Black box testing
Testing targeted at ensuring that a software object meets its interface requirements, without using any knowledge of the design internal to the object.

Boundary Conditions
The value of on object at the extreme of its possible values, e.g. for a 16 bit 2's complement integer, the boundary condition values would be a very high value (i.e. 32,767) or very low value (i.e. -32,768).

Concurrency
A technique whereby sections of code are permitted logically to execute in parallel with each other.

Critical Regions
A section of code during whose execution rescheduling is avoided. Usually applied to task rescheduling, which may be disabled by vendor supplied facilities or by direct access to the underlying hardware (e.g. disabling interrupts). All the code in critical regions will be executed in strict sequence without other tasks being able to interfere.

Deadlock
A situation in a multi-tasking system where a set of tasks is permanently unable to proceed as they are waiting for an unavailable resource or resources.

Glossary

Debugger
A program able to use the symbolic information constructed by a compiler and linker from Ada code to allow interaction with a running program using symbols used in the Ada code. For example it may allow locations of code to be expressed in terms of procedures and source code statement numbers, and variables to be known by their Ada identifier.

Deque
See 3.5

Double linked list
A data structure where by using pointers, a sequence of objects are linked, such that it is possible to reference successive items in the list in either direction.

Garbage collection
A process of retrieving heap memory that is no longer used and making it available for subsequent use. Normally performed by the RTS at irregular intervals.

Heap
Memory managed by the RTS which is used for certain purposes by a program. Memory is allocated from heap for particular purposes and may be deallocated in a different order.

Heap Creep
The process whereby heap space is progressively allocated but not deallocated, eventually becoming exhausted.

Heap Fragmentation
The process whereby heap space is allocated and deallocated but where the resulting space cannot easily be reused. Similar in nature to disc fragmentation.

Host Machine
The computer on which a program or system is developed.

Implementation Dependent Areas
Parts of the Ada language where the compiler vendors have freedom to implement even though the implementation is visible to the users. Most of it is in chapter 13 and appendix F of the ALRM.

Invariant
Mathematical formula which should still be true for machine held representations. For example, the union of any set and its complement will equal the full set.

Multi-Tasking Program
A program which makes use of Ada's tasking capability in order to establish section(s) of code which are able to run concurrently.

Object Oriented Design
An approach to design which focuses on information hiding by encapsulating the information about an object and the operations that can be performed on it.

Portability
The ease with which software developed on a host machine using one vendor's Ada compiler targeting to one target machine, is transferred to a different environment where it must continue to be developed or used with a different host, target, compiler or any combination of the three.

Precision
The granularity to which the underlying representation is able to store a value. The accuracy of a value will always be less than or equal to its precision.

Race Condition
A situation in concurrent processing systems where the result of a program is dependent upon the exact order of execution between tasks, which may vary. For example consider a program with two tasks, A and B running independently but sharing an integer object X initially set to 5. Task A reads the value of X, increments its local copy and write the result back to X. At the same time task B overwrites X with the value 10. The final value of X could be 6, 10 or 11 depending upon the exact order of execution of the tasks.

RAM
Random Access Memory.

Real time
A characteristic of some systems where the correctness of a result is dependent upon not only the value, but also the timeliness with which it is made available.

Glossary

Regression Testing
When source code is changed and tested, the final stage, regression testing, is that the full suite of tests are rerun to ensure that there are no side effects from the alterations.

Requirement specification
A document which states the requirement which a software item must meet. It describes the 'what' is needed, not the 'how' it is to be achieved.

RTS
See Run Time System

Run Time System
That part of the code inserted by an Ada compiler into the executable code which supports basic features by Ada, such as start up, elaboration, tasking, memory management

Single linked list
A data structure where by using pointers, a sequence of objects are linked, such that it is possible to reference successive items in the list, moving from the start to the end. Transit in the reverse direction is not possible.

Software Engineering
The use of engineering discipline, particularly via the use of standards methods and tools, when creating software.

State transition
A technique whereby a system or a part of a system moves from one state to another, in a strict order driven by external events, such as messages arriving, or invocations occurring.

Target Machine
The computer on which a program will run when in use. May or may not be the same as the host machine.

Threshold Conditions
The value of an object at the transition points within the possible values, for example for an integer, the threshold condition would be around the value zero (i.e. -1, 0, 1) as the transition from negative to positive or vice versa is a significant one in the range of integer values.

Through Life Costs
The cost of an item from conception through to decommissioning.

Validated
A process of establishing that a compiler adheres to the standard through a rigorous series of compile time and run time tests.

White box testing
Testing targeted at stressing the design of a software item in the knowledge of the potential "weak" points, e.g. threshold or boundary conditions.

APPENDIX H   REFERENCES

[Abell 75]
Exploration of the Universe
By George O. Abell
Holt, Rinehart & Winston, New York, 3rd edition

[ALRM]
Reference Manual for the Ada Programming Language, ANSI/MIL-STD-1815A-1983
US Department of Defense, 1983

[Firesmith 87]
Ada Project Management
Presentation by Donald G. Firesmith, Magnavox Electronic Systems Co, Fort Wayne, Indiana, USA

[Fisher 84]
Universal Arithmetic Packages, Ada Letters, Volume III Number 6, May-June, pp 30-47
By Gerry Fisher
ACM SigAda, ACM Headquarters, 11 W 42nd Street, New York, NY 10036, USA

[Knuth 81]
The Art of Computer Programming, volume 2, Seminumerical Algorithms
By Donald E. Knuth
Addison-Wesley, Reading, Ma, USA, 2nd edition

[McIlroy 69]
Mass Produced Software Components
By M.D. McIlroy in Peter Naur, B. Randell & J.N. Buxton (Eds), Software Engineering Concepts and Techniques
Proceedings of NATO Conference on Software Engineering held at Garmisch in 1968, pp 88-98, Petrocelli/Charter, New York

[NAG 88]
NAG Ada Library, available from the Numerical Algorithms Group Ltd, NAG Central Office, Wilkinson House, Jordan Hill Road, Oxford OX2 8DR, U.K.

[Nissen 84]
Portability and Style in Ada
By John C.D. Nissen & Peter Wallis
Cambridge University Press

[Orme 86]
Project Management Experience of Ada
By Antony W. Orme
Ada User, volume 7 number 2

[Parise 82]
The Book of Calendars
By Frank Parise (Ed)
Facts on File, New York.

[Tajima 84]
Inside the Japanese Software Industry
By D. Tajima & T. Matsubara
IEEE Computer pp 34-43, March 1984

[Wichmann 90]
UI0052 (approved June 1990 by Working Group WG9 of the ISO)
Brian A. Wichmann (Ed)
Obtainable from the National Physical Laboratory, London, TW11 OLW, U.K.

[Wirth 76]
Algorithms plus Data Structures = Programs
By Niklaus Wirth
Prentice-Hall, Englewood Cliffs, NJ 07632, USA

APPENDIX I INDEX

A
abstract data type, 4, 253
Ada 9X, viii
Ada machine, 3
automated testing, 242, 246

B
bag, 202
balanced tree, 147ff
black box testing, 242
bounded tasks, 170ff

C
catalogue, vi, 238
checksum, 222ff
complexity, vi, 8, 237, 257
component entry, 261ff
configuration control, 5, 222
configuration management, 238
cost benefit, 237
critical region, 11, 260

D
date & time, 26ff
deadlock, 176
dependency, 9, 237
deques, 86
description, 9
design authority, 236
disc, x
documentation, 5, 7, 237
dynamic tasking, 170ff

E
efficiency, 3, 10, 251
encapsulation, 242
example of use, 10
exceptions, 9, 176, 243, 259

F

flexible queues, 86ff
floating point arithmetic, 66
floppy disc, x
format of components, 8ff
functionality, 241

G

garbage collection, 95
generics, vi, 3, 253, 260
generics - nested, 90
glossary, 266ff

H

heap, 86, 115, 140, 256
heap creep, 95, 256
heap fragmentation, 256
heterogeneous task, 170, 187ff
homogeneous task, 170, 172ff

I

identification of components for reuse, 5
implementation dependent, 255, 256
implementation points, 10
inconsistency, 11
Input/Output, 257
integer arithmetic, 42ff
intellectual property rights, 236
internal state, 11, 226
I/O, 257

L

lexicographic order, 215
librarian, 7, 235ff
libraries, vi, 3, 4, 5, 235, 238, 241
library maintenance, 5, 237
lists, 134ff
logical tests, 244

M

maintenance, 5, 7, 242
management, 4, 7, 235, 236
mass-produced software components, 1

Index

mathematical algorithms, vi, 1
memory management, see heap
minimum implementable package, 9
modularity, 256
multi-tasking, 10, 259

N
novice programmer, 8
NUMERIC_ERROR, 260

O
object class, 2
options, 9
order, 251

P
packages, 4
parameterisation, vi
performance, vi, 237, 251
permutations, 214ff
pipe, 86
portability, 3, 4, 5, 32, 42, 66, 90, 255ff
pragmatics, 9
productivity, 4

Q
quality, 5, 241
quality assurance, 237, 238
queues, 86

R
race condition, 10
real arithmetic, 66ff
recompilation, 4, 242
recovery, 6
recycling of memory, 94, 115, 140, 257
references, 271
regression testing, 244
reliability, 2, 5
requirements, 241, 242
rescheduling, 11
resource locking, 11
restrictions on use, 9

retrieval, 238
reusability management, 4, 235ff
right to reuse, ix

S
sets, 202ff
shared data, 10
site standards, 3, 7, 236, 237
software engineering, v, 2
stacks, 86
standards, 3, 236, 237, 264
statistics, 86
strings - variable length, 12
submission to reusable library, 5, 237

T
tasking, 4, 10, 170ff, 258, 260
test code, x, 5, 6, 7, 241, 250, 260, 264
testing, 241ff
text handler, 12ff
time & date, 26ff
training, 8
tree, 108ff, 146
tree - balanced, 146
tree terminology, 115, 116

U
unbounded tasks, 170ff
understandability, 3, 6
universal integer, 42ff
universal real, 66ff
universality, 4
utility, 6

V
validation, 2, 5, 255
variable length strings, 12
vendor supplied packages, 255

W
white box testing, 243